WRITER: RICARDO SANCHE

ART: POP MHAN

HISTORY OF TELARA ART: JOEL GOMEZ

COLORS: ZAC ATKINSON

HISTORY OF TELARA COLORS (3&4): WES HARTMA

LETTERS: DERON BENNETT

BASED ON THE VIDEO GAME: RIFT™

COLLECTED EDITION COVER AND ORIGINAL SERIES COVERS 1-2
BY DREW JOHNSON & LIZZY JOHN

COVERS 3-4 BY DREW JOHNSON & CARRIE STRACHAN

COVER ZERO BY DUSTIN NGUYEN

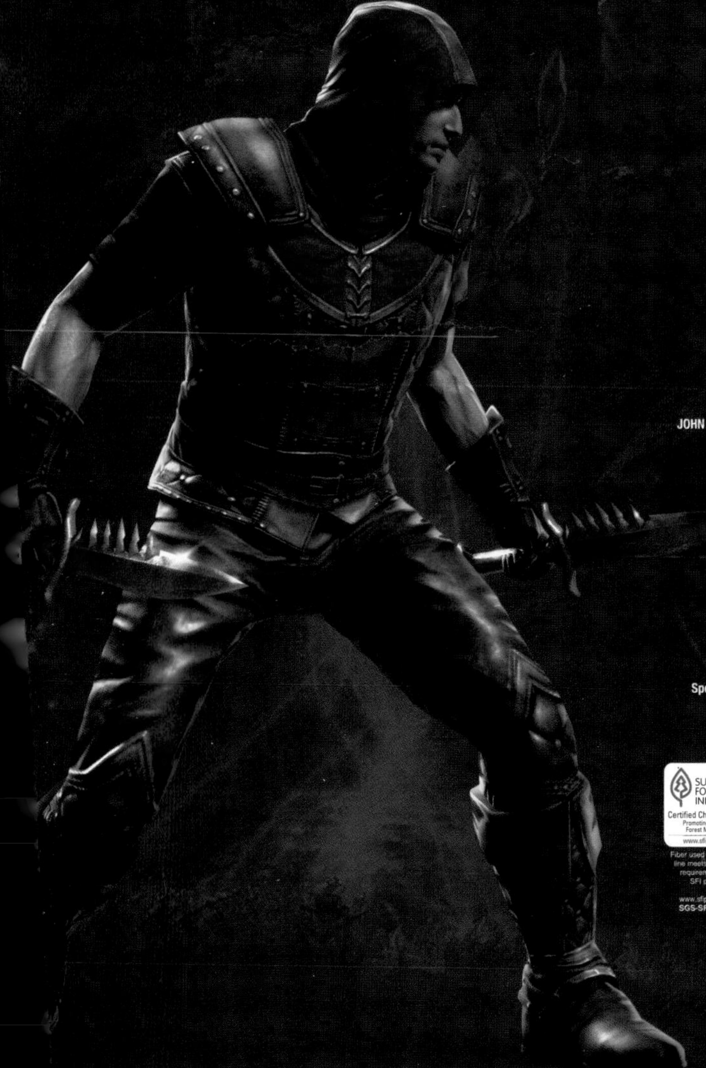

DC C
JIM CHADWIC
CHYNNA CLUGSTON FLORES Assista
BOB HARRAS Group Editor–Collected
ROBBIN BROSTERMAN Design Directo
ED ROEDER Art

DIANE NELSON P
DAN DIDIO and JIM LEE Co-P
GEOFF JOHNS Chief Creati
JOHN ROOD Executive Vice President–Sales, Marketing and Business Dev
PATRICK CALDON Executive Vice President–Finance and Adm
AMY GENKINS Senior VP–Business and L
STEVE ROTTERDAM Senior VP–Sales and
JOHN CUNNINGHAM VP
TERRI CUNNINGHAM VP–Man
ALISON GILL VP–M
DAVID HYDE
SUE POHJA VP–Boo
ALYSSE SOLL VP–Advertising and Cust
BOB W
MARK CHIARE

T
Publ
Story by R
with MORGAN LOCKHART, NICHOLAS MCDOWELL

Special Thanks GREG BAUMAN, JORDAN ROSENBAUM, SCOT
BROWN, DARREN PATTENDEN

SUSTAINABLE FORESTRY INITIATIVE
Certified Chain of Custody
Promoting Sustainable Forest Management
www.sfiprogram.org
Fiber used in this product line meets the sourcing requirements of the SFI program.
www.sfiprogram.org
SGS-SFICOC-130

DC Comics, a Warner Bros. E

SoftCover ISBN: 97

TELARA CHRONICLES

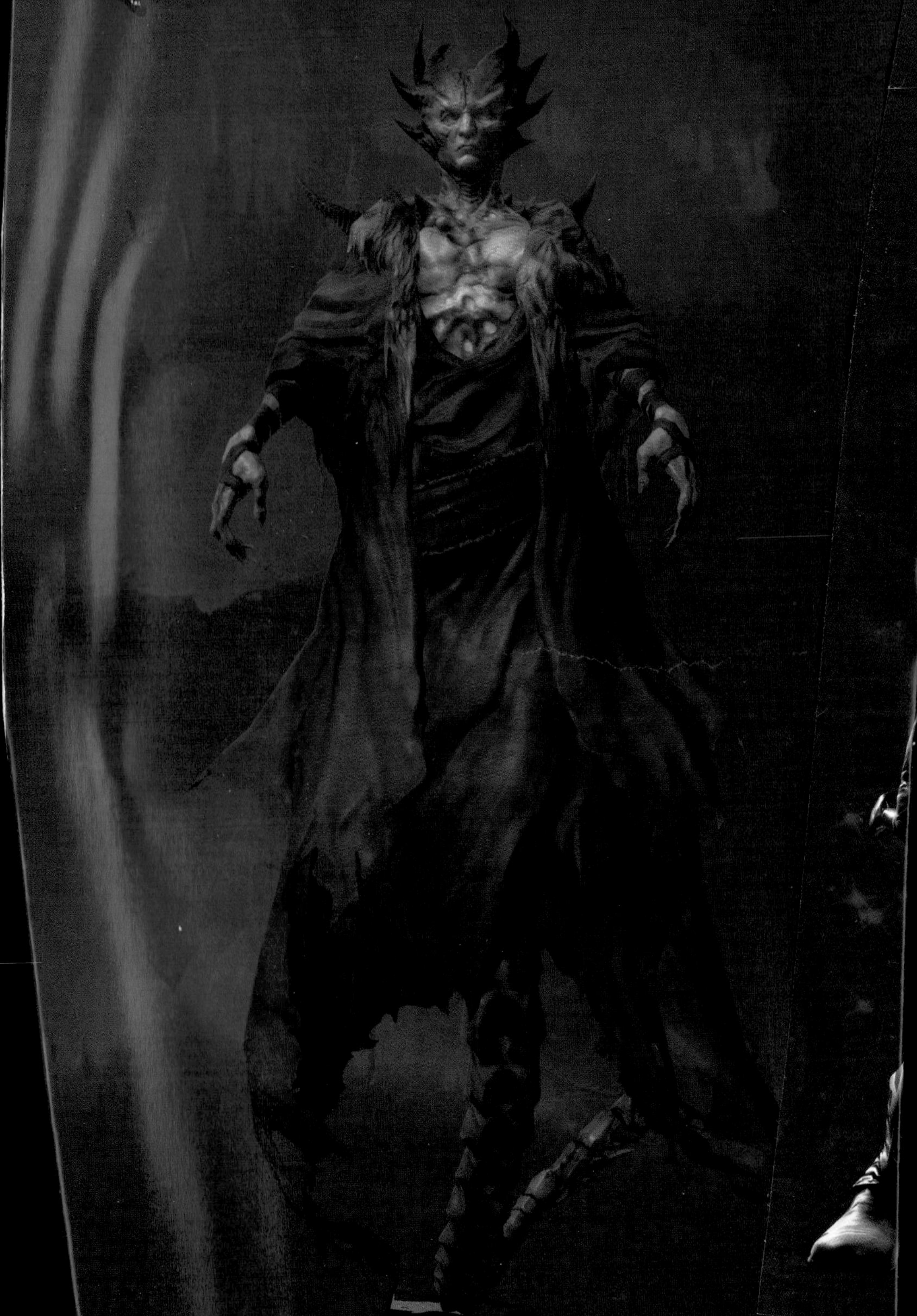

CHAPTER ONE

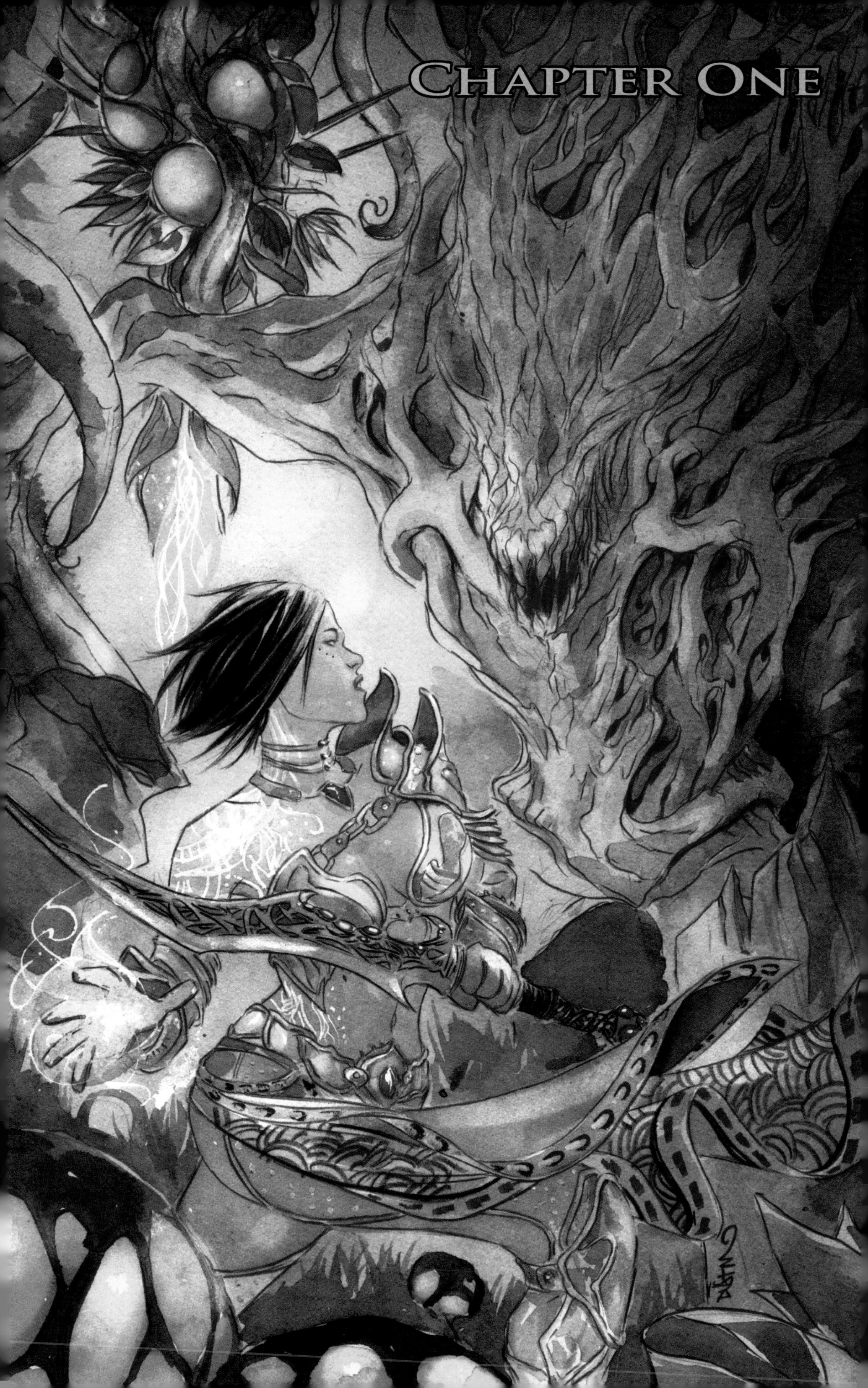

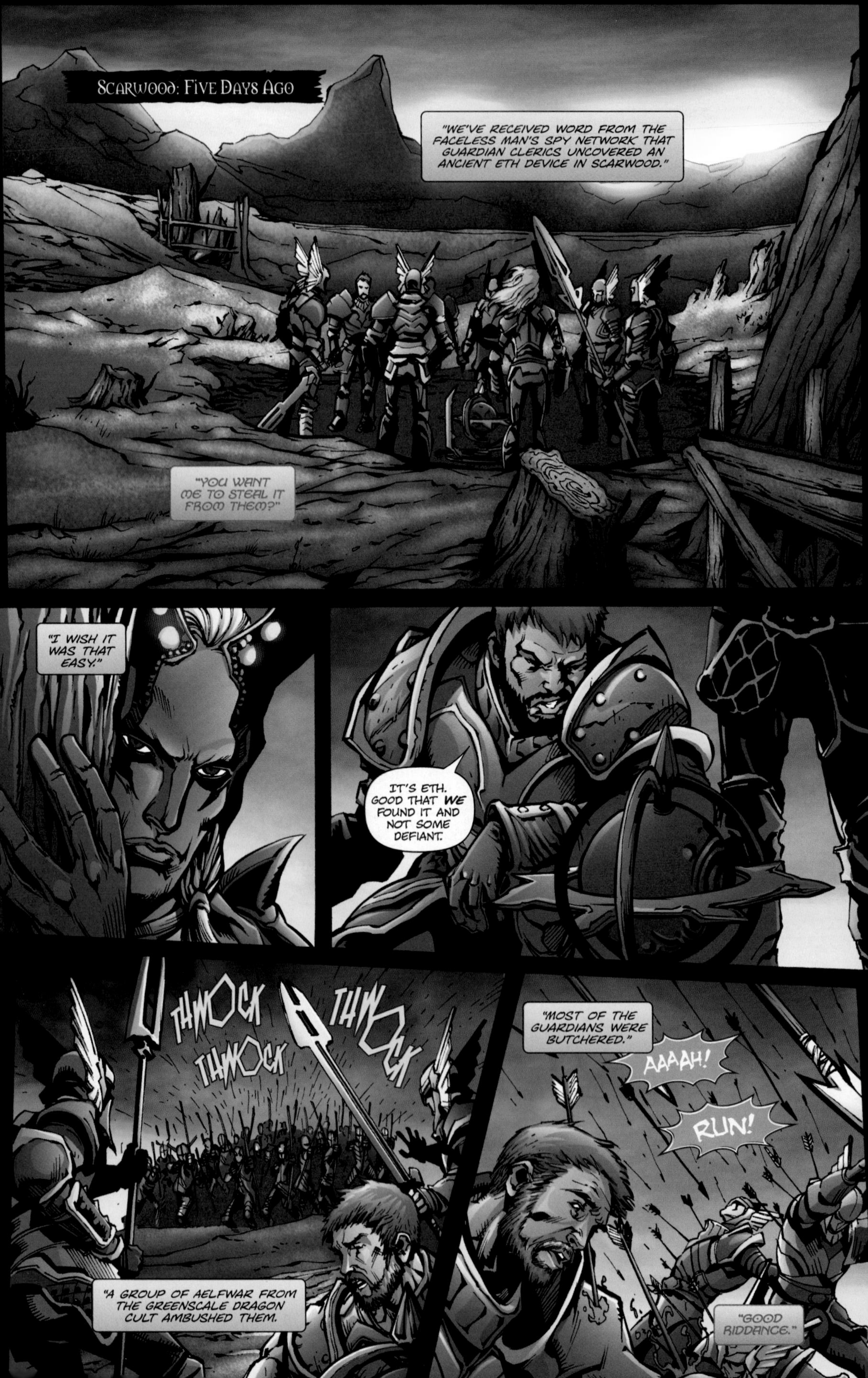
Scarwood: Five Days Ago
"We've received word from the Faceless Man's spy network that Guardian Clerics uncovered an ancient Eth device in Scarwood."
"You want me to steal it from them?"
"I wish it was that easy."
It's Eth. Good that *we* found it and not some Defiant.
THWOCK
THWOCK
THWOCK
"A group of Aelfwar from the Greenscale Dragon Cult ambushed them.
"Most of the Guardians were butchered."
AAAAH!
RUN!
"Good riddance."

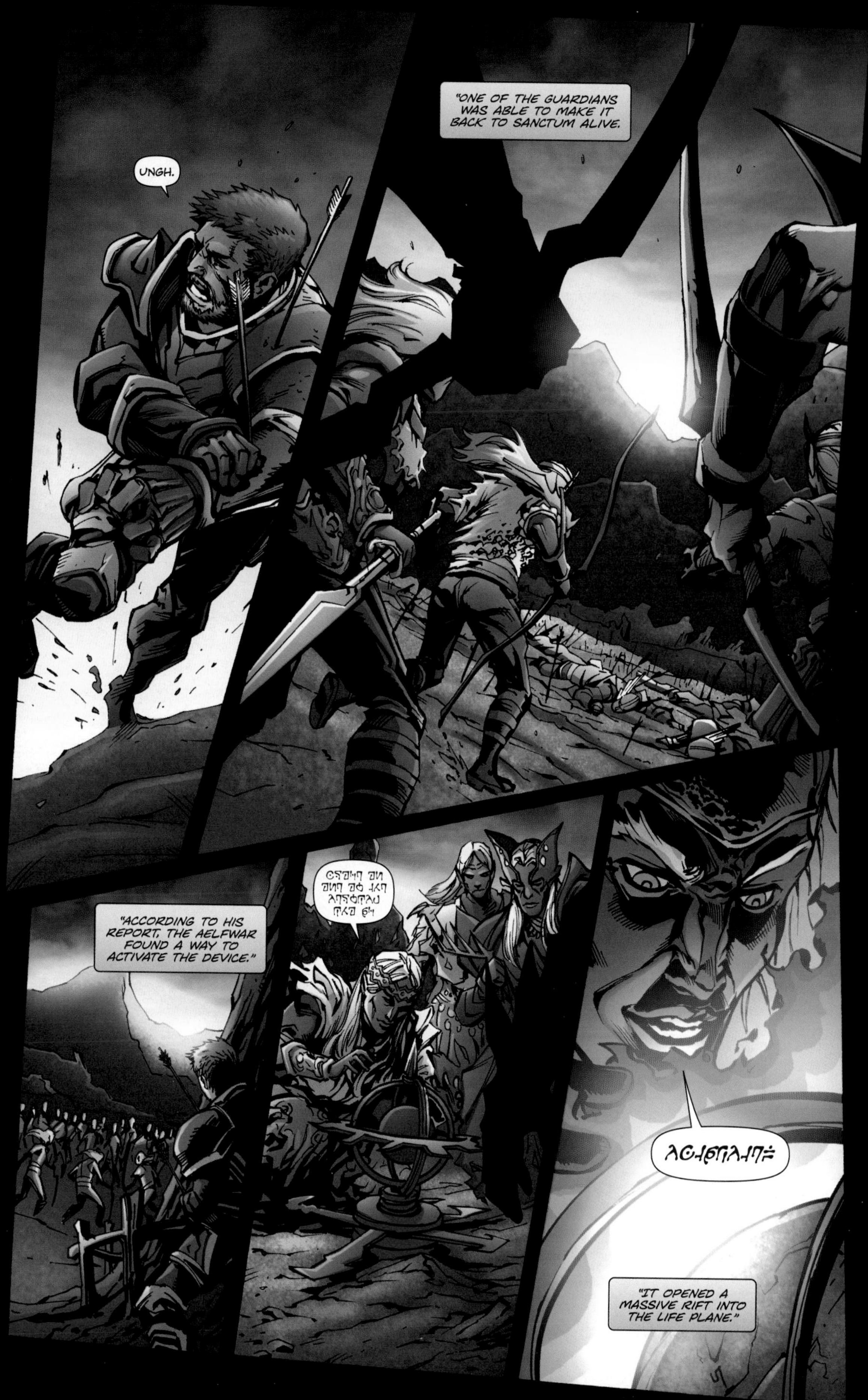
"ONE OF THE GUARDIANS WAS ABLE TO MAKE IT BACK TO SANCTUM ALIVE.
UNGH.
"ACCORDING TO HIS REPORT, THE AELFWAR FOUND A WAY TO ACTIVATE THE DEVICE."
"IT OPENED A MASSIVE RIFT INTO THE LIFE PLANE."

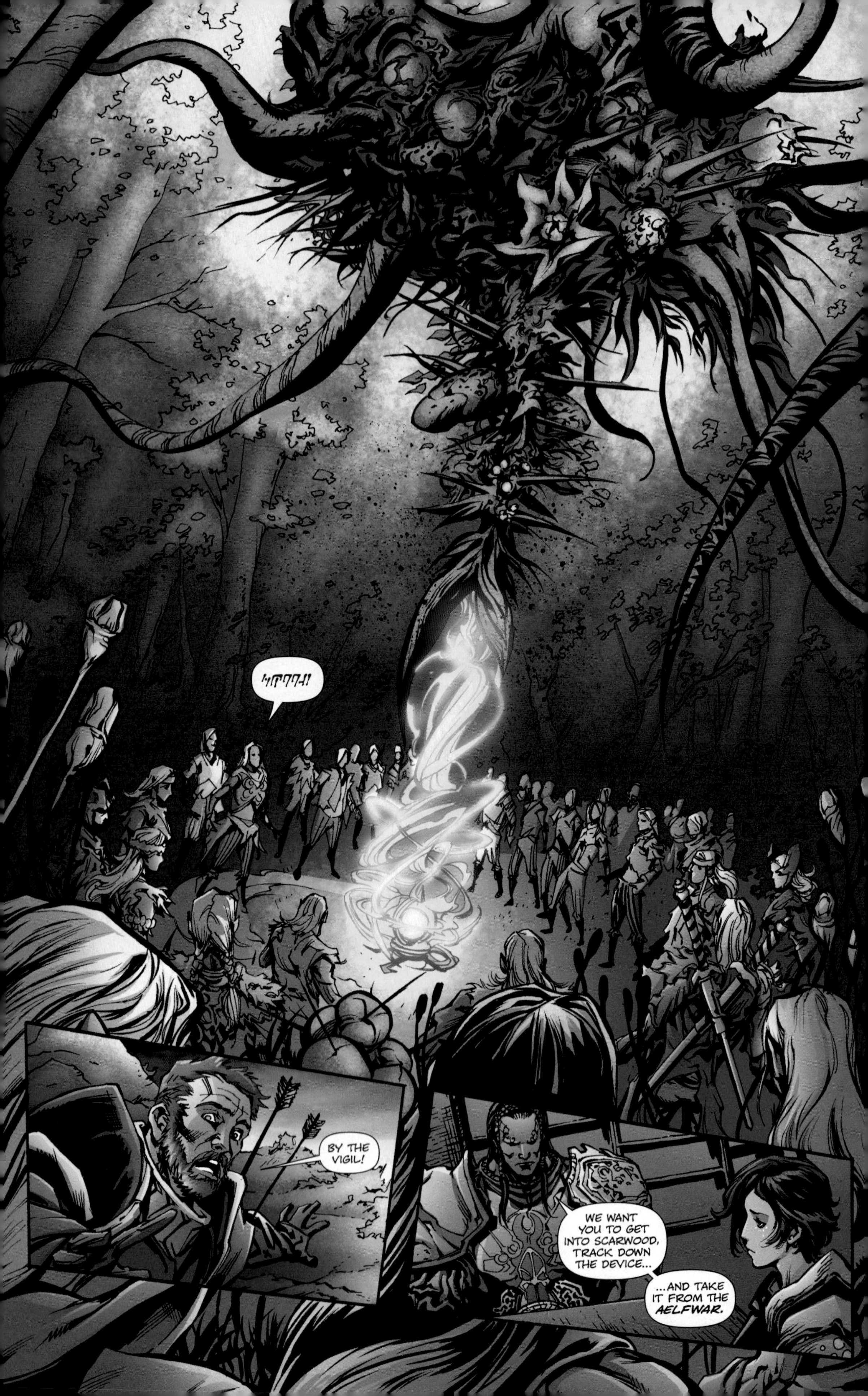

BY THE VIGIL!
WE WANT YOU TO GET INTO SCARWOOD, TRACK DOWN THE DEVICE...
...AND TAKE IT FROM THE *AELFWAR.*

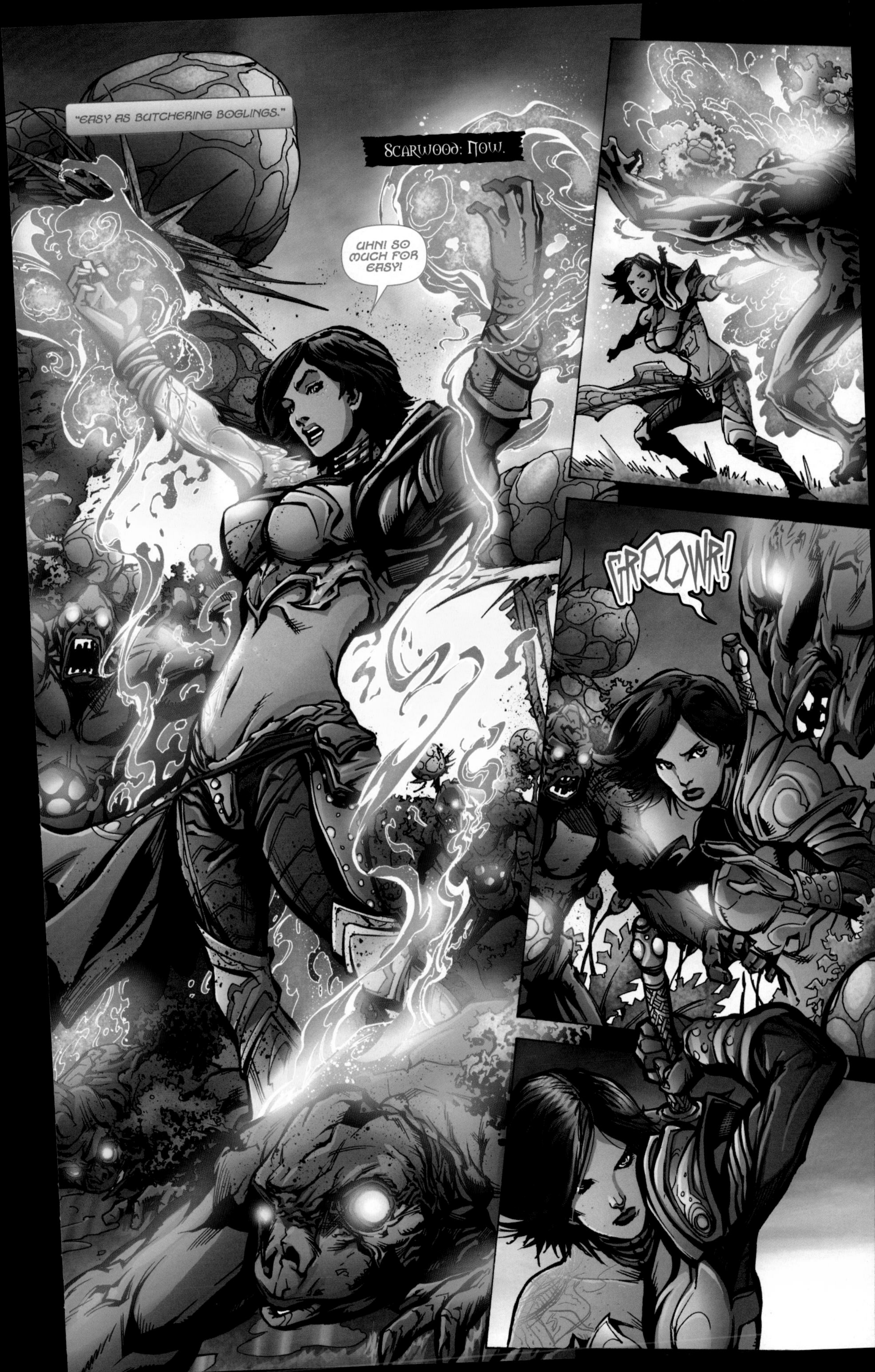
"EASY AS BUTCHERING BOGLINGS."
SCARWOOD: NOW.
UHN! SO MUCH FOR EASY!
GROOWR!

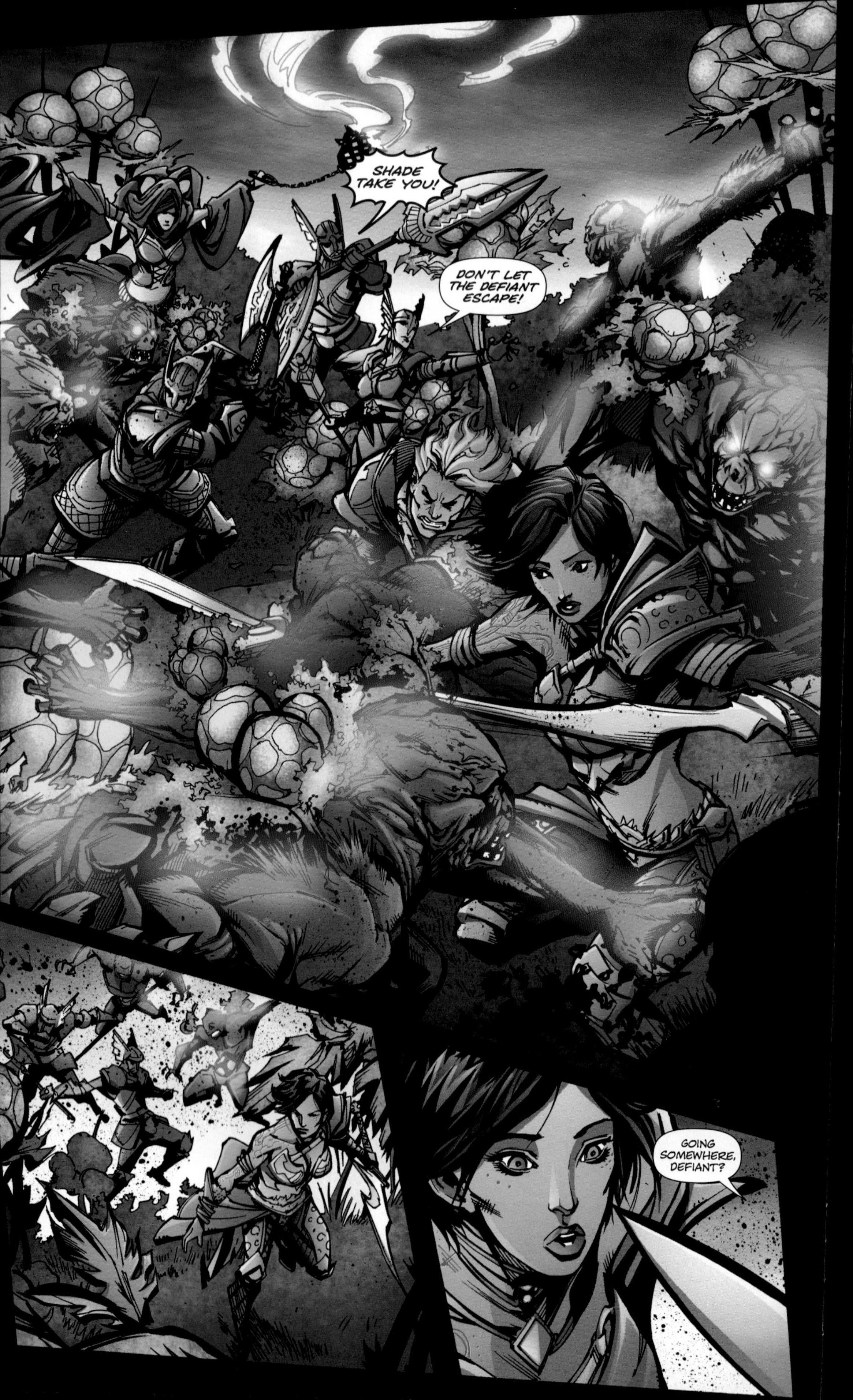
SHADE TAKE YOU!
DON'T LET THE DEFIANT ESCAPE!
GOING SOMEWHERE, DEFIANT?

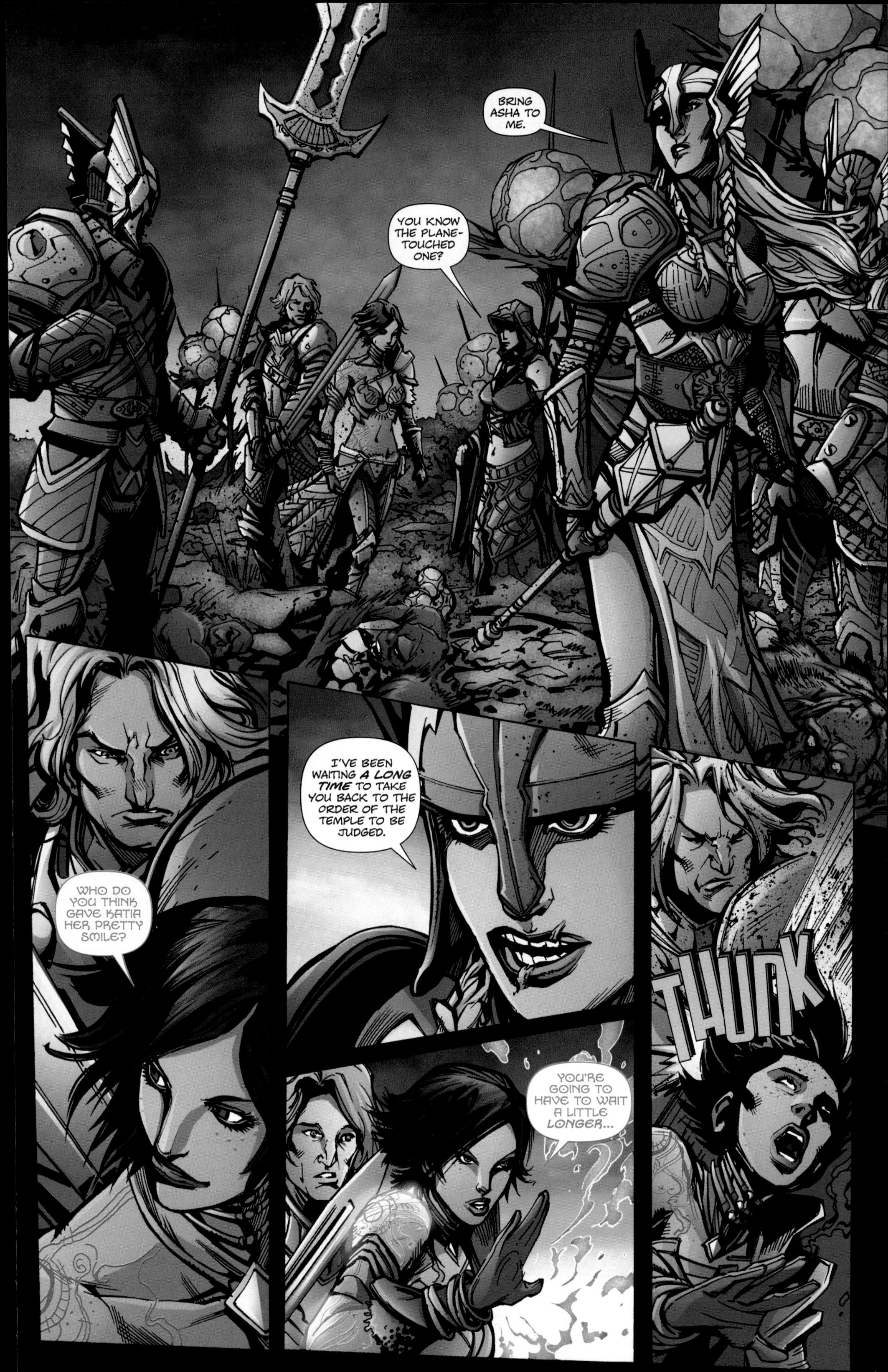
BRING ASHA TO ME.
YOU KNOW THE PLANE-TOUCHED ONE?
WHO DO YOU THINK GAVE KATIA HER PRETTY SMILE?
I'VE BEEN WAITING A LONG TIME TO TAKE YOU BACK TO THE ORDER OF THE TEMPLE TO BE JUDGED.
YOU'RE GOING TO HAVE TO WAIT A LITTLE LONGER...
THUNK

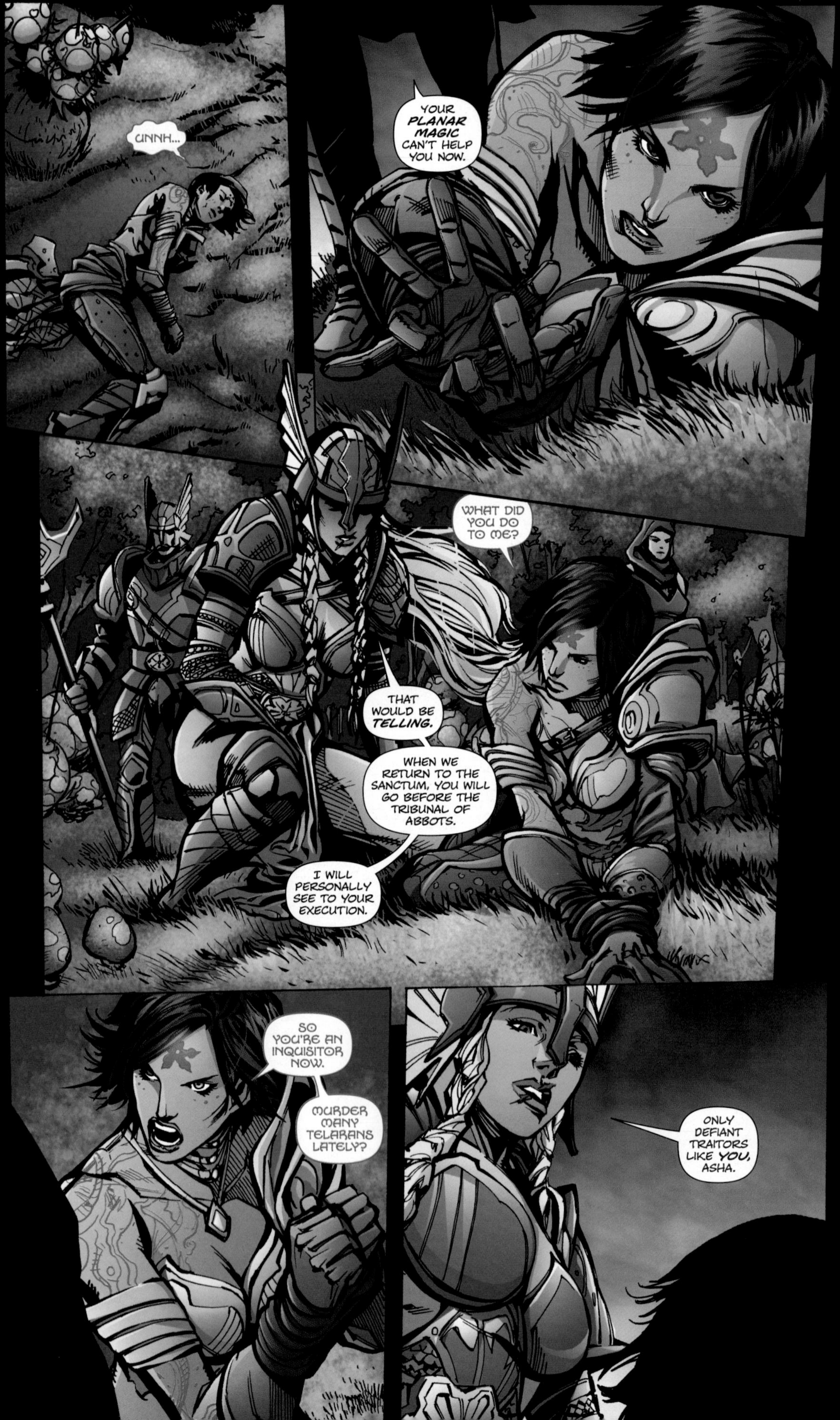
UNNH...
YOUR PLANAR MAGIC CAN'T HELP YOU NOW.
WHAT DID YOU DO TO ME?
THAT WOULD BE TELLING.
WHEN WE RETURN TO THE SANCTUM, YOU WILL GO BEFORE THE TRIBUNAL OF ABBOTS.
I WILL PERSONALLY SEE TO YOUR EXECUTION.
SO YOU'RE AN INQUISITOR NOW.
MURDER MANY TELARANS LATELY?
ONLY DEFIANT TRAITORS LIKE YOU, ASHA.

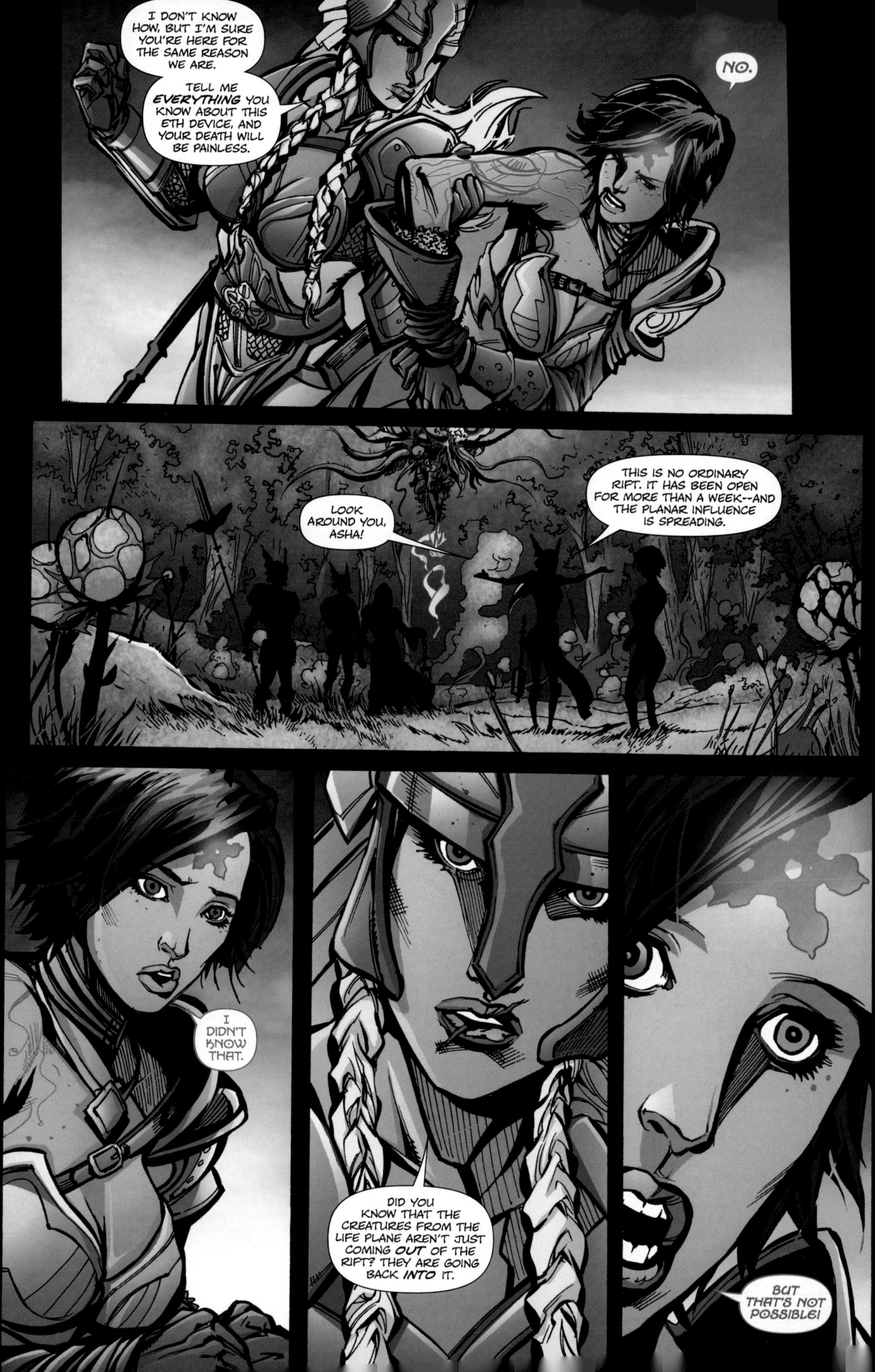
I DON'T KNOW HOW, BUT I'M SURE YOU'RE HERE FOR THE SAME REASON WE ARE.
TELL ME EVERYTHING YOU KNOW ABOUT THIS ETH DEVICE, AND YOUR DEATH WILL BE PAINLESS.
NO.
LOOK AROUND YOU, ASHA!
THIS IS NO ORDINARY RIFT. IT HAS BEEN OPEN FOR MORE THAN A WEEK--AND THE PLANAR INFLUENCE IS SPREADING.
I DIDN'T KNOW THAT.
DID YOU KNOW THAT THE CREATURES FROM THE LIFE PLANE AREN'T JUST COMING OUT OF THE RIFT? THEY ARE GOING BACK INTO IT.
BUT THAT'S NOT POSSIBLE!

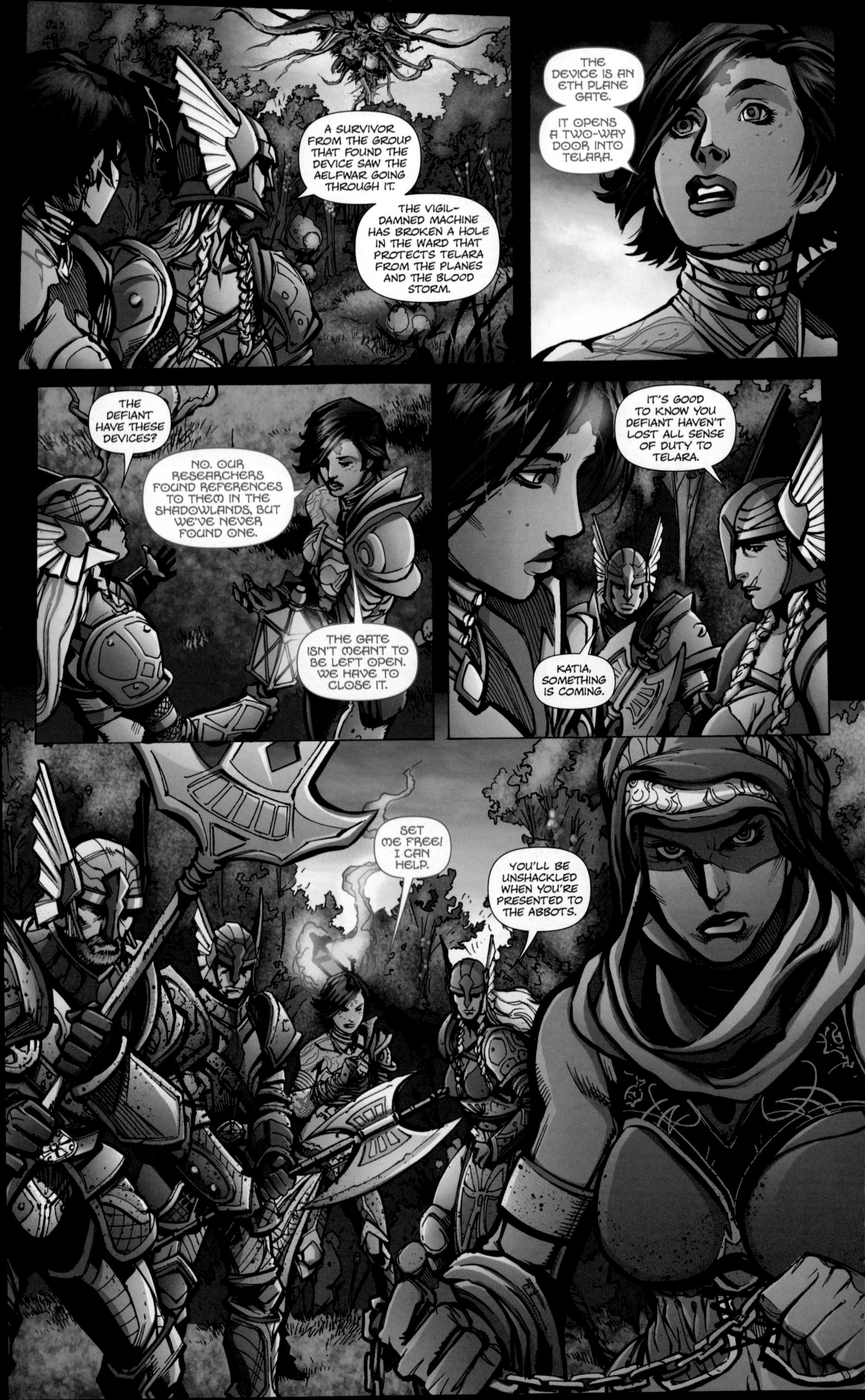
A SURVIVOR FROM THE GROUP THAT FOUND THE DEVICE SAW THE AELFWAR GOING THROUGH IT.
THE VIGIL-DAMNED MACHINE HAS BROKEN A HOLE IN THE WARD THAT PROTECTS TELARA FROM THE PLANES AND THE BLOOD STORM.
THE DEVICE IS AN ETH PLANE GATE.
IT OPENS A TWO-WAY DOOR INTO TELARA.
THE DEFIANT HAVE THESE DEVICES?
NO. OUR RESEARCHERS FOUND REFERENCES TO THEM IN THE SHADOWLANDS, BUT WE'VE NEVER FOUND ONE.
THE GATE ISN'T MEANT TO BE LEFT OPEN. WE HAVE TO CLOSE IT.
IT'S GOOD TO KNOW YOU DEFIANT HAVEN'T LOST ALL SENSE OF DUTY TO TELARA.
KATIA, SOMETHING IS COMING.
SET ME FREE! I CAN HELP.
YOU'LL BE UNSHACKLED WHEN YOU'RE PRESENTED TO THE ABBOTS.

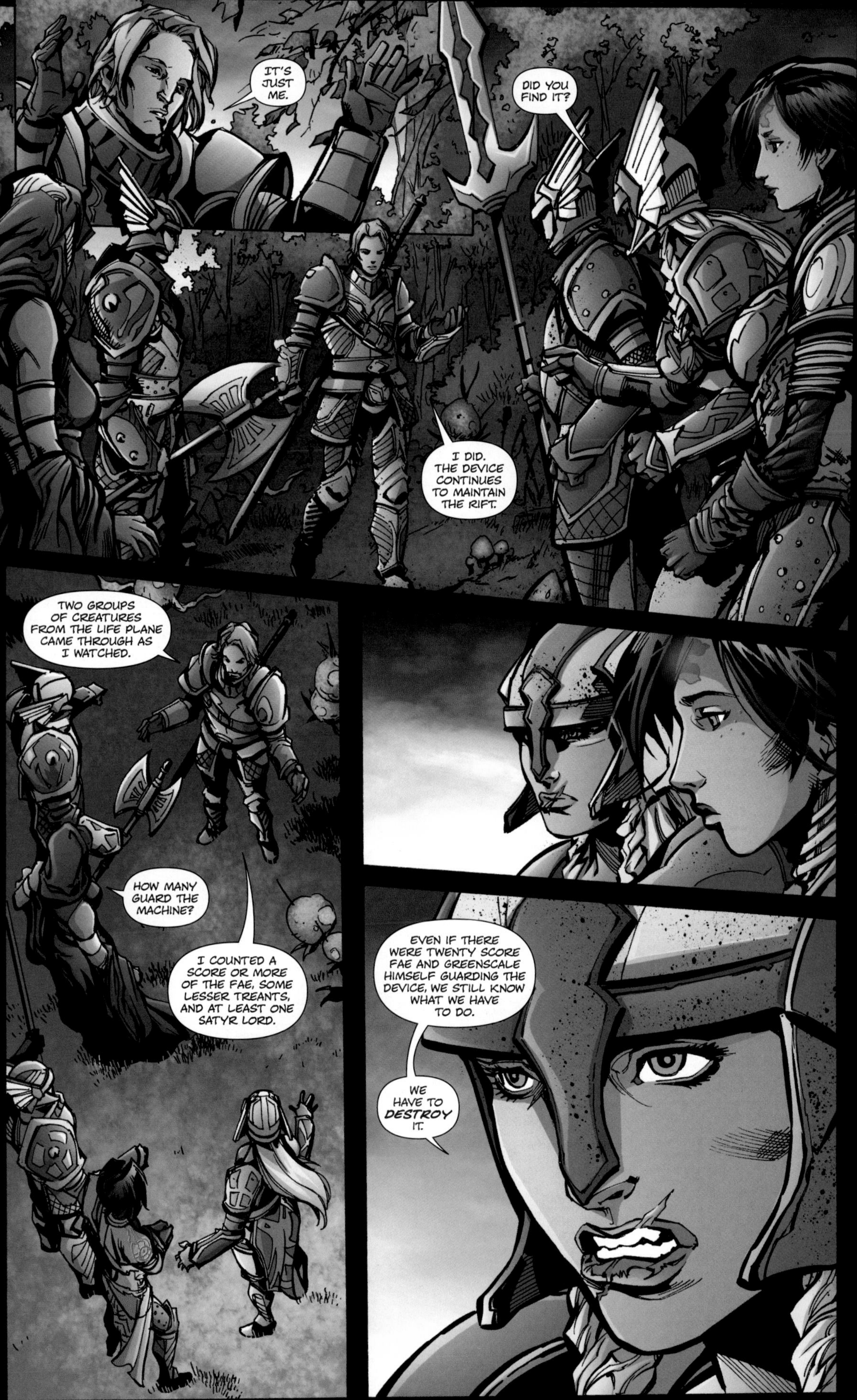
IT'S JUST ME.
DID YOU FIND IT?
I DID. THE DEVICE CONTINUES TO MAINTAIN THE RIFT.
TWO GROUPS OF CREATURES FROM THE LIFE PLANE CAME THROUGH AS I WATCHED.
HOW MANY GUARD THE MACHINE?
I COUNTED A SCORE OR MORE OF THE FAE, SOME LESSER TREANTS, AND AT LEAST ONE SATYR LORD.
EVEN IF THERE WERE TWENTY SCORE FAE AND GREENSCALE HIMSELF GUARDING THE DEVICE, WE STILL KNOW WHAT WE HAVE TO DO.
WE HAVE TO *DESTROY* IT.

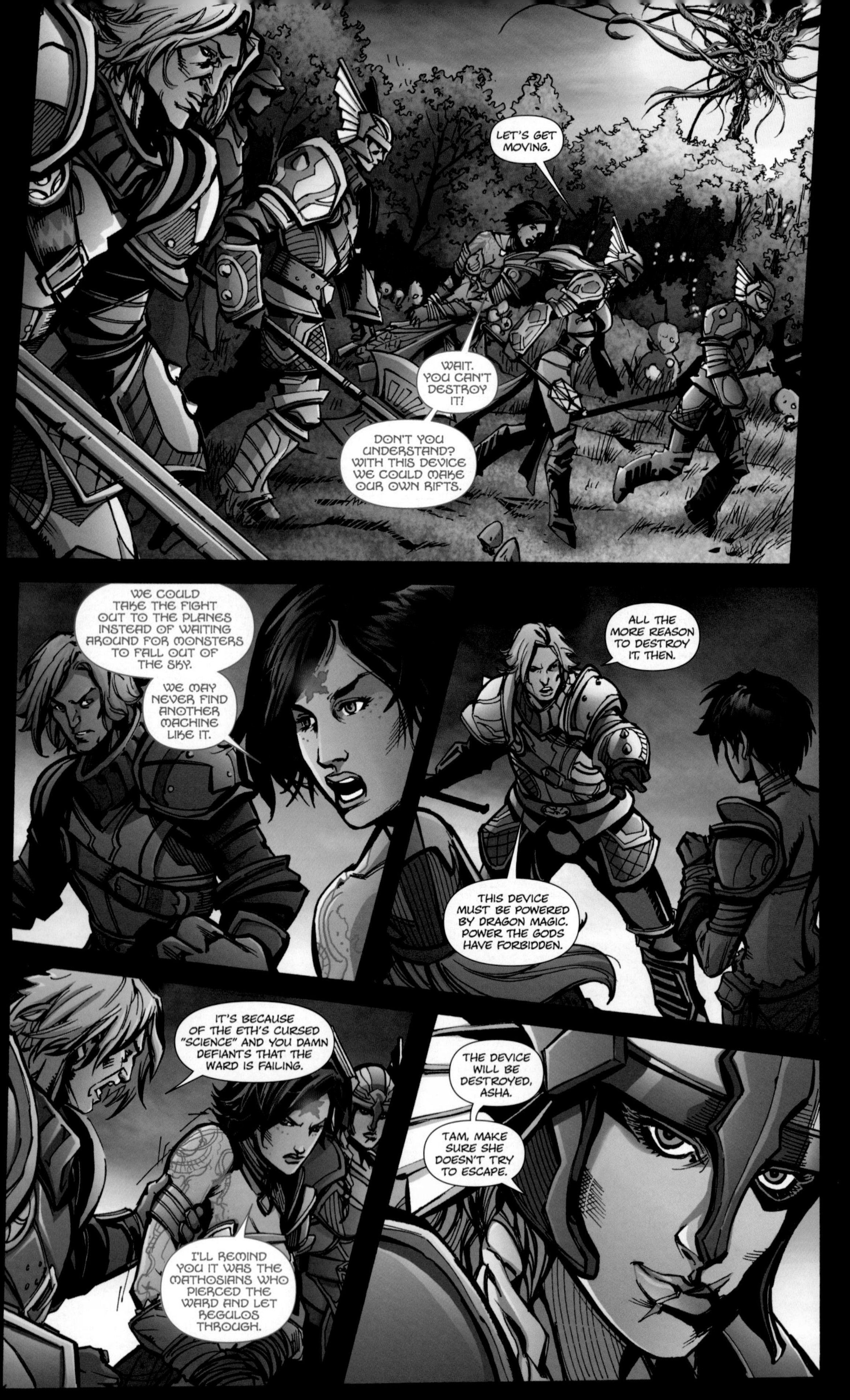
LET'S GET MOVING.
WAIT. YOU CAN'T DESTROY IT!
DON'T YOU UNDERSTAND? WITH THIS DEVICE WE COULD MAKE OUR OWN RIFTS.
WE COULD TAKE THE FIGHT OUT TO THE PLANES INSTEAD OF WAITING AROUND FOR MONSTERS TO FALL OUT OF THE SKY.
WE MAY NEVER FIND ANOTHER MACHINE LIKE IT.
ALL THE MORE REASON TO DESTROY IT, THEN.
THIS DEVICE MUST BE POWERED BY DRAGON MAGIC. POWER THE GODS HAVE FORBIDDEN.
IT'S BECAUSE OF THE ETH'S CURSED "SCIENCE" AND YOU DAMN DEFIANTS THAT THE WARD IS FAILING.
I'LL REMIND YOU IT WAS THE MATHOSIANS WHO PIERCED THE WARD AND LET REGULOS THROUGH.
THE DEVICE WILL BE DESTROYED, ASHA.
TAM, MAKE SURE SHE DOESN'T TRY TO ESCAPE.

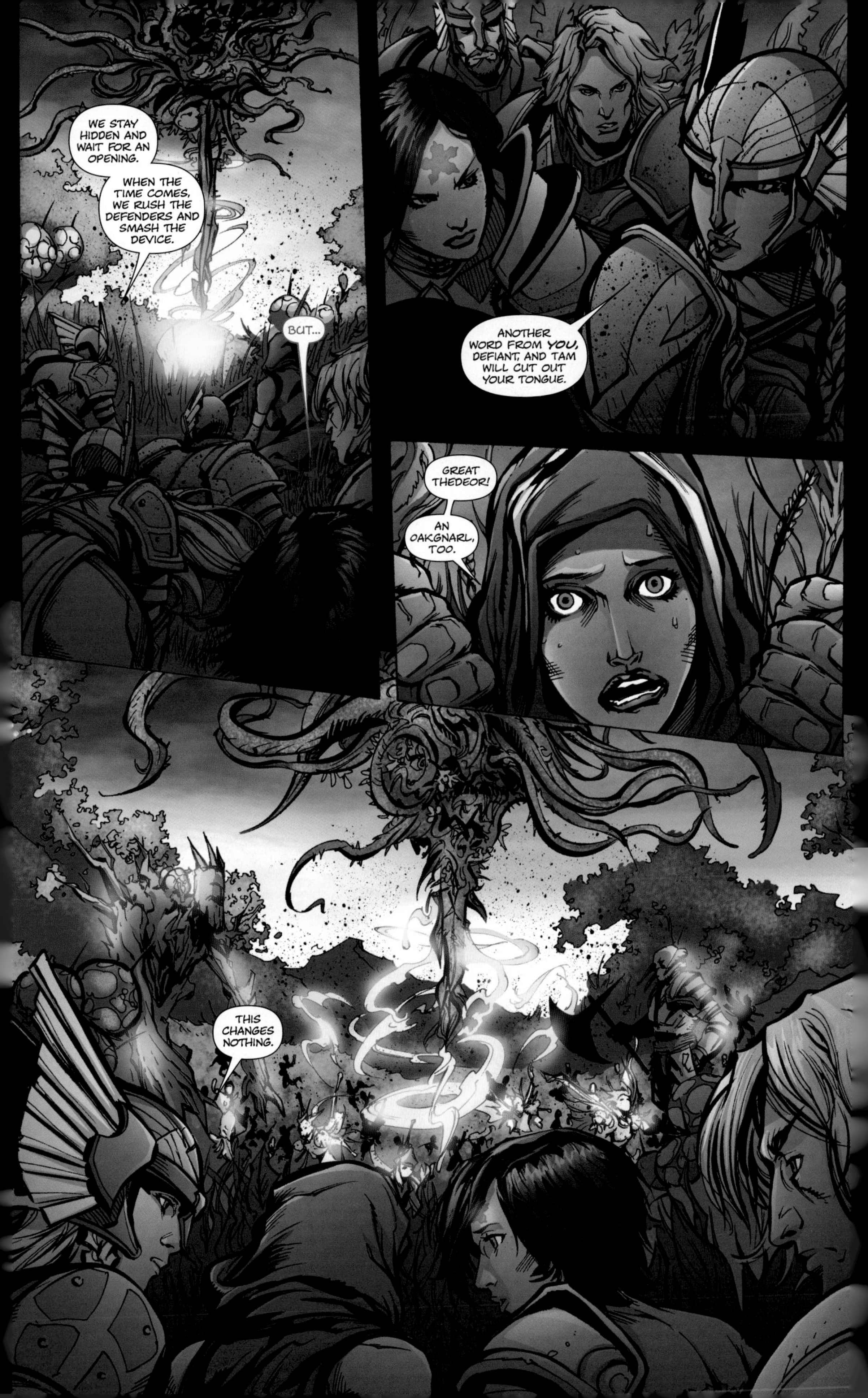
WE STAY HIDDEN AND WAIT FOR AN OPENING.
WHEN THE TIME COMES, WE RUSH THE DEFENDERS AND SMASH THE DEVICE.
BUT...
ANOTHER WORD FROM YOU, DEFIANT, AND TAM WILL CUT OUT YOUR TONGUE.
GREAT THEDEOR!
AN OAKGNARL, TOO.
THIS CHANGES NOTHING.

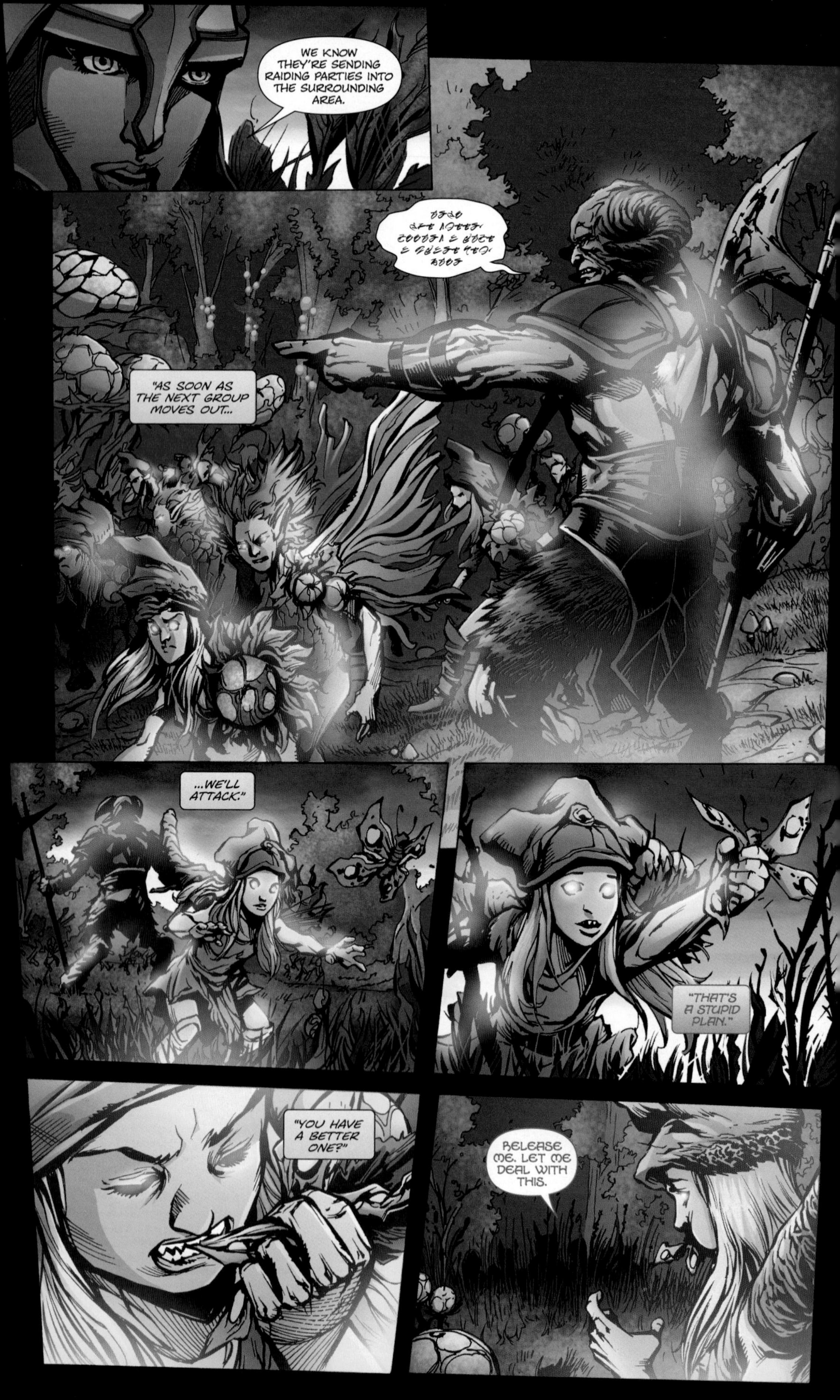
WE KNOW THEY'RE SENDING RAIDING PARTIES INTO THE SURROUNDING AREA.
"AS SOON AS THE NEXT GROUP MOVES OUT...
...WE'LL ATTACK."
"THAT'S A STUPID PLAN."
"YOU HAVE A BETTER ONE?"
RELEASE ME. LET ME DEAL WITH THIS.

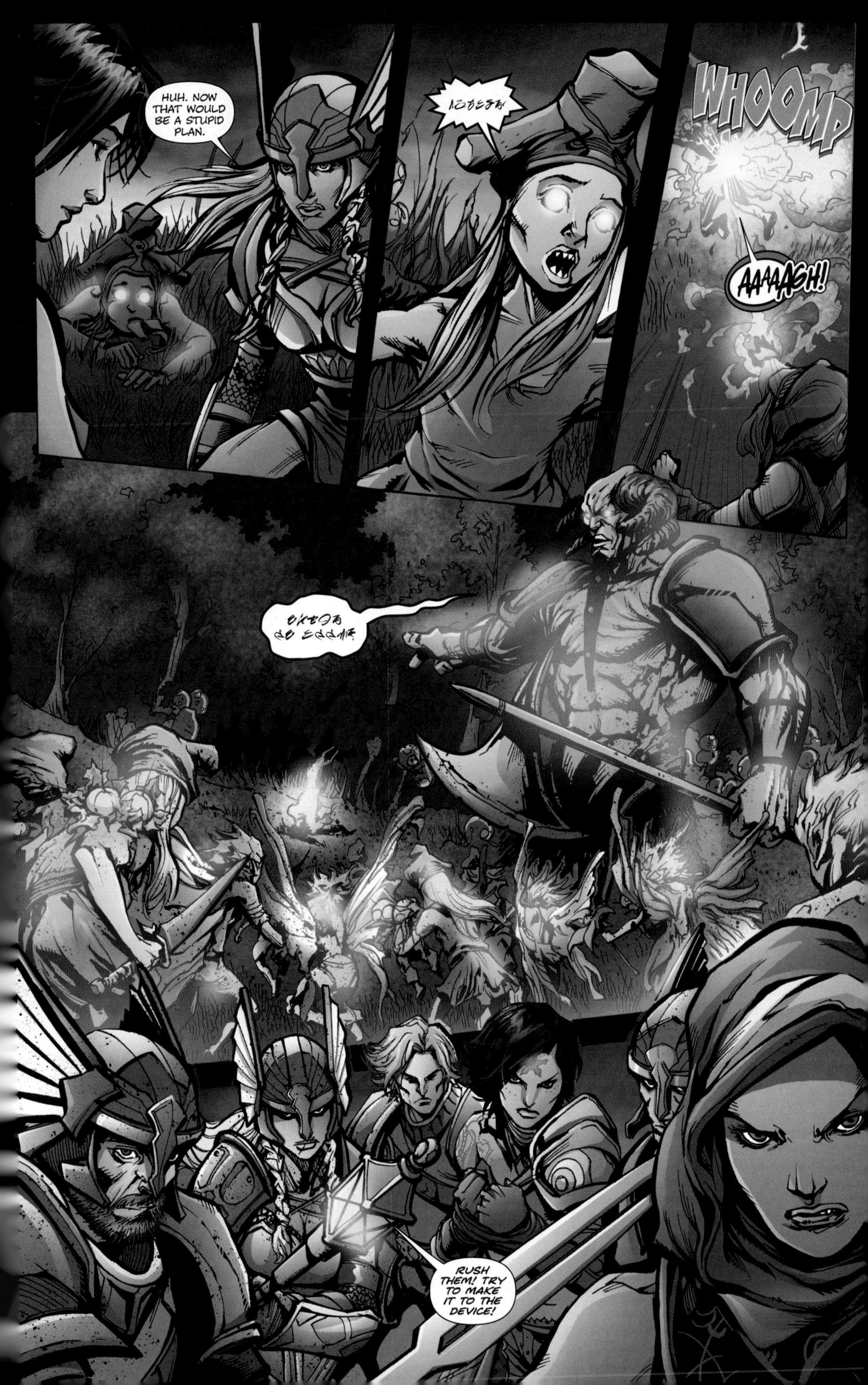
HUH. NOW THAT WOULD BE A STUPID PLAN.
WHOOMP
AAAAAGH!
RUSH THEM! TRY TO MAKE IT TO THE DEVICE!

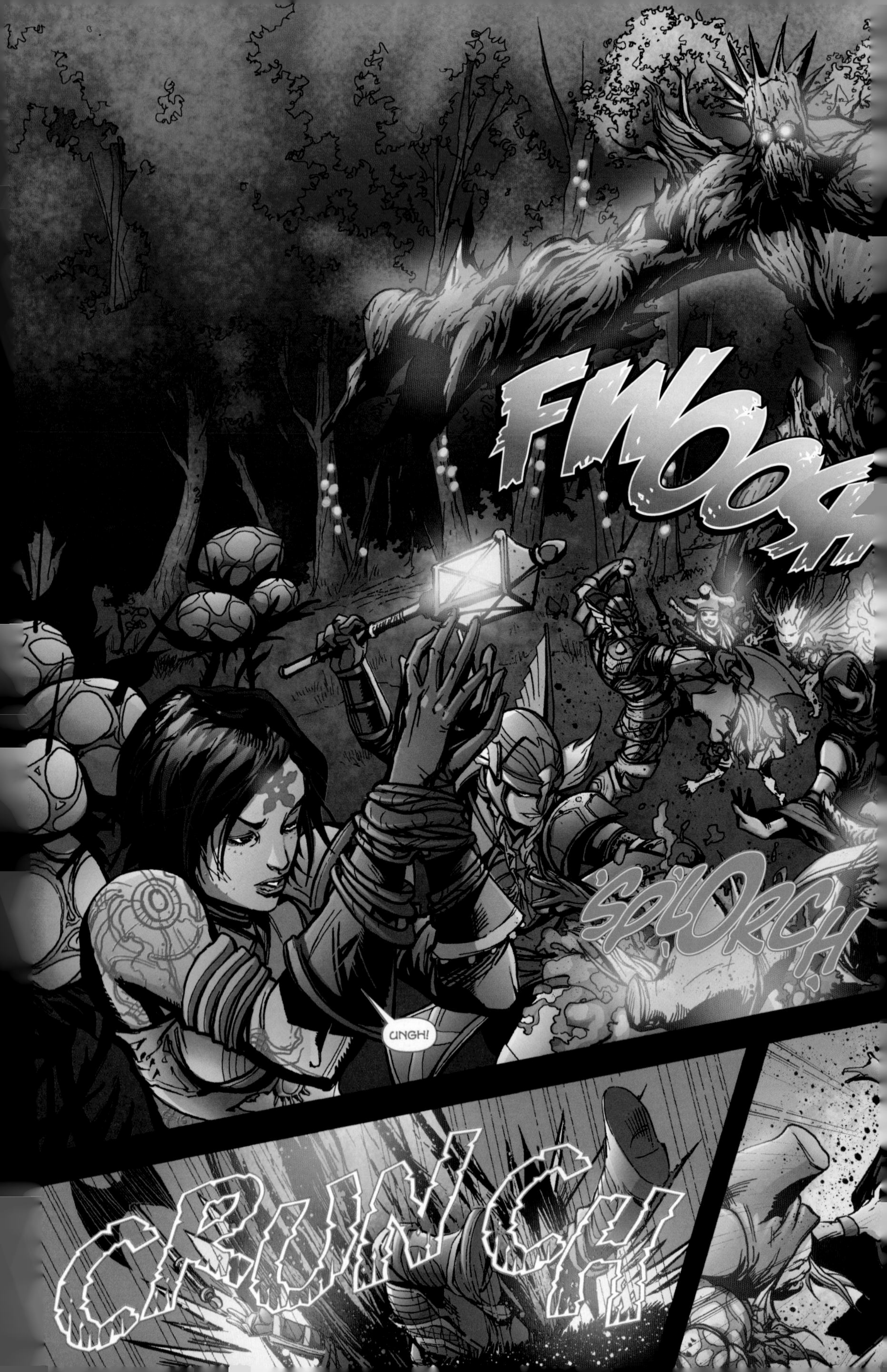
FWOOOSH
SPLORCH
UNGH!
CRUNCH

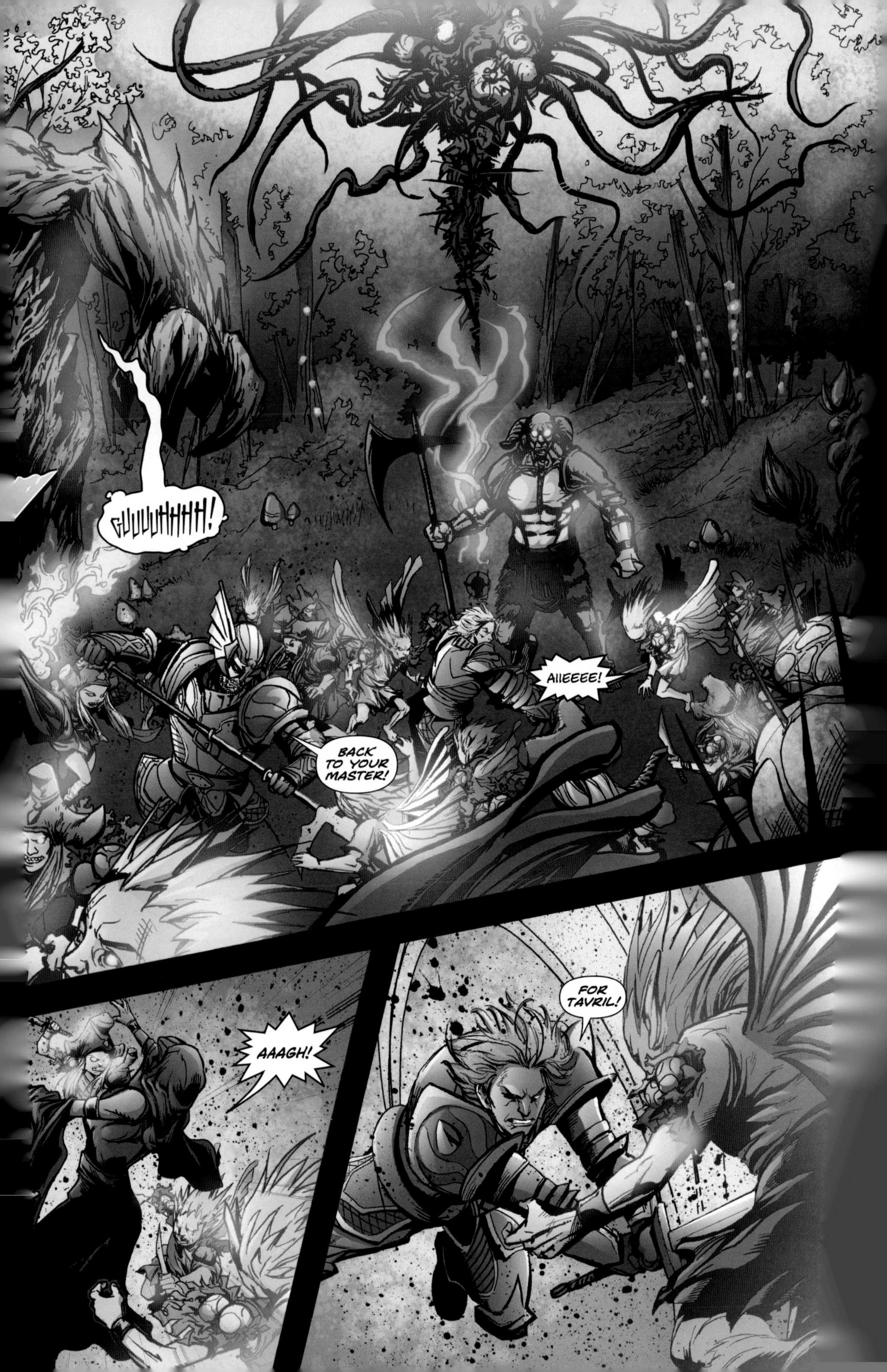
GUUUUHHHH!
AIIEEEE!
BACK TO YOUR MASTER!
AAAGH!
FOR TAVRIL!

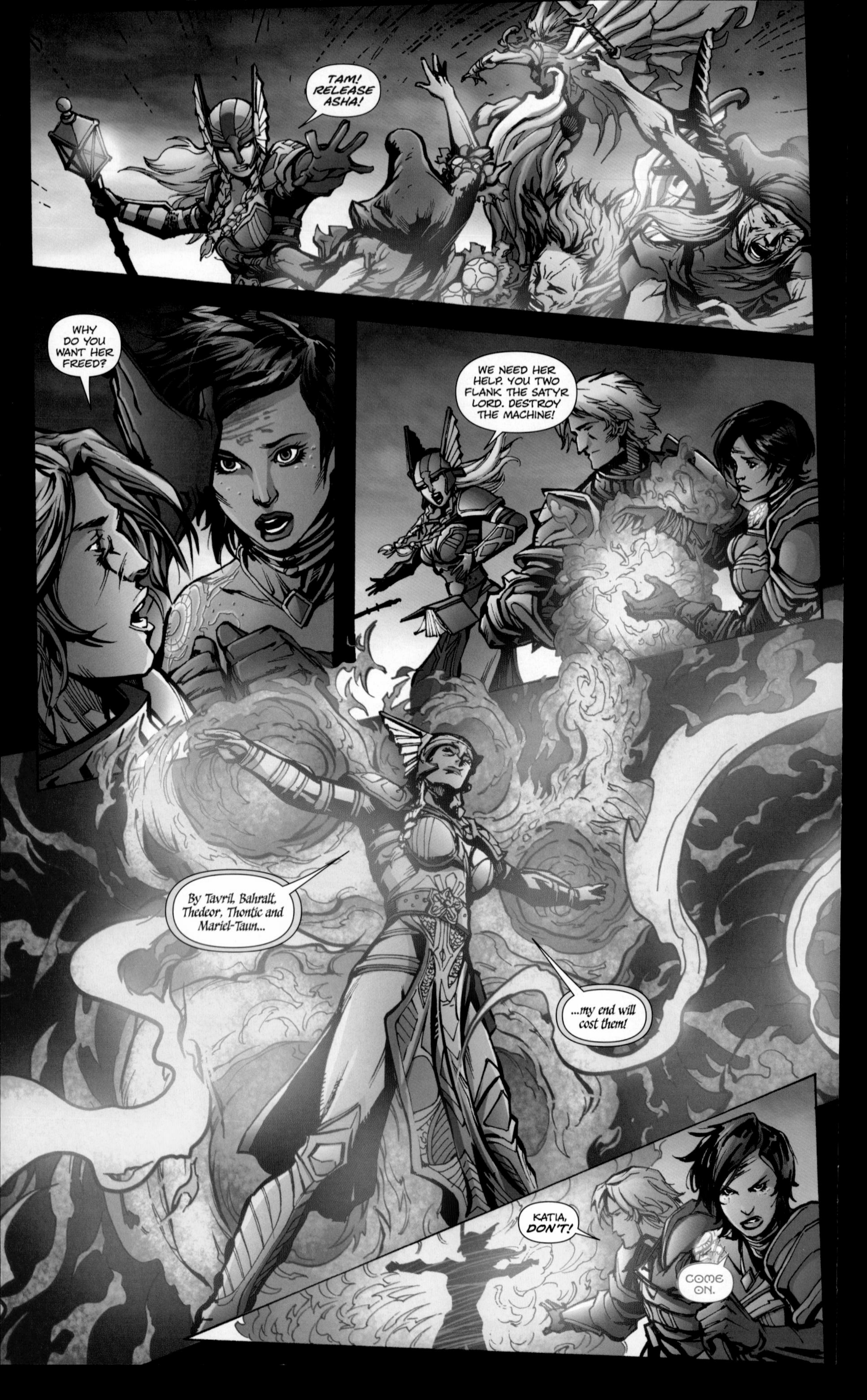
TAM! RELEASE ASHA!
WHY DO YOU WANT HER FREED?
WE NEED HER HELP. YOU TWO FLANK THE SATYR LORD. DESTROY THE MACHINE!
By Tavril, Bahralt, Thedeor, Thontic and Mariel-Taun...
...my end will cost them!
KATIA, DON'T!
COME ON.

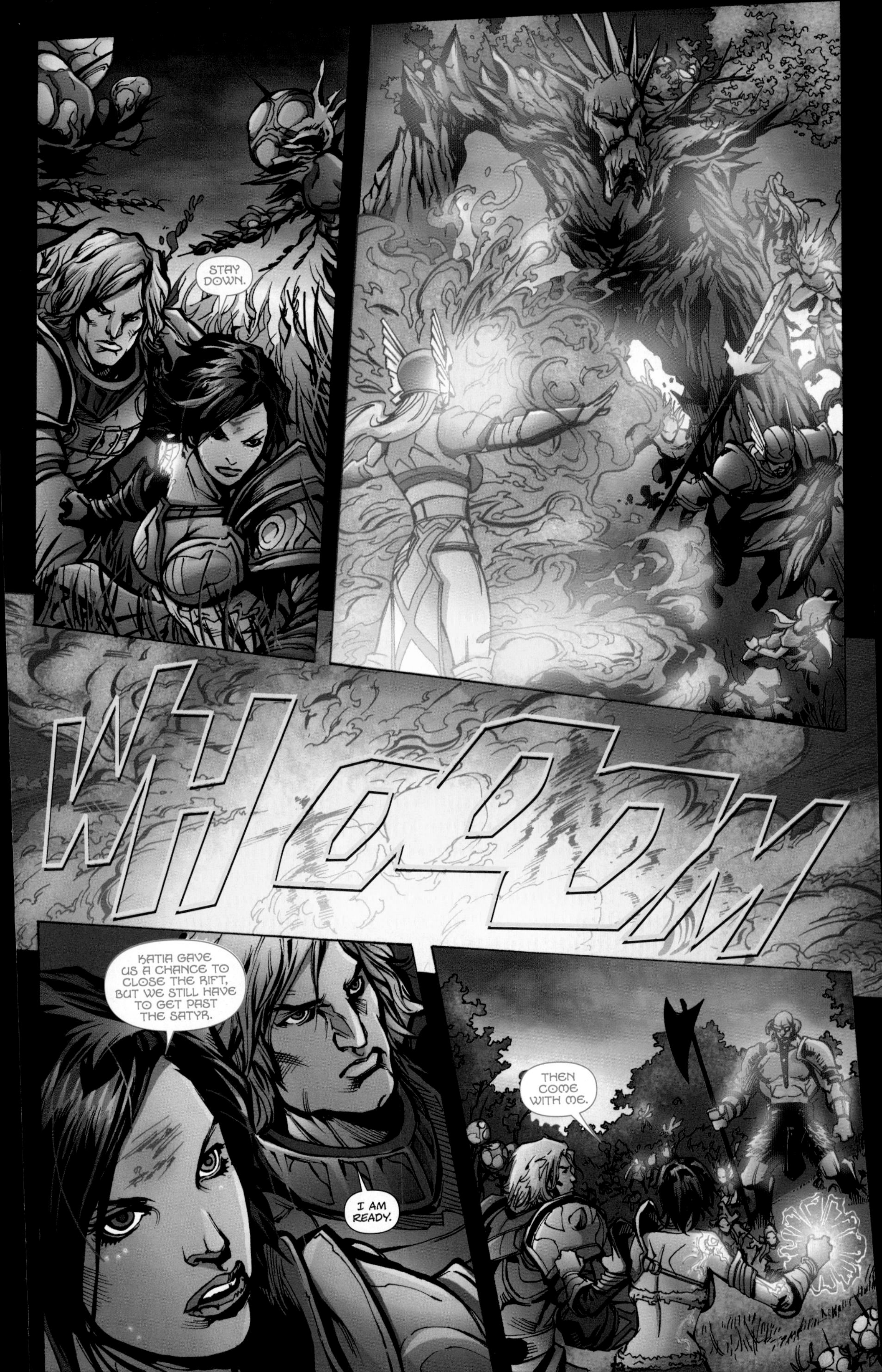
STAY DOWN.
WHOOM
KATIA GAVE US A CHANCE TO CLOSE THE RIFT, BUT WE STILL HAVE TO GET PAST THE SATYR.
I AM READY.
THEN COME WITH ME.

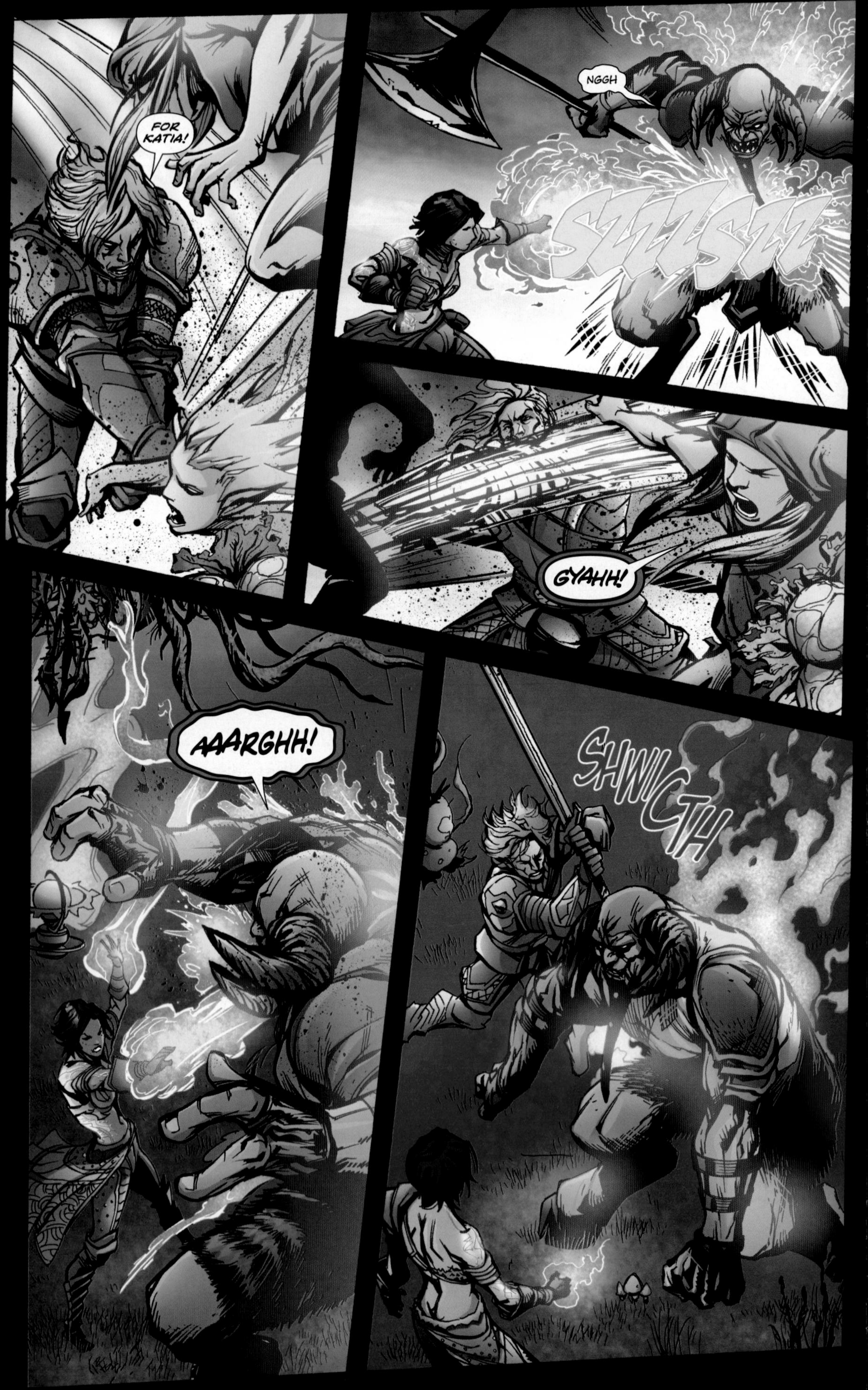
FOR KATIA!
NGGH
SZZZSZZZ
GYAHH!
AAARGHH!
SHWICTH

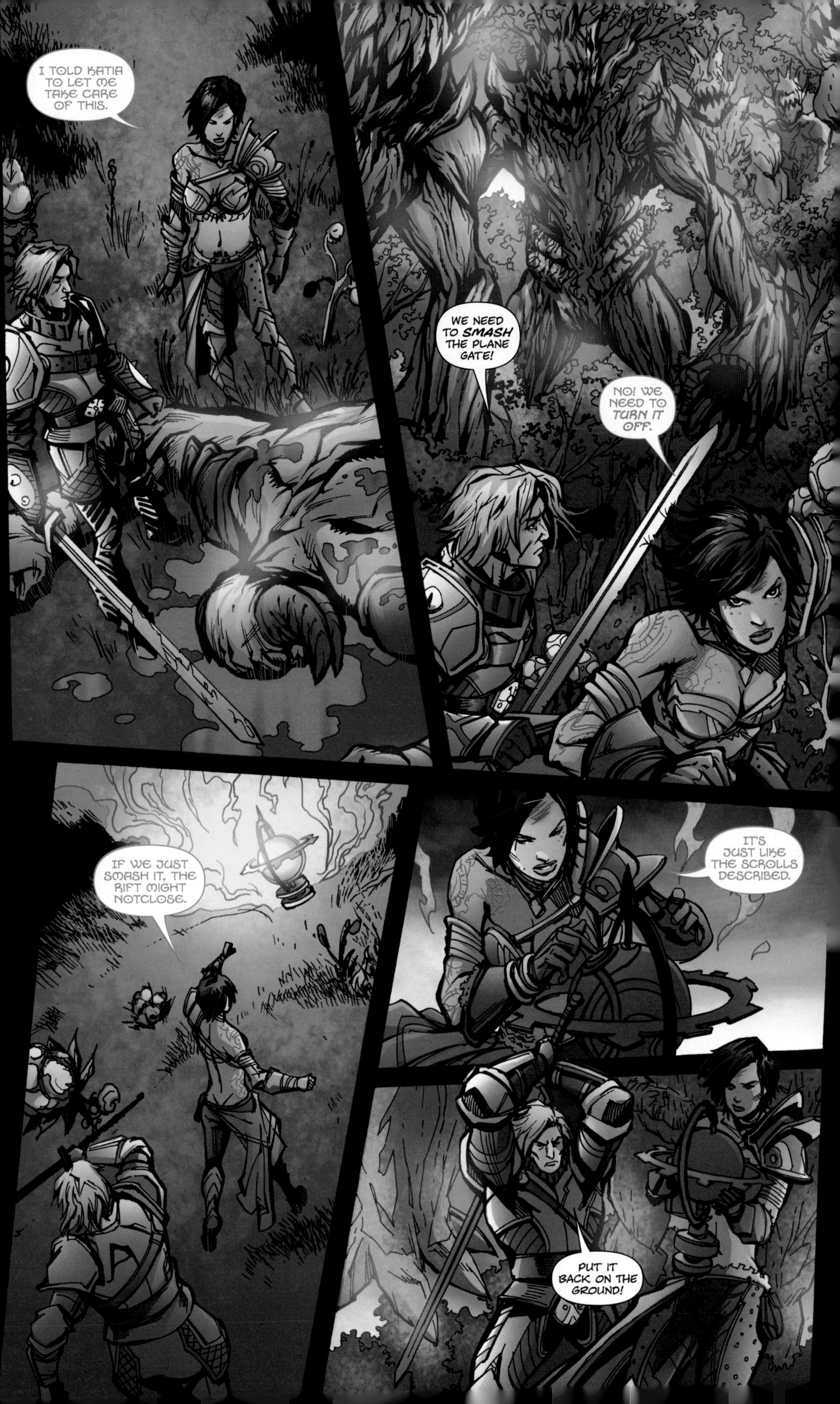
I TOLD KATIA TO LET ME TAKE CARE OF THIS.
WE NEED TO SMASH THE PLANE GATE!
NO! WE NEED TO TURN IT OFF.
IF WE JUST SMASH IT, THE RIFT MIGHT NOTCLOSE.
IT'S JUST LIKE THE SCROLLS DESCRIBED.
PUT IT BACK ON THE GROUND!

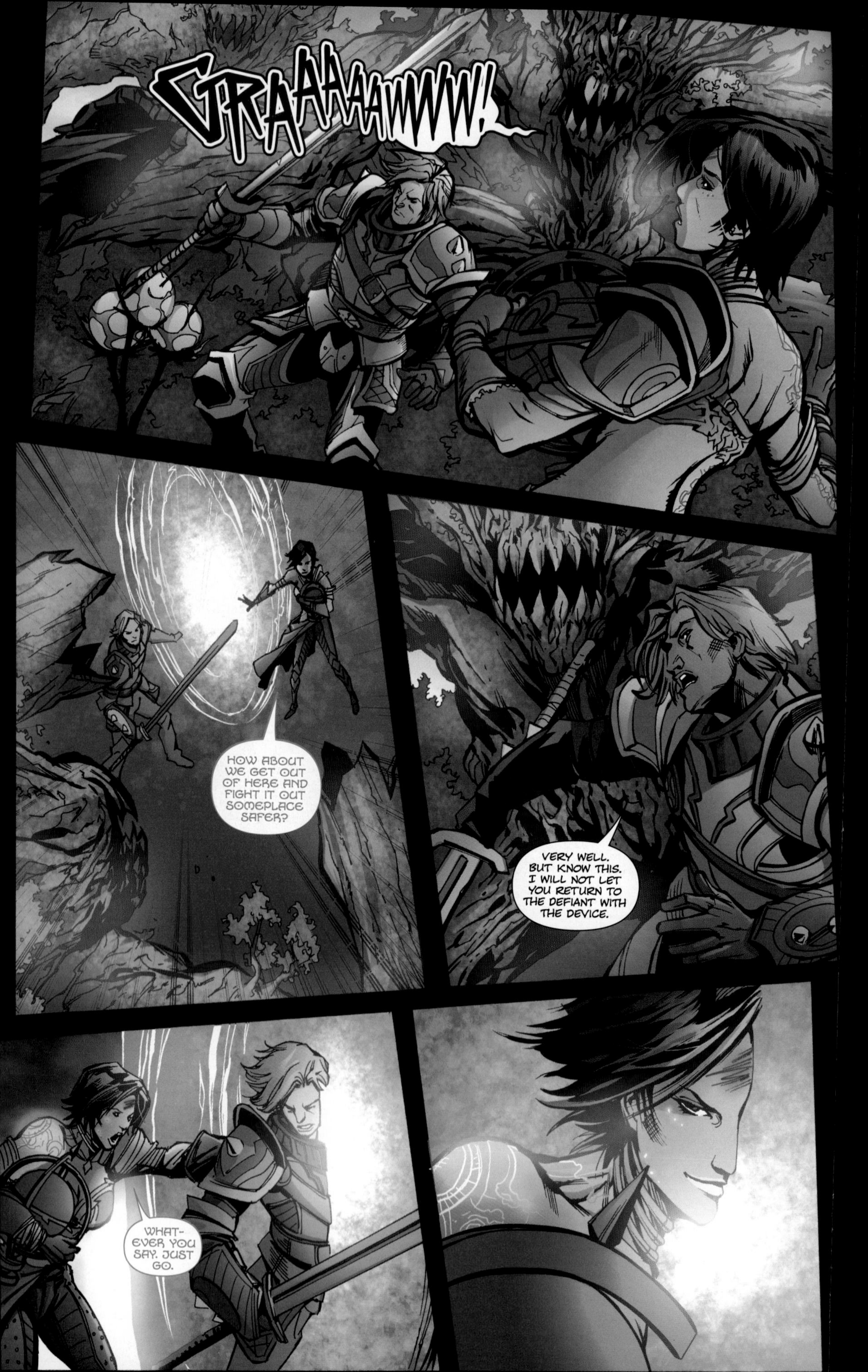
GRAAAAAWWW!
HOW ABOUT WE GET OUT OF HERE AND FIGHT IT OUT SOMEPLACE SAFER?
VERY WELL. BUT KNOW THIS. I WILL NOT LET YOU RETURN TO THE DEFIANT WITH THE DEVICE.
WHAT-EVER YOU SAY. JUST GO.

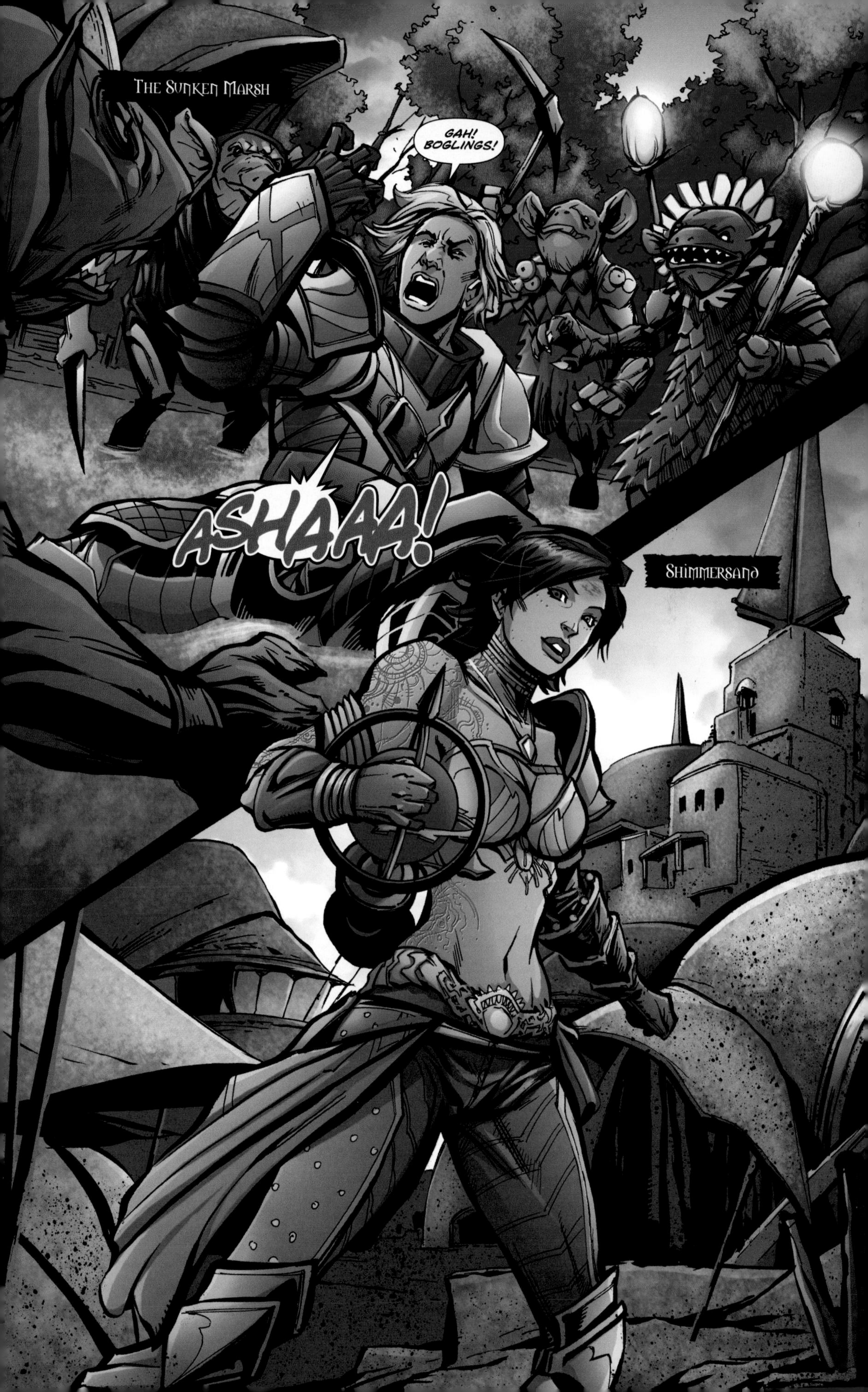
The Sunken Marsh
GAH! BOGLINGS!
ASHAAA!
Shimmersand

CHAPTER TWO

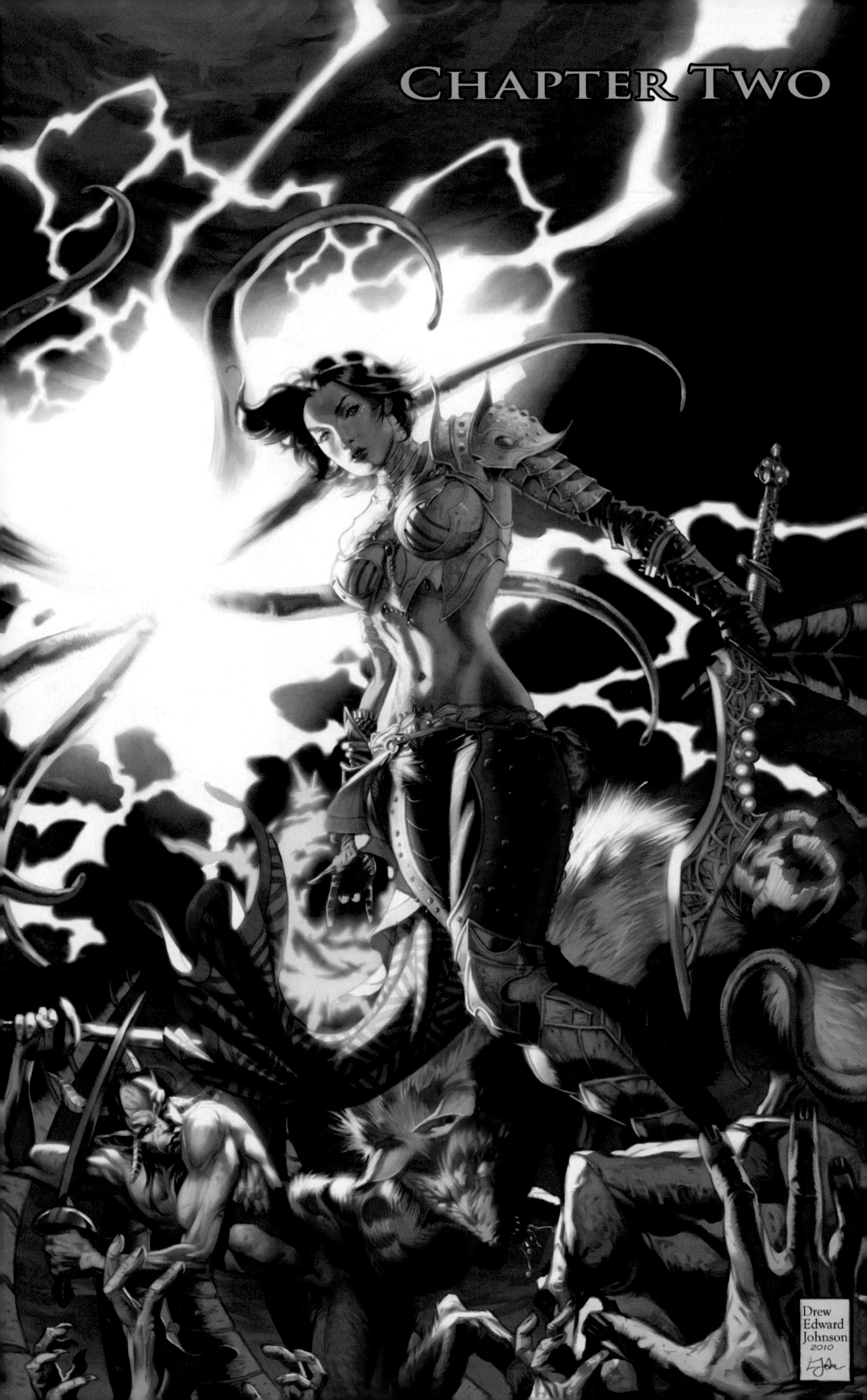
Drew
Edward
Johnson
2010

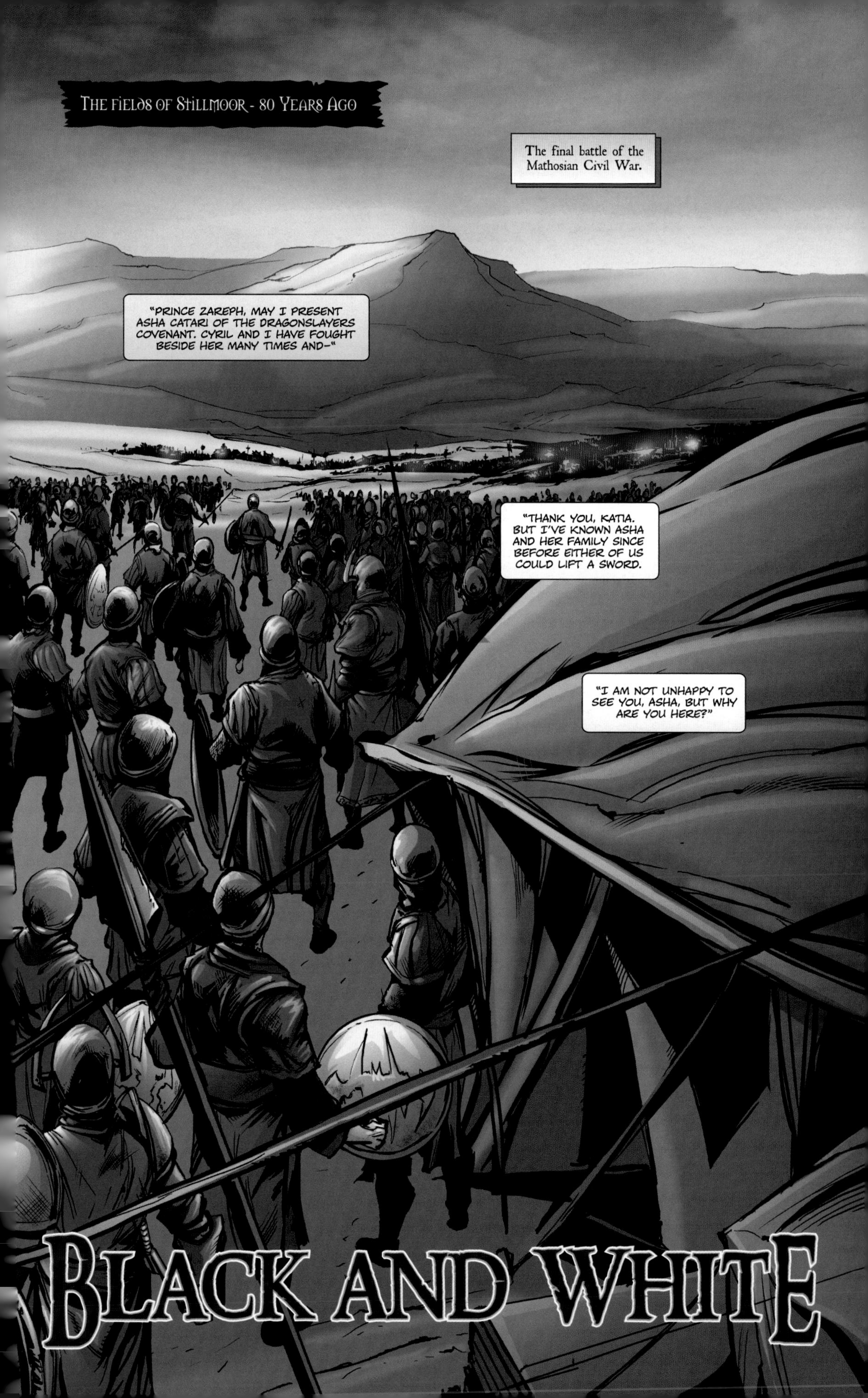
THE FIELDS OF STILLMOOR - 80 YEARS AGO
The final battle of the Mathosian Civil War.
"PRINCE ZAREPH, MAY I PRESENT ASHA CATARI OF THE DRAGONSLAYERS COVENANT. CYRIL AND I HAVE FOUGHT BESIDE HER MANY TIMES AND-"
"THANK YOU, KATIA. BUT I'VE KNOWN ASHA AND HER FAMILY SINCE BEFORE EITHER OF US COULD LIFT A SWORD.
"I AM NOT UNHAPPY TO SEE YOU, ASHA, BUT WHY ARE YOU HERE?"
BLACK AND WHITE

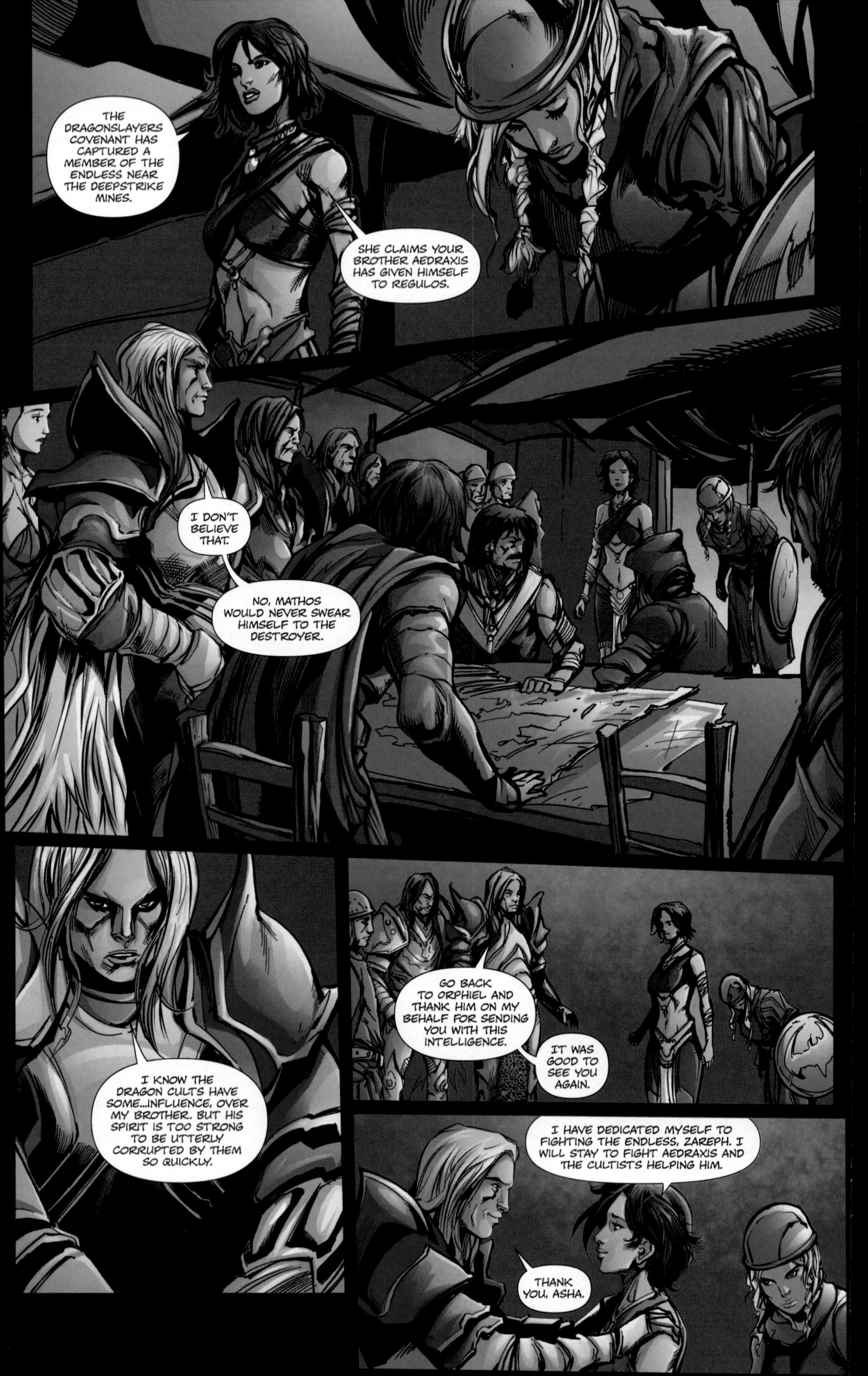
THE DRAGONSLAYERS COVENANT HAS CAPTURED A MEMBER OF THE ENDLESS NEAR THE DEEPSTRIKE MINES.
SHE CLAIMS YOUR BROTHER AEDRAXIS HAS GIVEN HIMSELF TO REGULOS.
I DON'T BELIEVE THAT.
NO, MATHOS WOULD NEVER SWEAR HIMSELF TO THE DESTROYER.
I KNOW THE DRAGON CULTS HAVE SOME...INFLUENCE, OVER MY BROTHER. BUT HIS SPIRIT IS TOO STRONG TO BE UTTERLY CORRUPTED BY THEM SO QUICKLY.
GO BACK TO ORPHIEL AND THANK HIM ON MY BEHALF FOR SENDING YOU WITH THIS INTELLIGENCE.
IT WAS GOOD TO SEE YOU AGAIN.
I HAVE DEDICATED MYSELF TO FIGHTING THE ENDLESS, ZAREPH. I WILL STAY TO FIGHT AEDRAXIS AND THE CULTISTS HELPING HIM.
THANK YOU, ASHA.

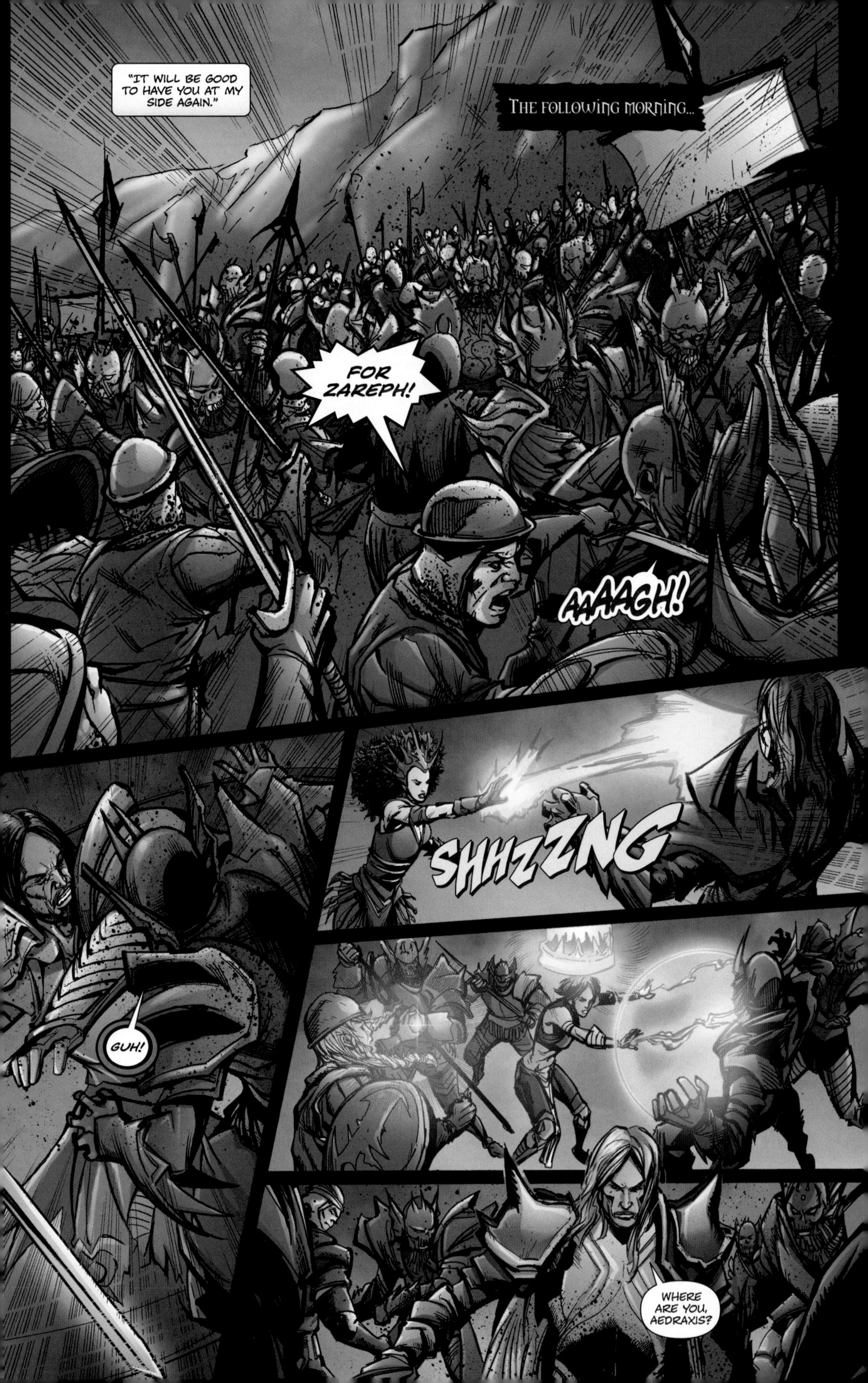
"IT WILL BE GOOD TO HAVE YOU AT MY SIDE AGAIN."
THE FOLLOWING MORNING...
FOR ZAREPH!
AAAAGH!
GUH!
SHHZZNG
WHERE ARE YOU, AEDRAXIS?

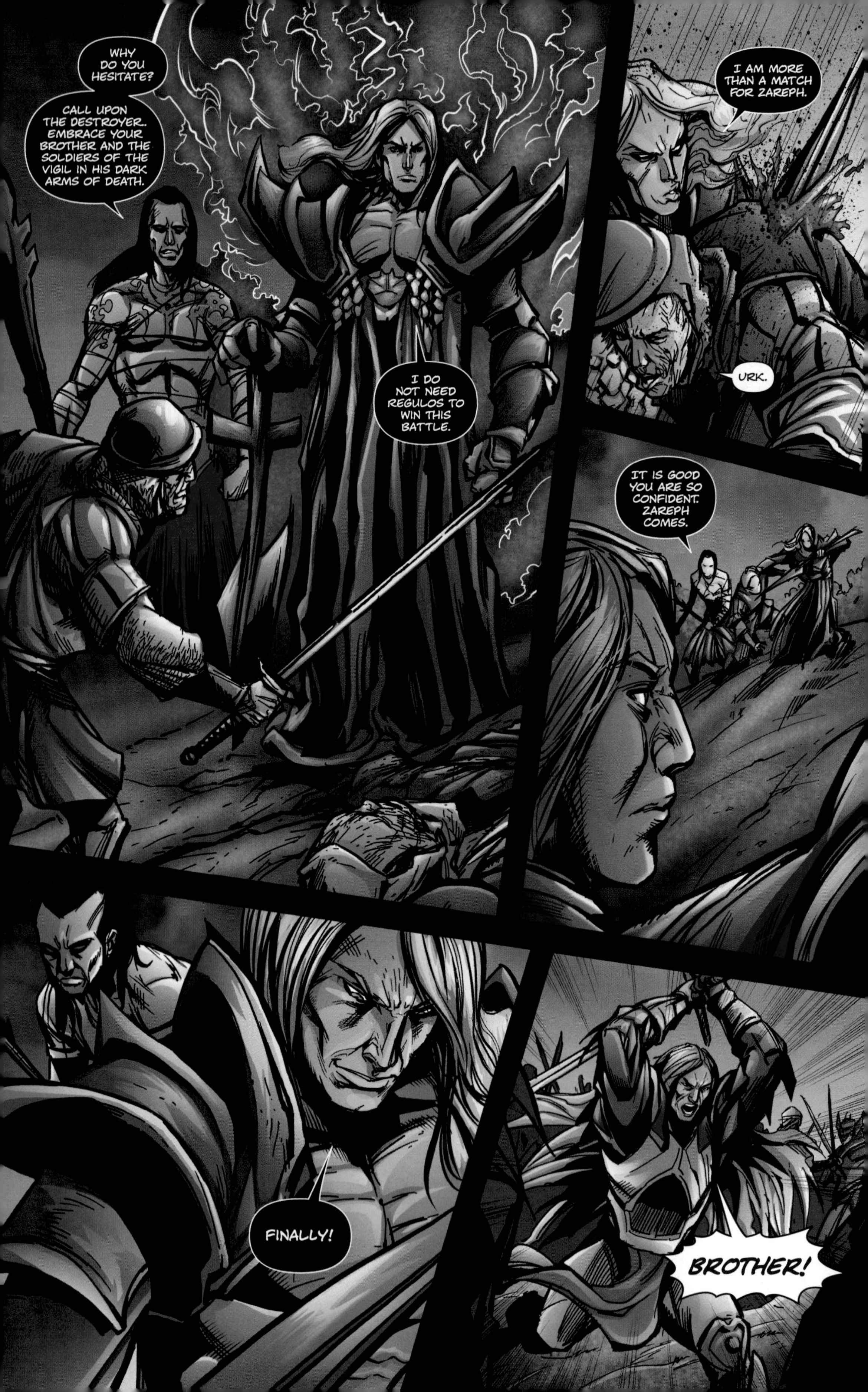
WHY DO YOU HESITATE?
CALL UPON THE DESTROYER. EMBRACE YOUR BROTHER AND THE SOLDIERS OF THE VIGIL IN HIS DARK ARMS OF DEATH.
I DO NOT NEED REGULOS TO WIN THIS BATTLE.
I AM MORE THAN A MATCH FOR ZAREPH.
URK.
IT IS GOOD YOU ARE SO CONFIDENT. ZAREPH COMES.
FINALLY!
BROTHER!

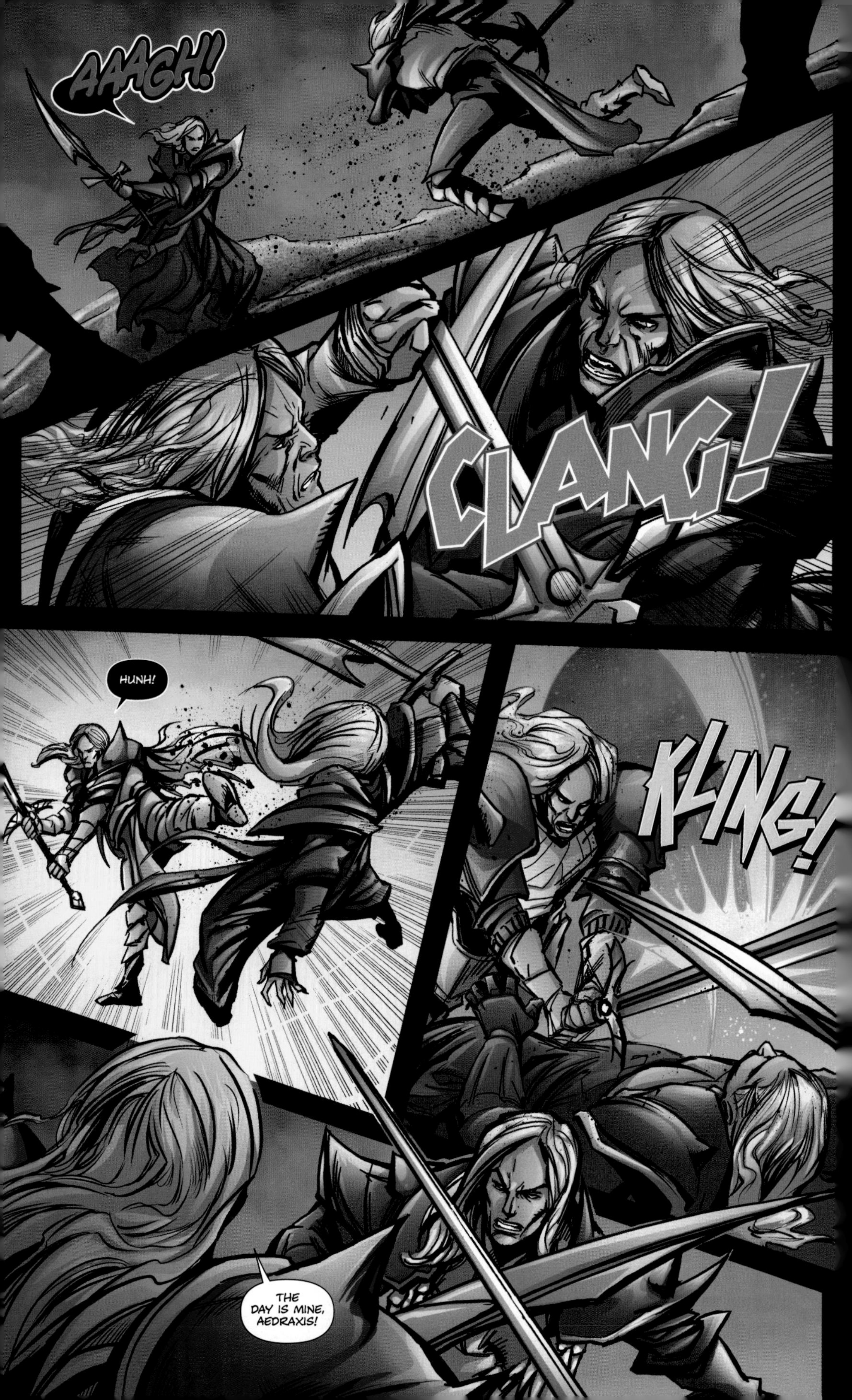
AAAGH!
CLANG!
HUNH!
KLING!
THE DAY IS MINE, AEDRAXIS!

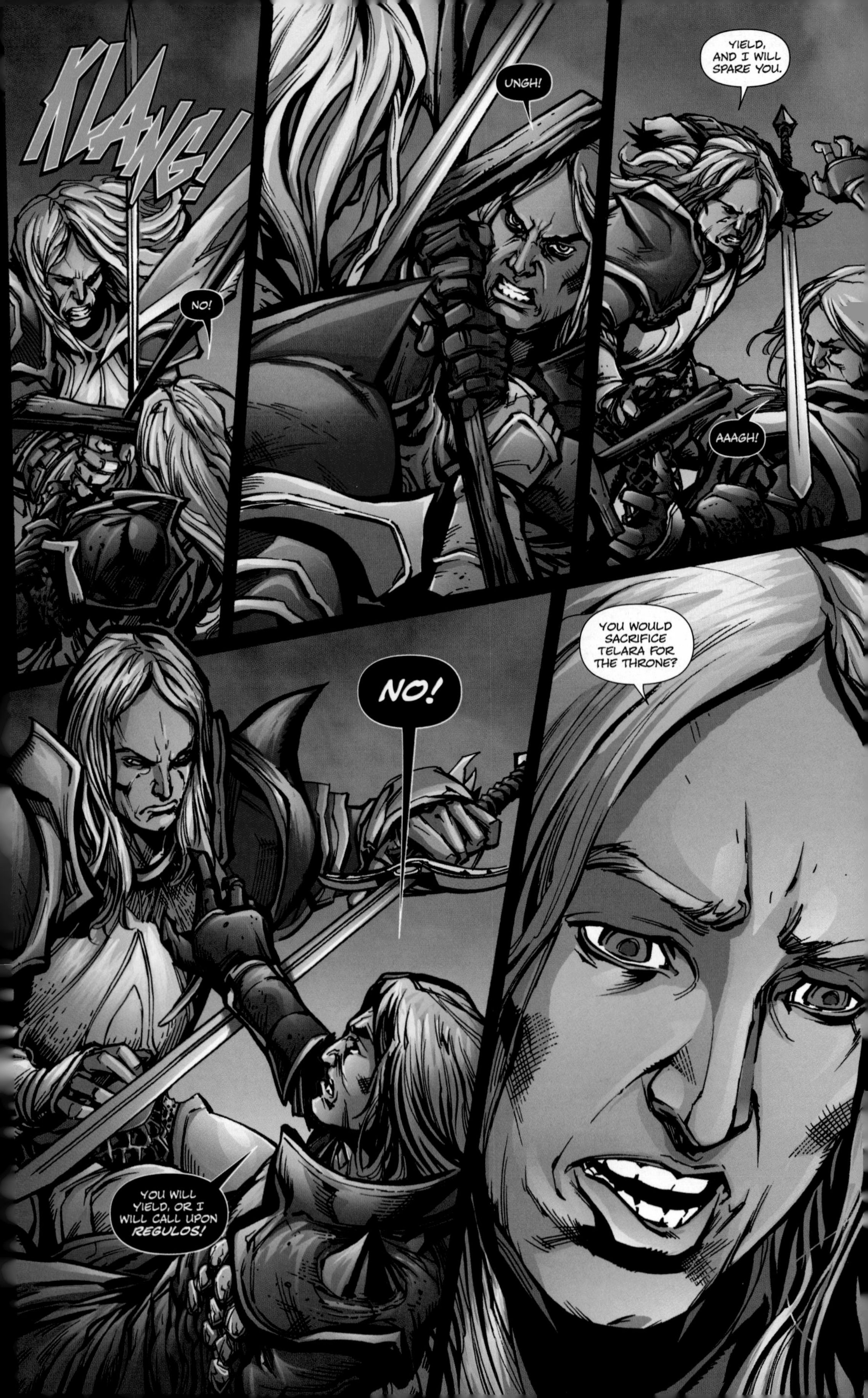
KLANG!
NO!
UNGH!
YIELD, AND I WILL SPARE YOU.
AAAGH!
NO!
YOU WILL YIELD, OR I WILL CALL UPON REGULOS!
YOU WOULD SACRIFICE TELARA FOR THE THRONE?

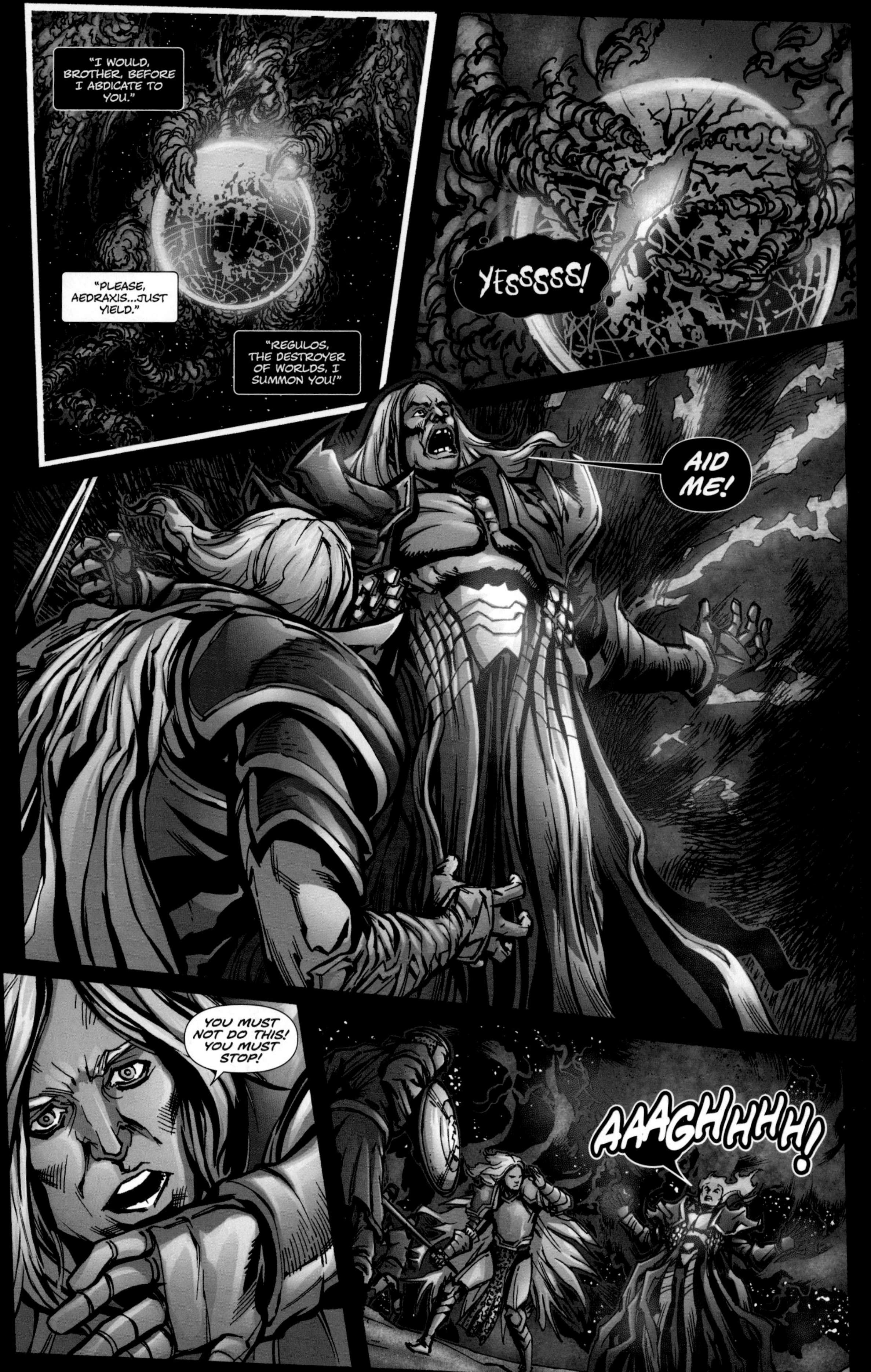
"I WOULD, BROTHER, BEFORE I ABDICATE TO YOU."
"PLEASE, AEDRAXIS...JUST YIELD."
"REGULOS, THE DESTROYER OF WORLDS, I SUMMON YOU!"
YESSSSS!
AID ME!
YOU MUST NOT DO THIS! YOU MUST STOP!
AAAGHHHH!

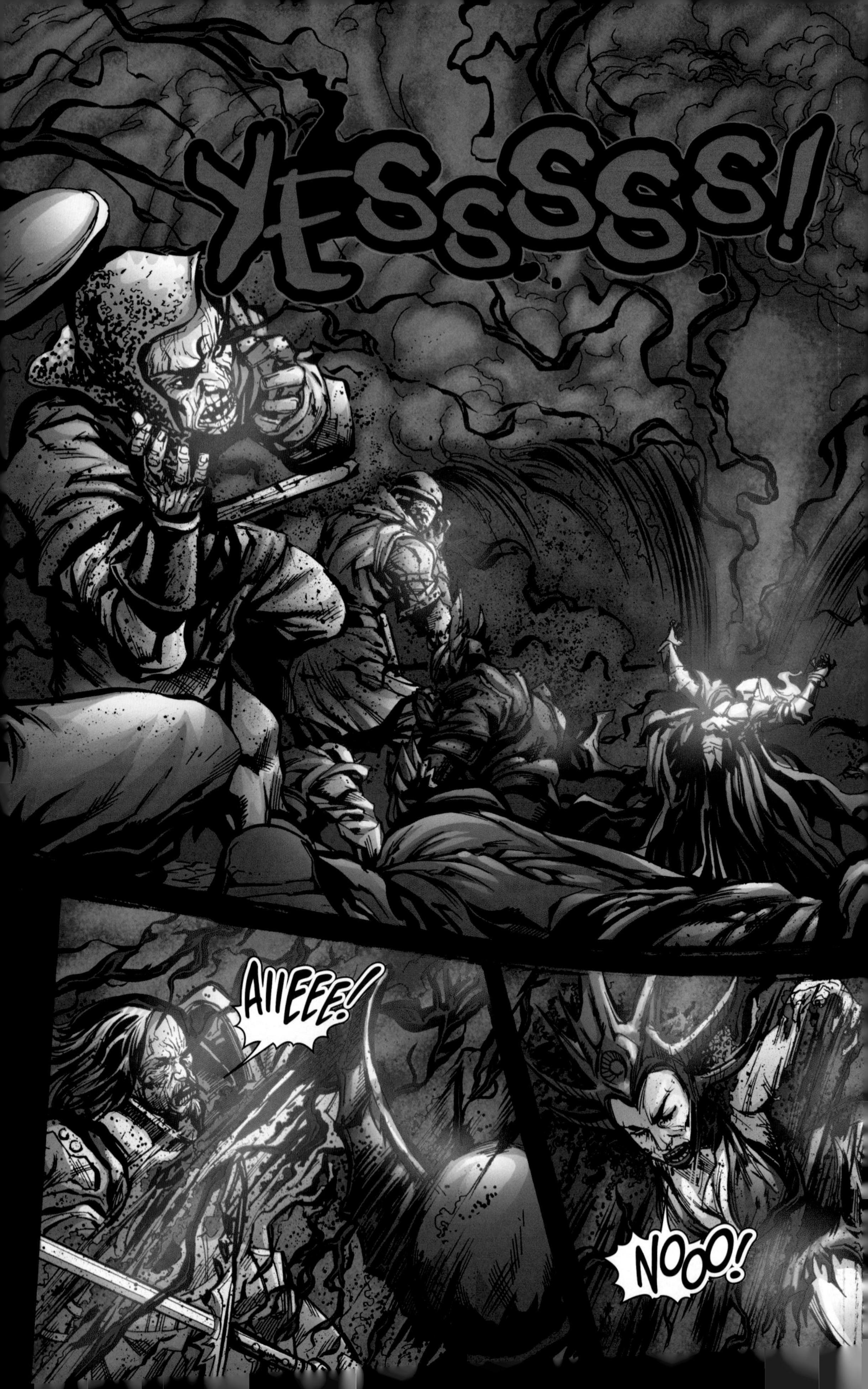
YESSSSS!
AIIEEE!
NOOO!

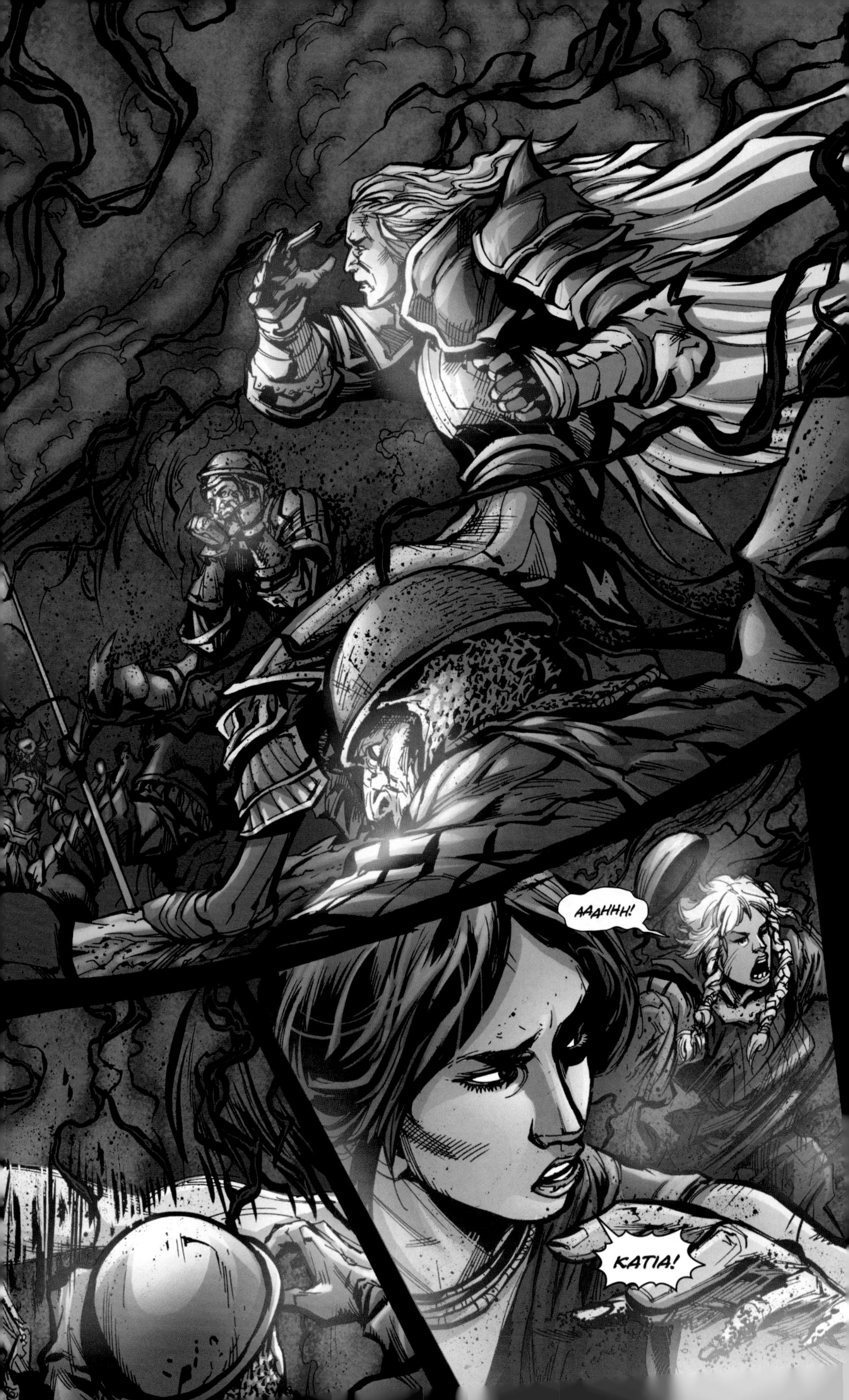
AADHHH!
KATIA!

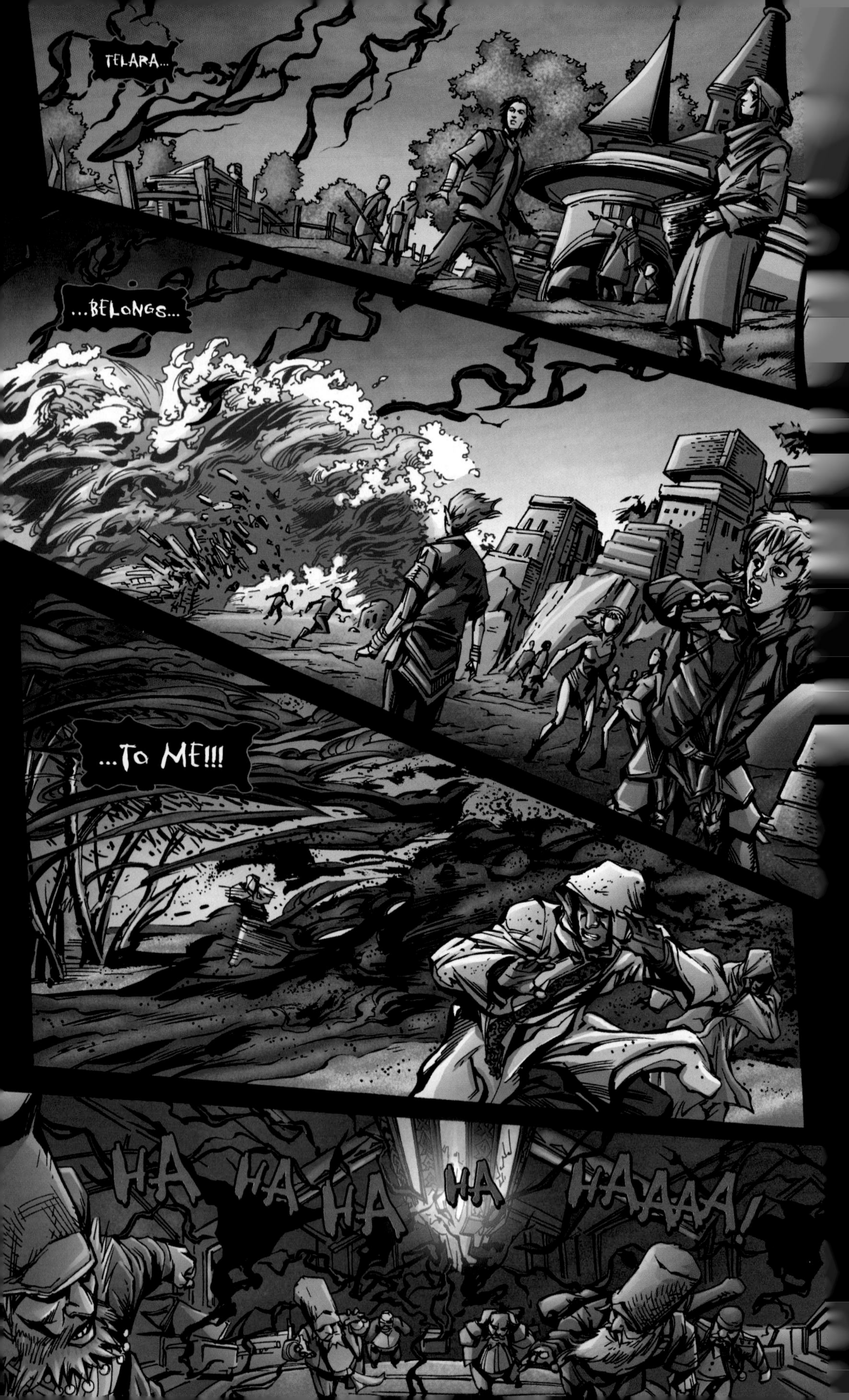
TELARA...
...BELONGS...
...TO ME!!!
HA HA HA HA HAAAA!

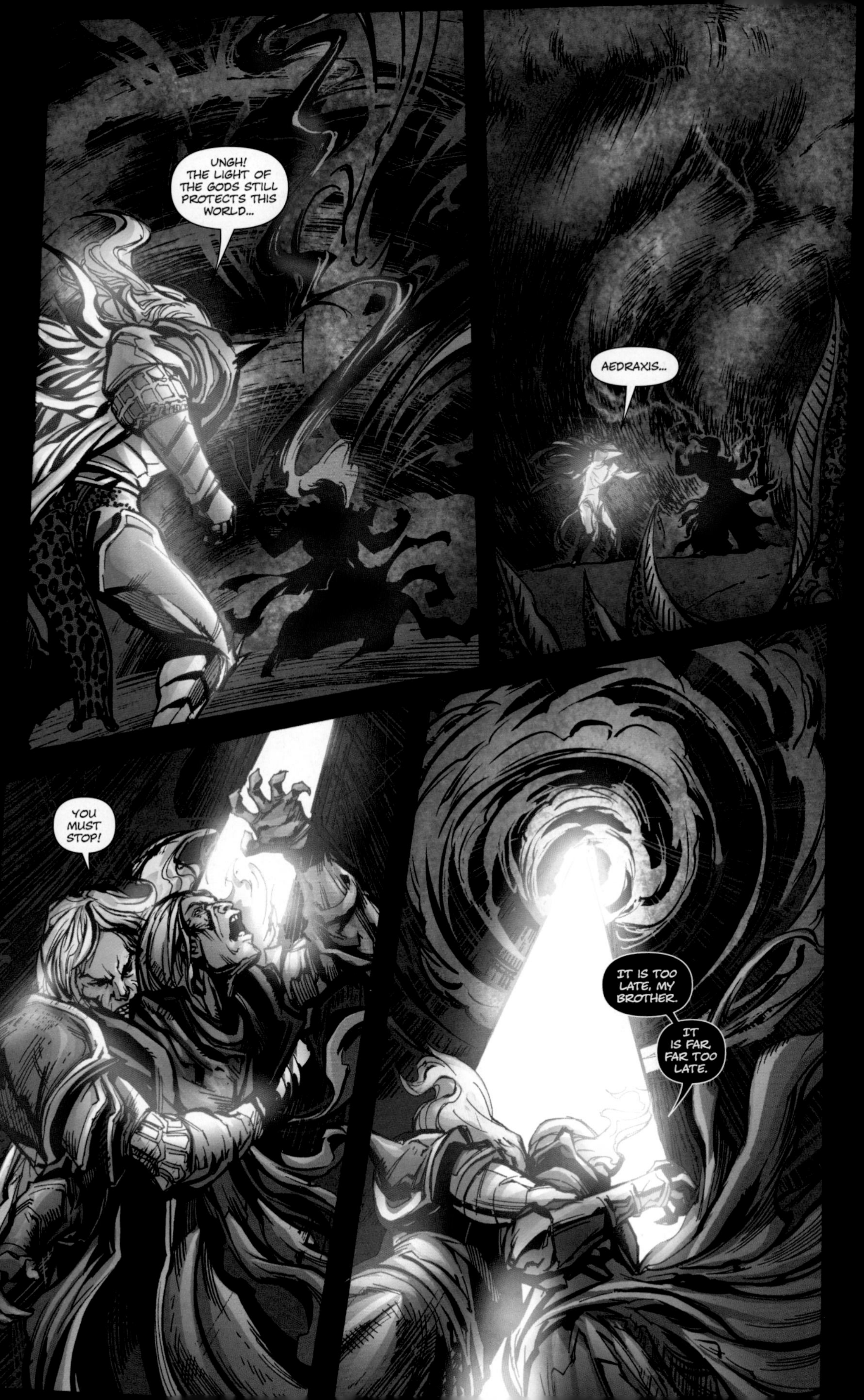
UNGH! THE LIGHT OF THE GODS STILL PROTECTS THIS WORLD...
AEDRAXIS...
YOU MUST STOP!
IT IS TOO LATE, MY BROTHER.
IT IS FAR FAR TOO LATE.

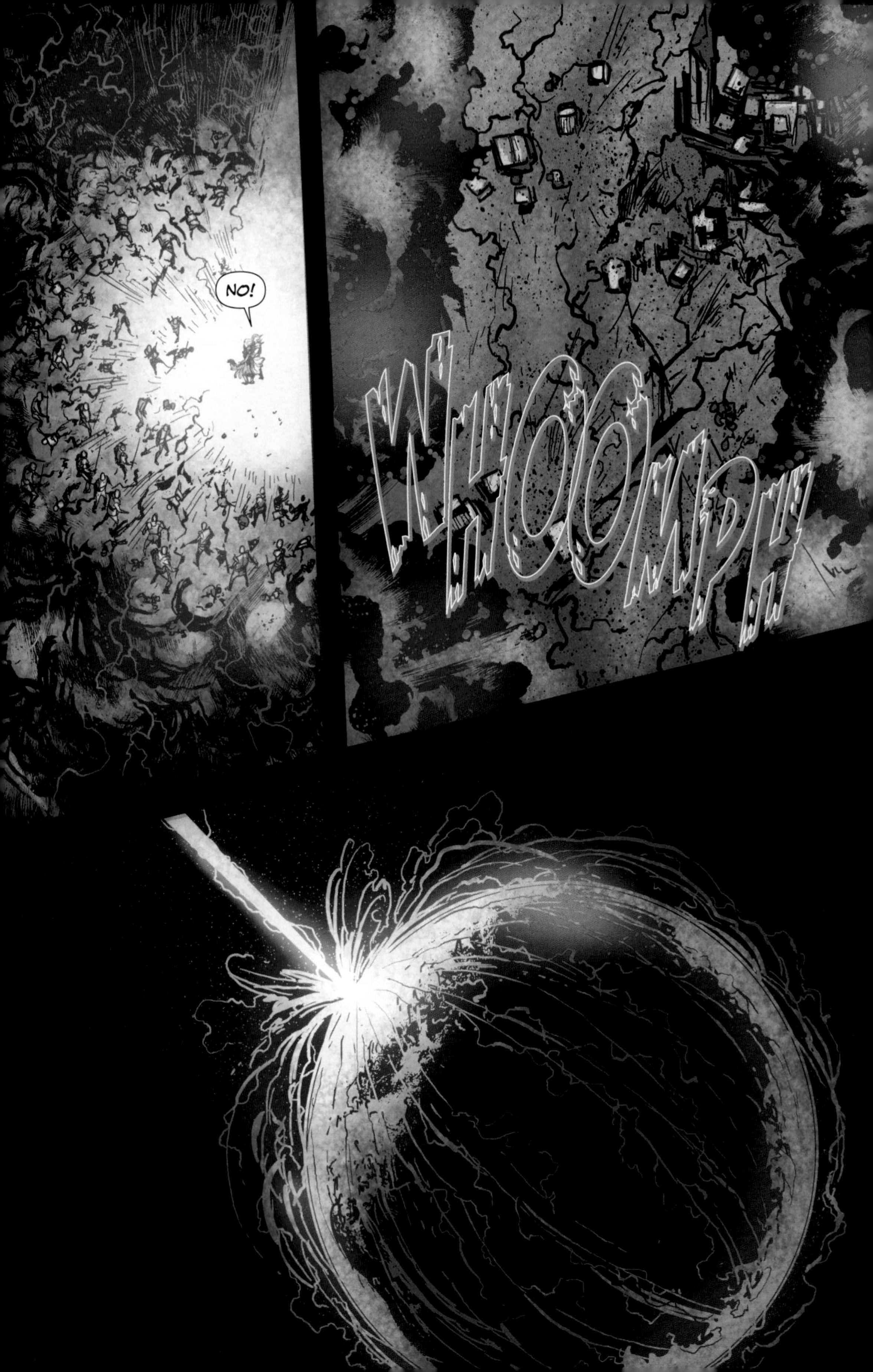
NO!
WHOOMPH

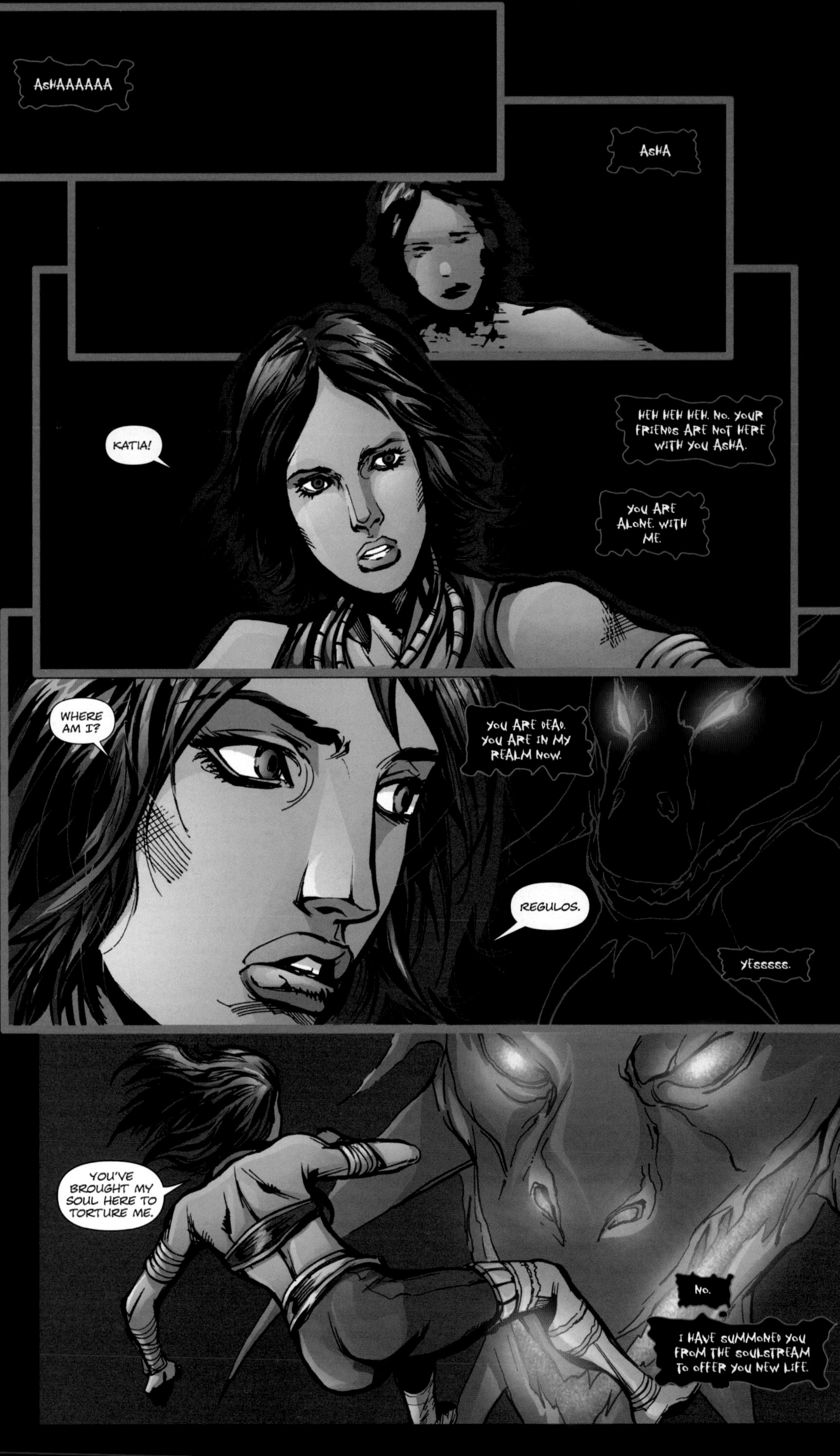
AsHAAAAAA
AsHA
KATIA!
HEH HEH HEH. No. YOUR FRIENDS ARE NOT HERE WITH YOU AsHA.
YOU ARE ALONE. WITH ME.
WHERE AM I?
YOU ARE DEAD. YOU ARE IN MY REALM NOW.
REGULOS.
YESSSSS.
YOU'VE BROUGHT MY SOUL HERE TO TORTURE ME.
No.
I HAVE SUMMONED YOU FROM THE SOULSTREAM TO OFFER YOU NEW LIFE.

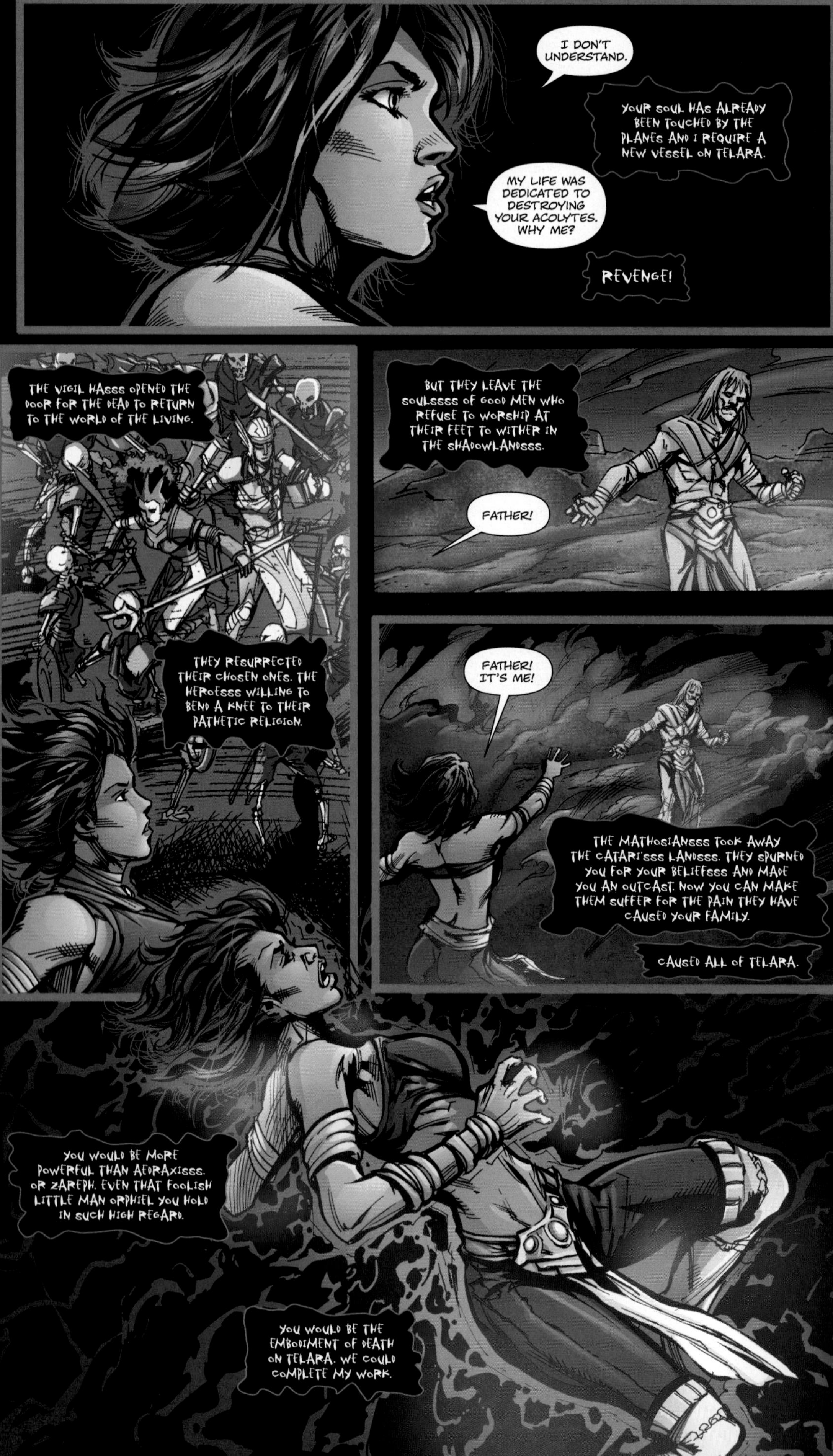
I DON'T UNDERSTAND.
YOUR SOUL HAS ALREADY BEEN TOUCHED BY THE PLANES AND I REQUIRE A NEW VESSEL ON TELARA.
MY LIFE WAS DEDICATED TO DESTROYING YOUR ACOLYTES. WHY ME?
REVENGE!
THE VIGIL HASSS OPENED THE DOOR FOR THE DEAD TO RETURN TO THE WORLD OF THE LIVING.
THEY RESURRECTED THEIR CHOSEN ONES. THE HEROESSS WILLING TO BEND A KNEE TO THEIR PATHETIC RELIGION.
BUT THEY LEAVE THE SOULSSSS OF GOOD MEN WHO REFUSE TO WORSHIP AT THEIR FEET TO WITHER IN THE SHADOWLANDSSS.
FATHER!
FATHER! IT'S ME!
THE MATHOSIANSSS TOOK AWAY THE CATARI'SSS LANDSSS. THEY SPURNED YOU FOR YOUR BELIEFSSS AND MADE YOU AN OUTCAST. NOW YOU CAN MAKE THEM SUFFER FOR THE PAIN THEY HAVE CAUSED YOUR FAMILY.
CAUSED ALL OF TELARA.
YOU WOULD BE MORE POWERFUL THAN AEDRAXISSS. OR ZAREPH. EVEN THAT FOOLISH LITTLE MAN ORPHIEL YOU HOLD IN SUCH HIGH REGARD.
YOU WOULD BE THE EMBODIMENT OF DEATH ON TELARA. WE COULD COMPLETE MY WORK.

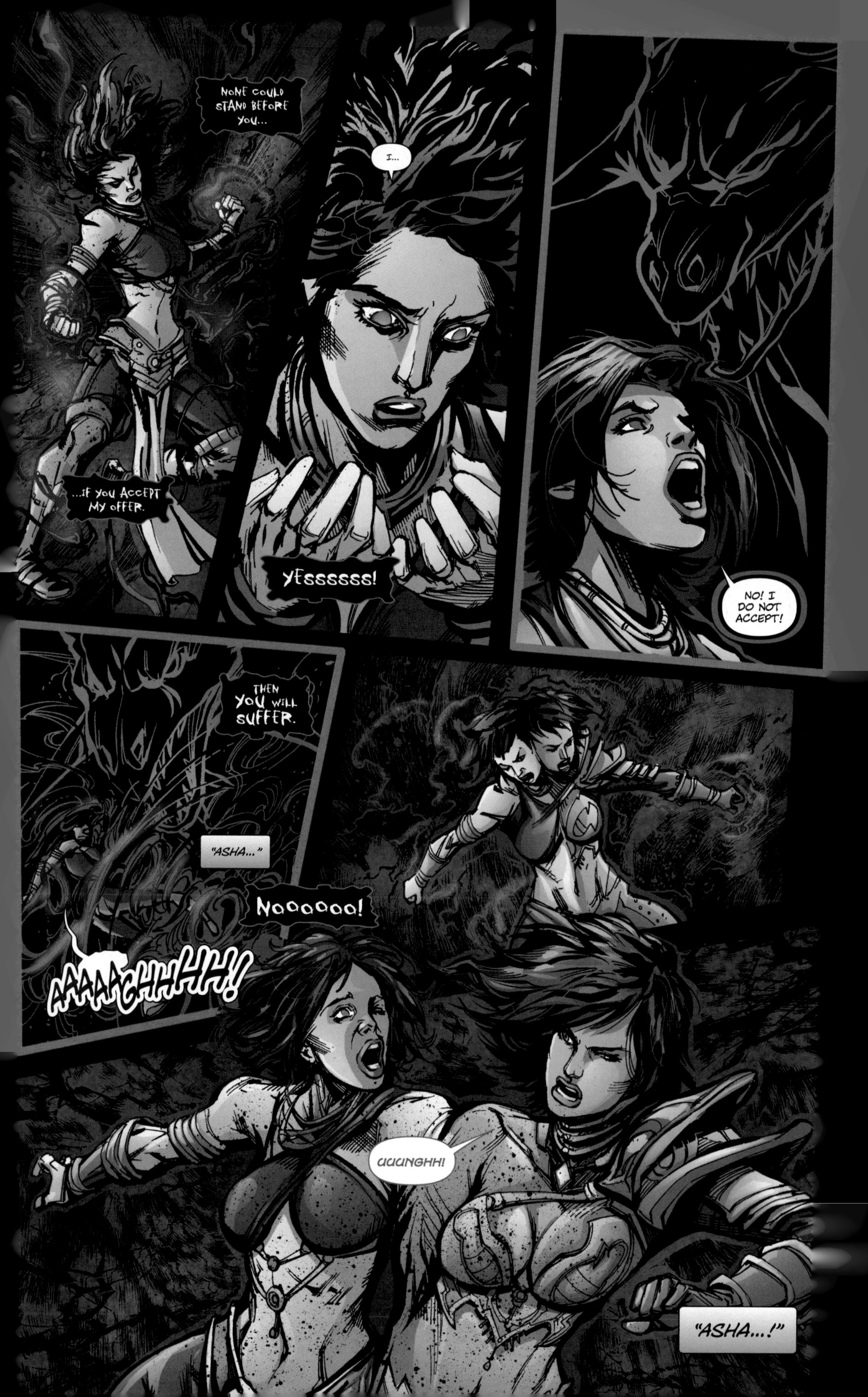
NONE COULD STAND BEFORE YOU...
...IF YOU ACCEPT MY OFFER.
I...
YESSSSSS!
NO! I DO NOT ACCEPT!
THEN YOU WILL SUFFER.
"ASHA..."
AAAAACHHHHH!
Nooooooo!
UUUNGHH!
"ASHA...!"

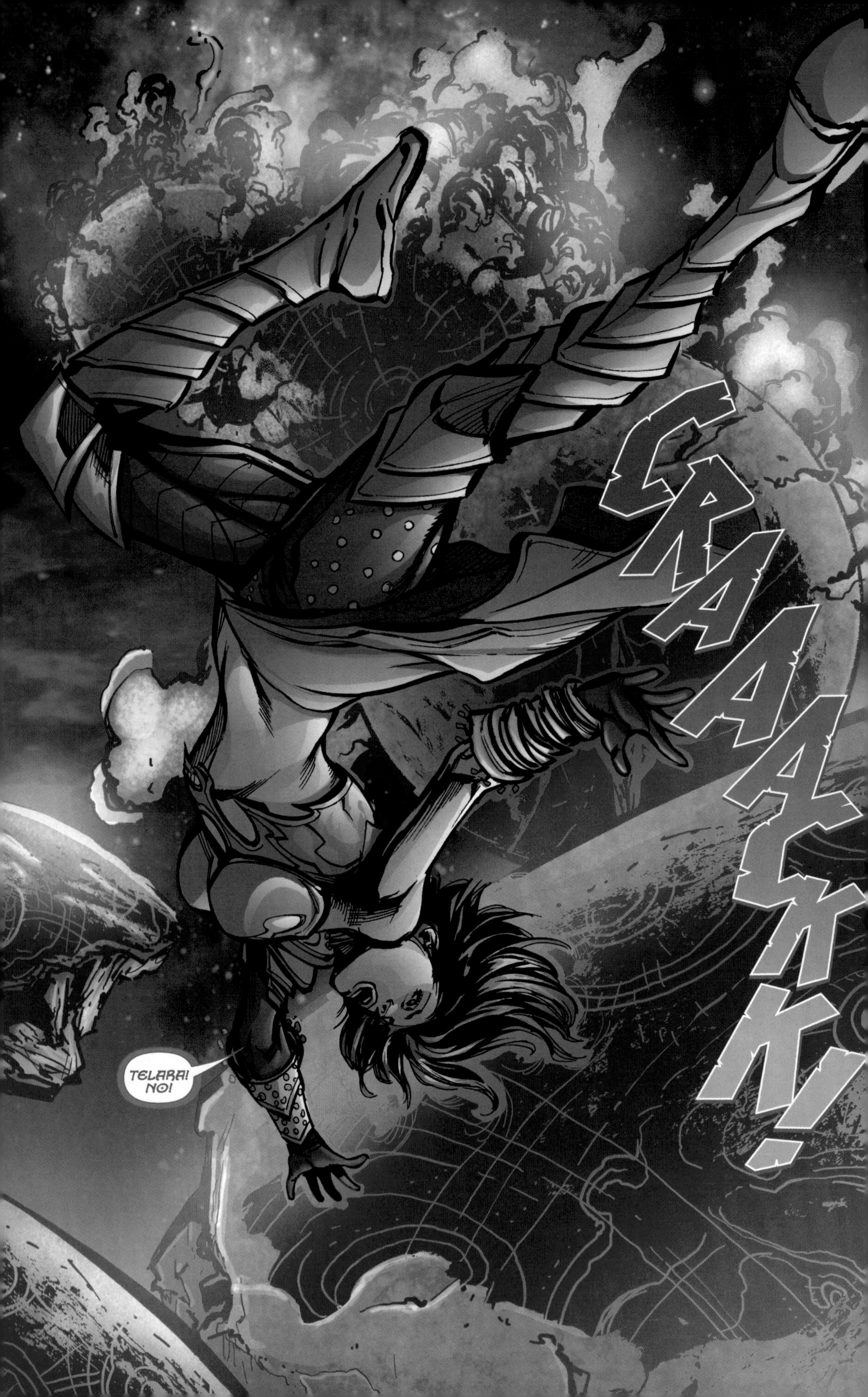
TELARA! NO!
CRAAACKK!

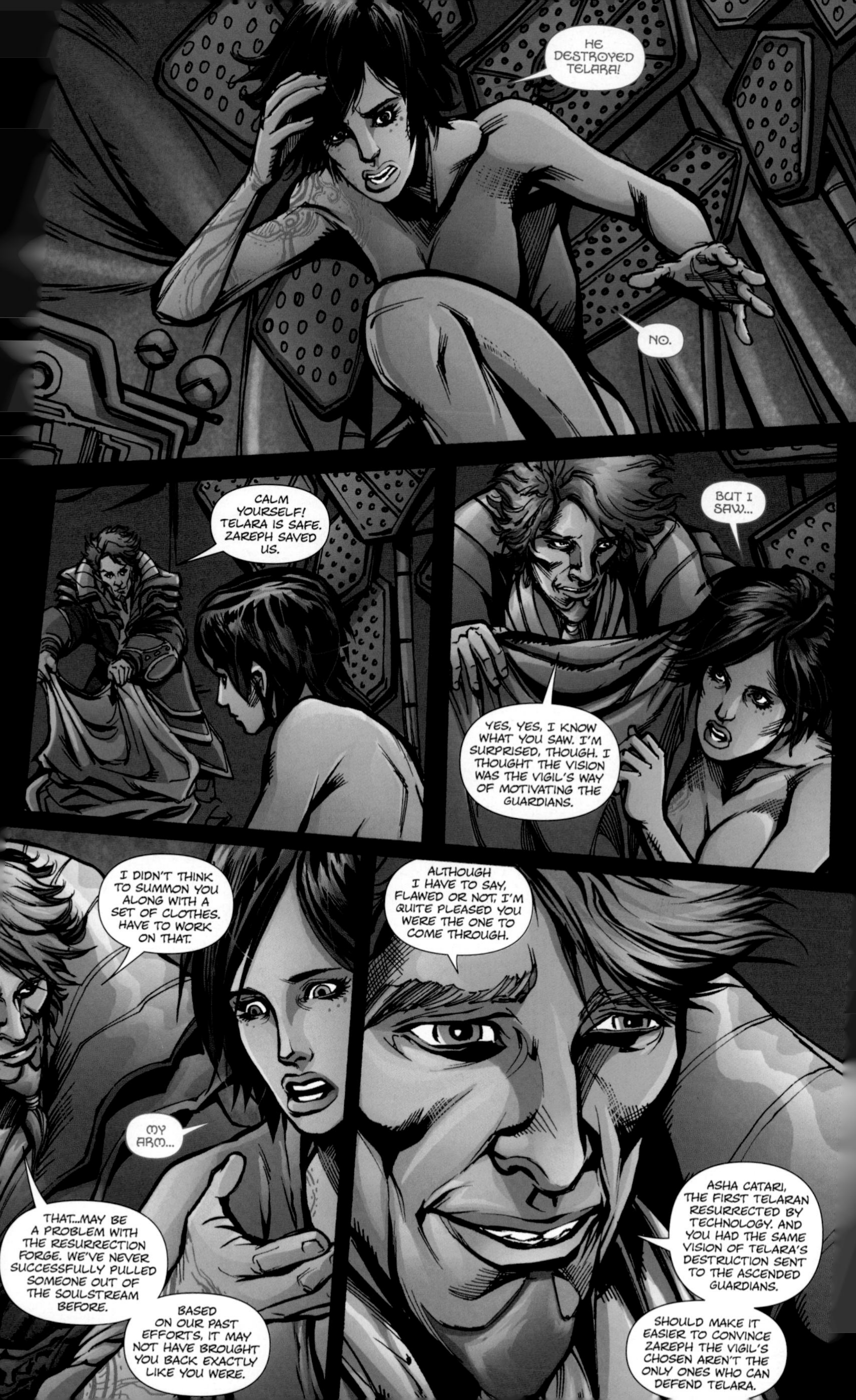
HE DESTROYED TELARA!
NO.
CALM YOURSELF! TELARA IS SAFE. ZAREPH SAVED US.
BUT I SAW...
YES, YES, I KNOW WHAT YOU SAW. I'M SURPRISED, THOUGH. I THOUGHT THE VISION WAS THE VIGIL'S WAY OF MOTIVATING THE GUARDIANS.
I DIDN'T THINK TO SUMMON YOU ALONG WITH A SET OF CLOTHES. HAVE TO WORK ON THAT.
MY ARM...
THAT...MAY BE A PROBLEM WITH THE RESURRECTION FORGE. WE'VE NEVER SUCCESSFULLY PULLED SOMEONE OUT OF THE SOULSTREAM BEFORE.
BASED ON OUR PAST EFFORTS, IT MAY NOT HAVE BROUGHT YOU BACK EXACTLY LIKE YOU WERE.
ALTHOUGH I HAVE TO SAY, FLAWED OR NOT, I'M QUITE PLEASED YOU WERE THE ONE TO COME THROUGH.
ASHA CATARI, THE FIRST TELARAN RESURRECTED BY TECHNOLOGY. AND YOU HAD THE SAME VISION OF TELARA'S DESTRUCTION SENT TO THE ASCENDED GUARDIANS.
SHOULD MAKE IT EASIER TO CONVINCE ZAREPH THE VIGIL'S CHOSEN AREN'T THE ONLY ONES WHO CAN DEFEND TELARA.

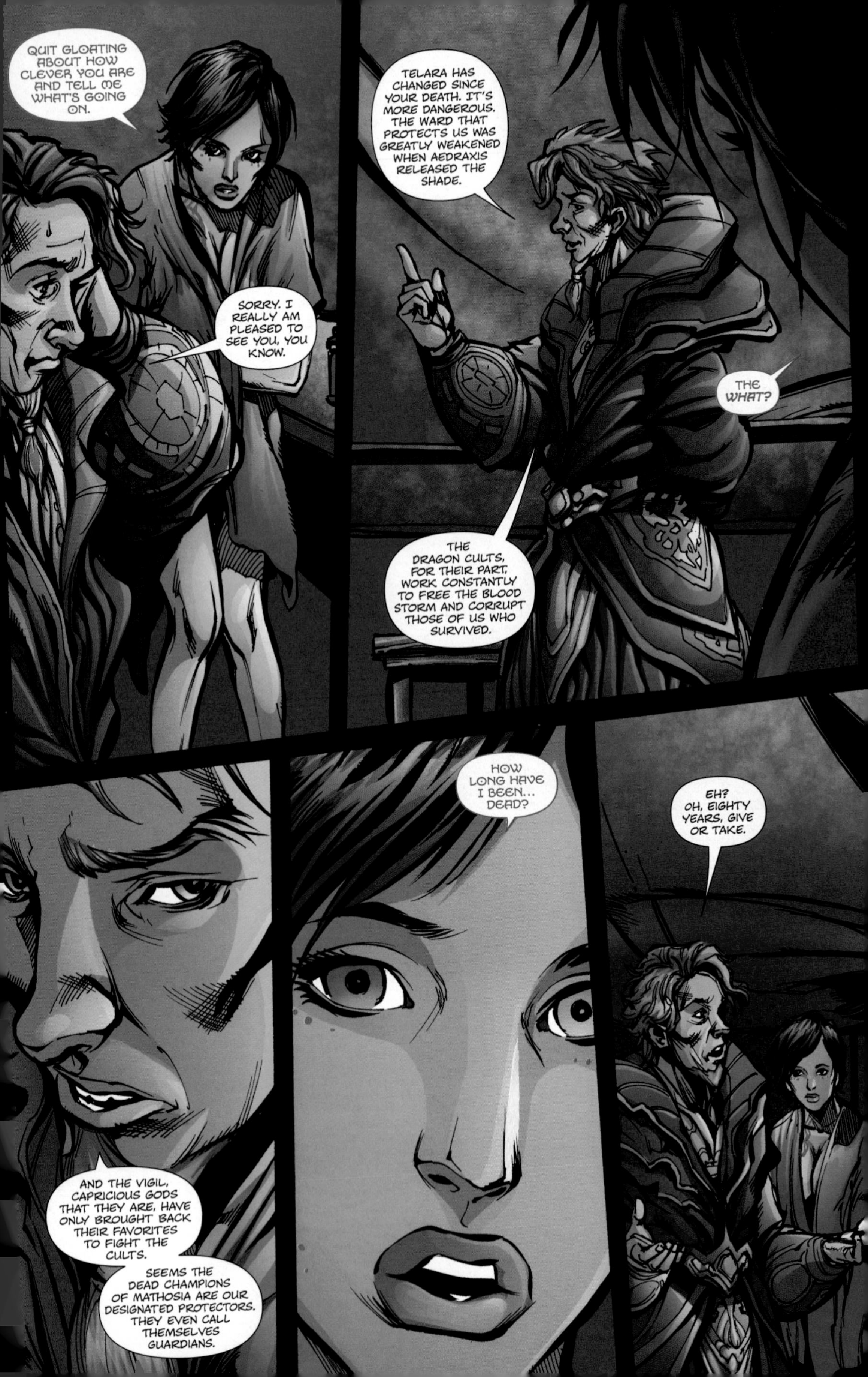
QUIT GLOATING ABOUT HOW CLEVER YOU ARE AND TELL ME WHAT'S GOING ON.
SORRY. I REALLY AM PLEASED TO SEE YOU, YOU KNOW.
TELARA HAS CHANGED SINCE YOUR DEATH. IT'S MORE DANGEROUS. THE WARD THAT PROTECTS US WAS GREATLY WEAKENED WHEN AEDRAXIS RELEASED THE SHADE.
THE WHAT?
THE DRAGON CULTS, FOR THEIR PART, WORK CONSTANTLY TO FREE THE BLOOD STORM AND CORRUPT THOSE OF US WHO SURVIVED.
AND THE VIGIL, CAPRICIOUS GODS THAT THEY ARE, HAVE ONLY BROUGHT BACK THEIR FAVORITES TO FIGHT THE CULTS.
SEEMS THE DEAD CHAMPIONS OF MATHOSIA ARE OUR DESIGNATED PROTECTORS. THEY EVEN CALL THEMSELVES GUARDIANS.
HOW LONG HAVE I BEEN... DEAD?
EH? OH, EIGHTY YEARS, GIVE OR TAKE.

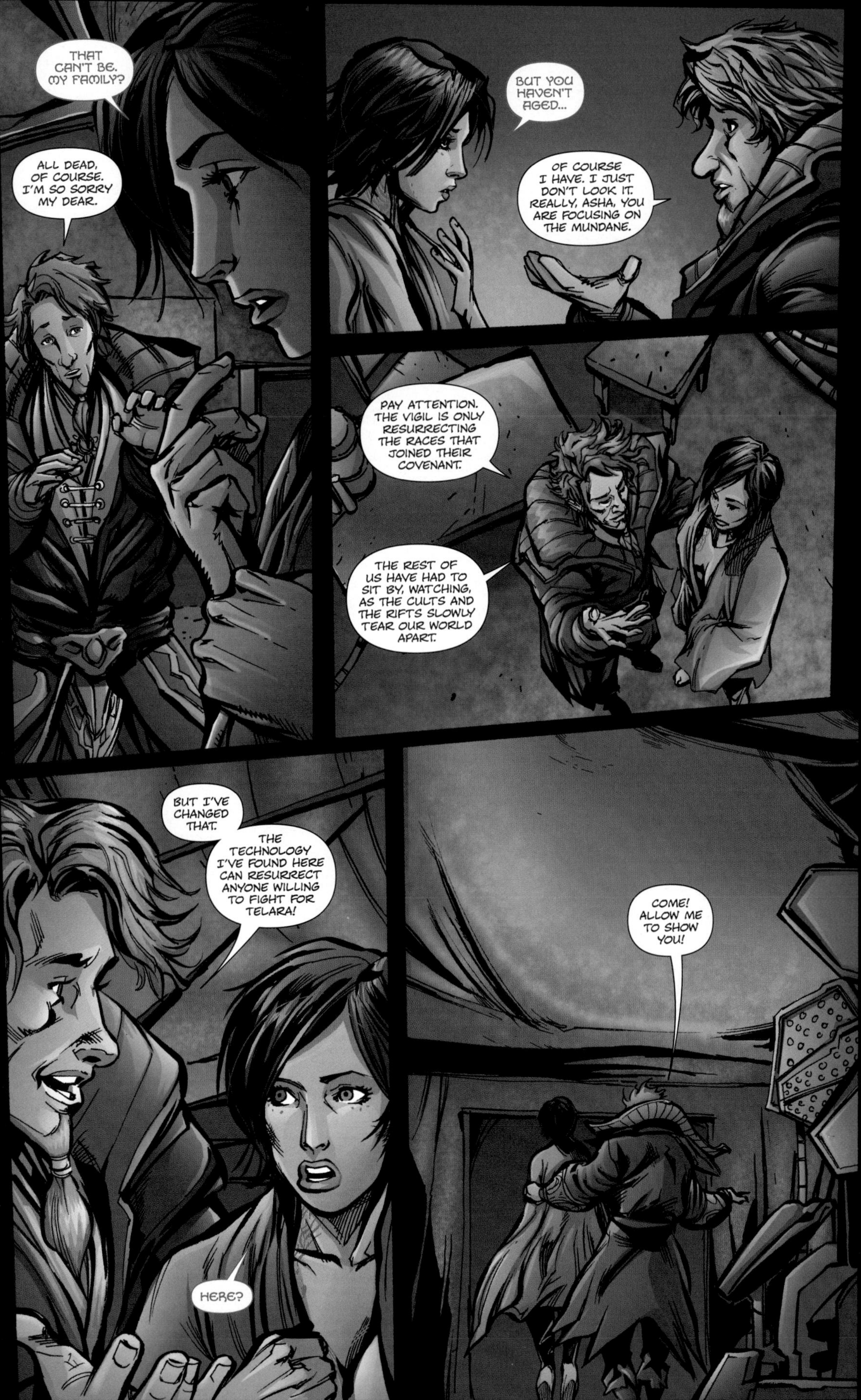
THAT CAN'T BE. MY FAMILY?
ALL DEAD, OF COURSE. I'M SO SORRY MY DEAR.
BUT YOU HAVEN'T AGED...
OF COURSE I HAVE. I JUST DON'T LOOK IT. REALLY, ASHA, YOU ARE FOCUSING ON THE MUNDANE.
PAY ATTENTION. THE VIGIL IS ONLY RESURRECTING THE RACES THAT JOINED THEIR COVENANT.
THE REST OF US HAVE HAD TO SIT BY, WATCHING, AS THE CULTS AND THE RIFTS SLOWLY TEAR OUR WORLD APART.
BUT I'VE CHANGED THAT.
THE TECHNOLOGY I'VE FOUND HERE CAN RESURRECT ANYONE WILLING TO FIGHT FOR TELARA!
HERE?
COME! ALLOW ME TO SHOW YOU!

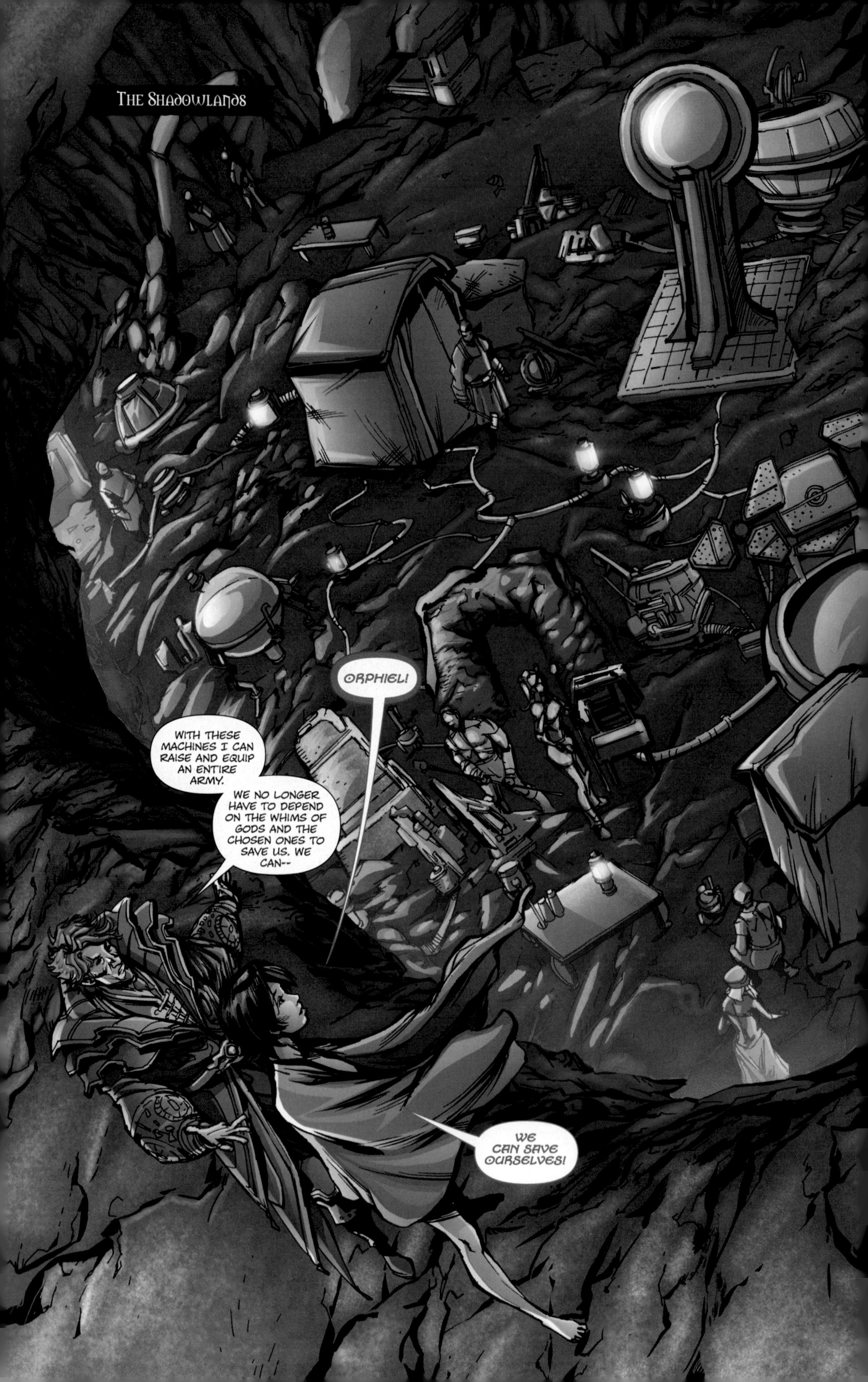
The Shadowlands
WITH THESE MACHINES I CAN RAISE AND EQUIP AN ENTIRE ARMY.
WE NO LONGER HAVE TO DEPEND ON THE WHIMS OF GODS AND THE CHOSEN ONES TO SAVE US. WE CAN--
ORPHIEL!
WE CAN SAVE OURSELVES!

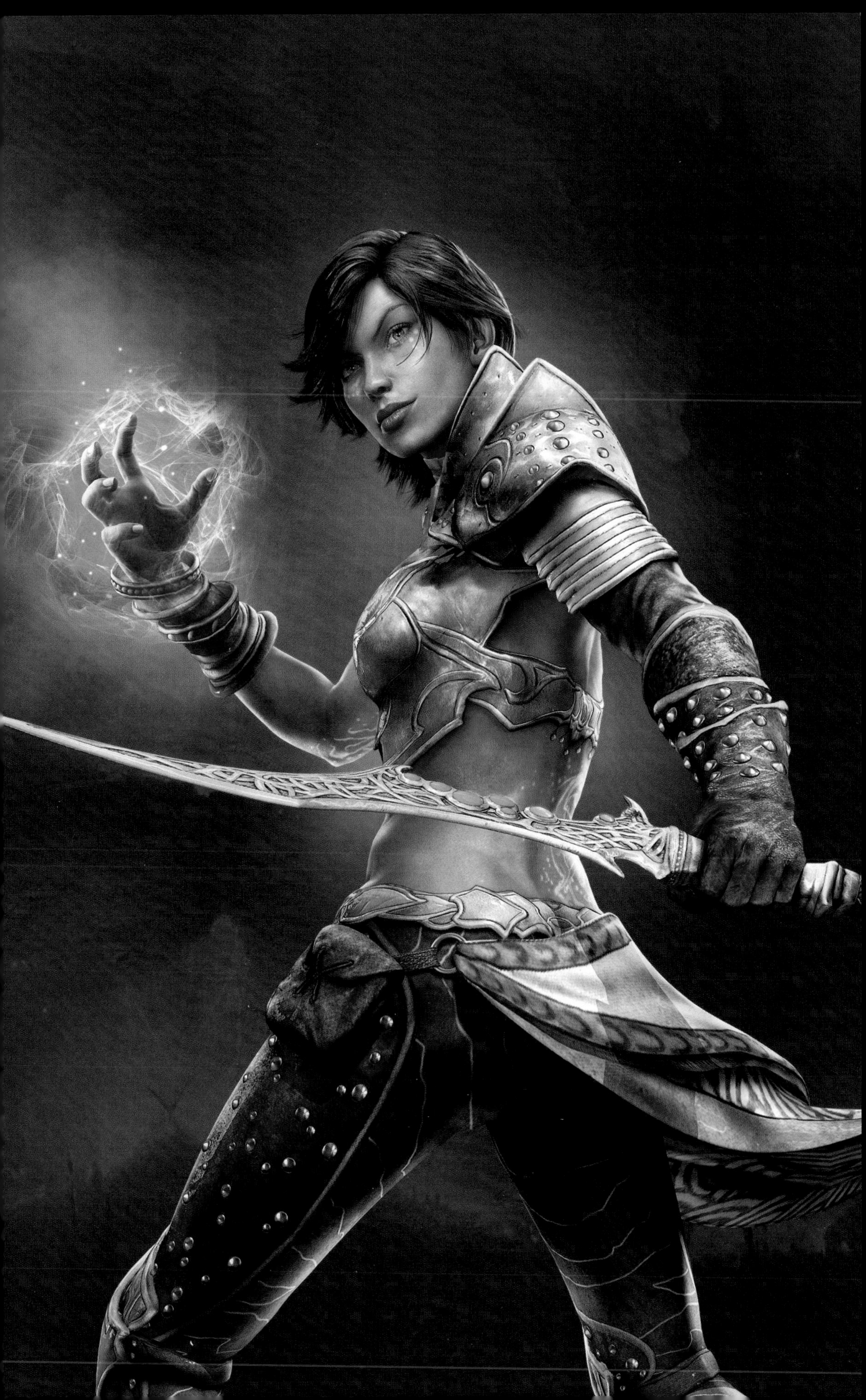

CHAPTER THREE

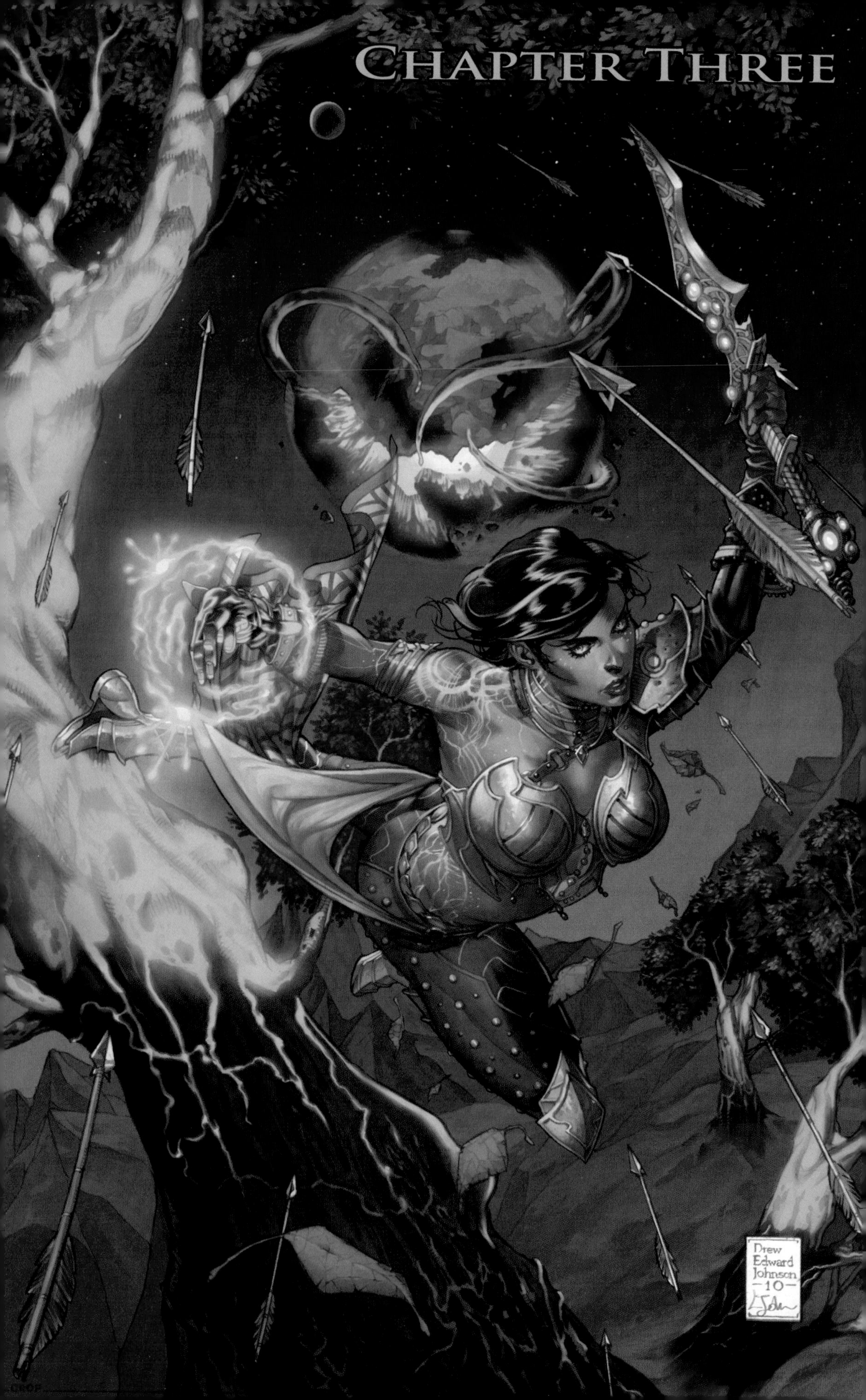
Drew Edward Johnson -10-

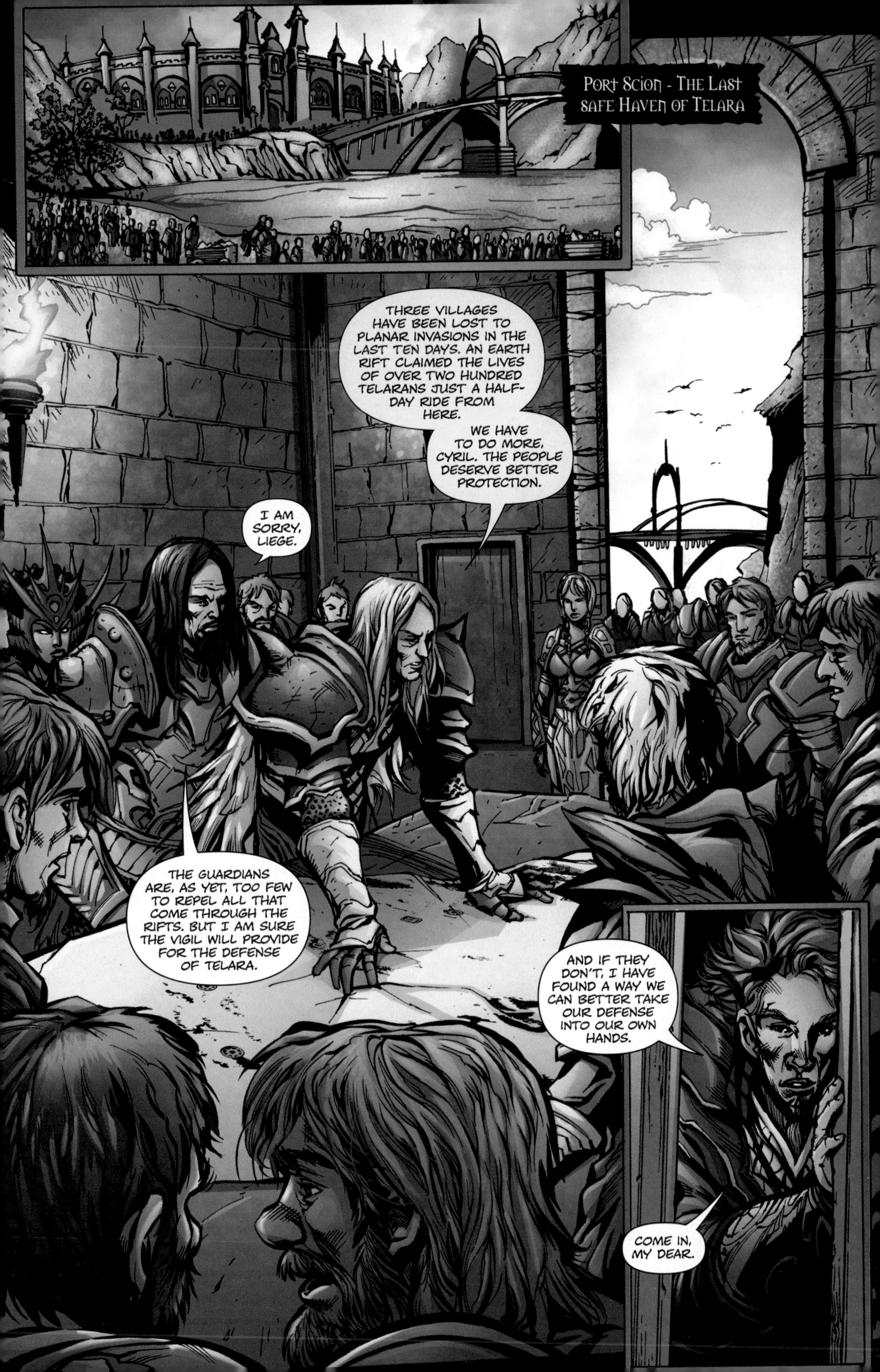
Port Scion - The Last safe Haven of Telara
THREE VILLAGES HAVE BEEN LOST TO PLANAR INVASIONS IN THE LAST TEN DAYS. AN EARTH RIFT CLAIMED THE LIVES OF OVER TWO HUNDRED TELARANS JUST A HALF-DAY RIDE FROM HERE.
WE HAVE TO DO MORE, CYRIL. THE PEOPLE DESERVE BETTER PROTECTION.
I AM SORRY, LIEGE.
THE GUARDIANS ARE, AS YET, TOO FEW TO REPEL ALL THAT COME THROUGH THE RIFTS. BUT I AM SURE THE VIGIL WILL PROVIDE FOR THE DEFENSE OF TELARA.
AND IF THEY DON'T, I HAVE FOUND A WAY WE CAN BETTER TAKE OUR DEFENSE INTO OUR OWN HANDS.
COME IN, MY DEAR.

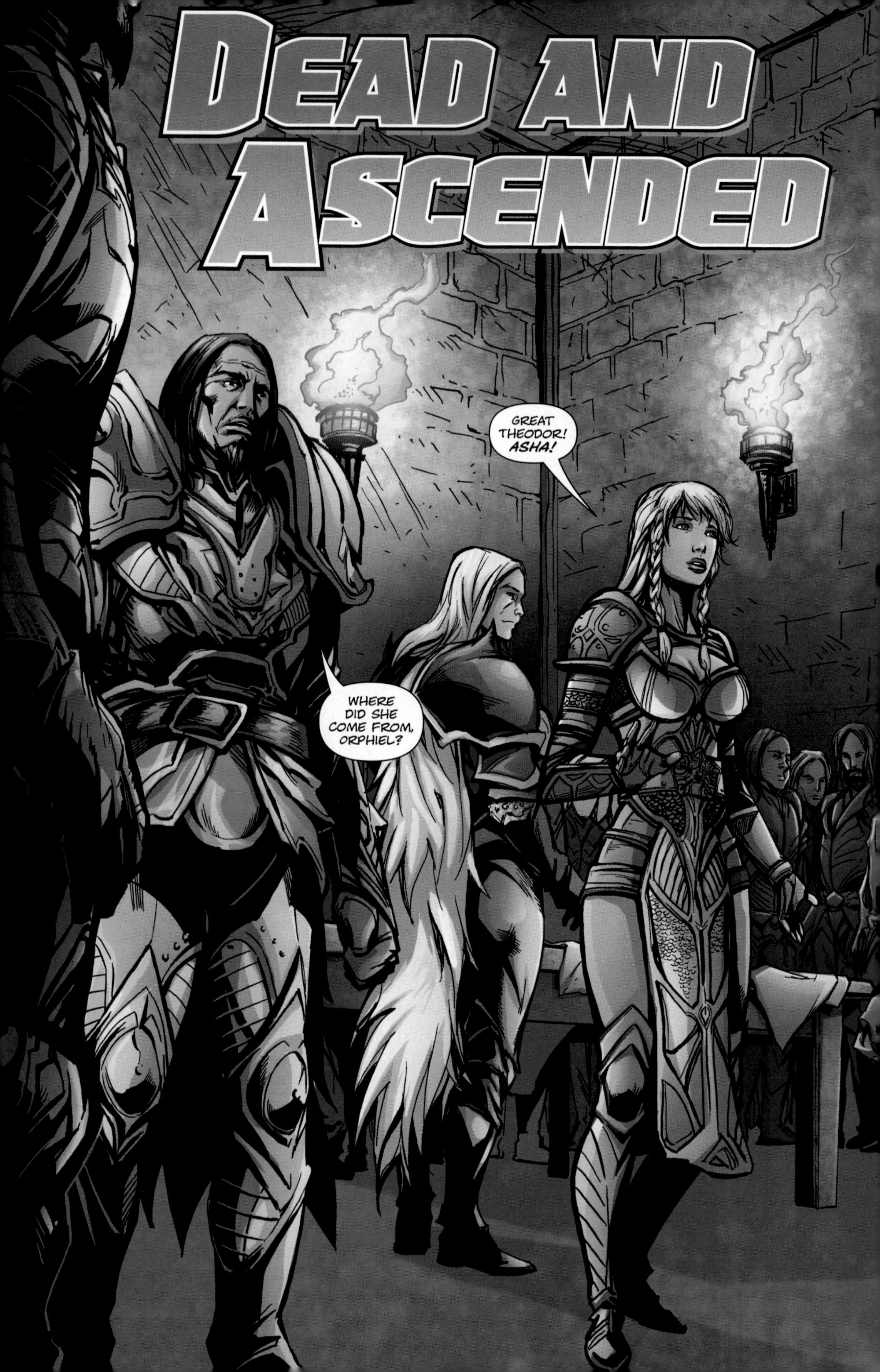
DEAD AND ASCENDED
GREAT THEODOR! ASHA!
WHERE DID SHE COME FROM, ORPHIEL?

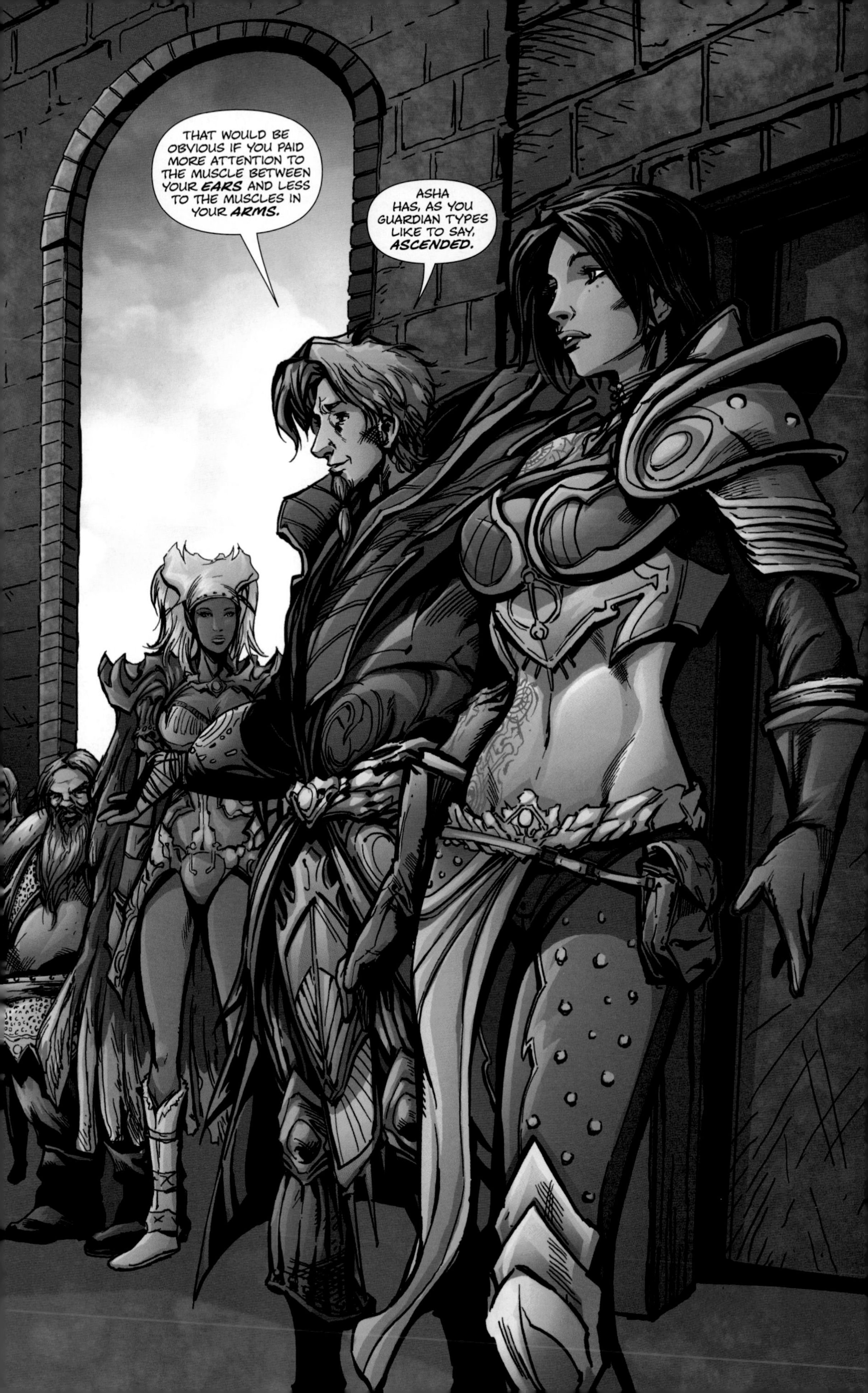
THAT WOULD BE OBVIOUS IF YOU PAID MORE ATTENTION TO THE MUSCLE BETWEEN YOUR **EARS** AND LESS TO THE MUSCLES IN YOUR **ARMS.**
ASHA HAS, AS YOU GUARDIAN TYPES LIKE TO SAY, **ASCENDED.**

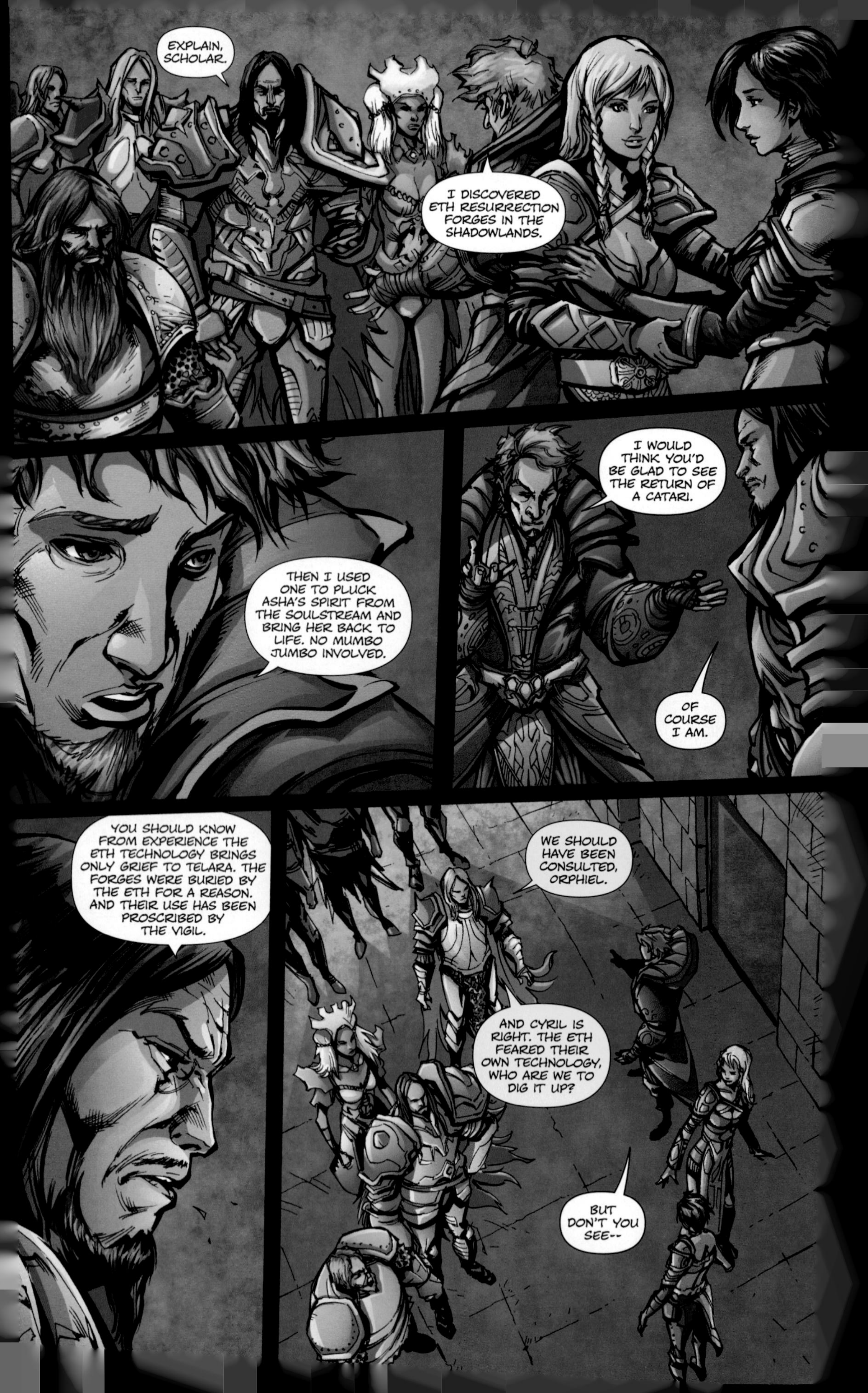
EXPLAIN, SCHOLAR.
I DISCOVERED ETH RESURRECTION FORGES IN THE SHADOWLANDS.
THEN I USED ONE TO PLUCK ASHA'S SPIRIT FROM THE SOULSTREAM AND BRING HER BACK TO LIFE. NO MUMBO JUMBO INVOLVED.
I WOULD THINK YOU'D BE GLAD TO SEE THE RETURN OF A CATARI.
OF COURSE I AM.
YOU SHOULD KNOW FROM EXPERIENCE THE ETH TECHNOLOGY BRINGS ONLY GRIEF TO TELARA. THE FORGES WERE BURIED BY THE ETH FOR A REASON. AND THEIR USE HAS BEEN PROSCRIBED BY THE VIGIL.
WE SHOULD HAVE BEEN CONSULTED, ORPHIEL.
AND CYRIL IS RIGHT. THE ETH FEARED THEIR OWN TECHNOLOGY, WHO ARE WE TO DIG IT UP?
BUT DON'T YOU SEE--

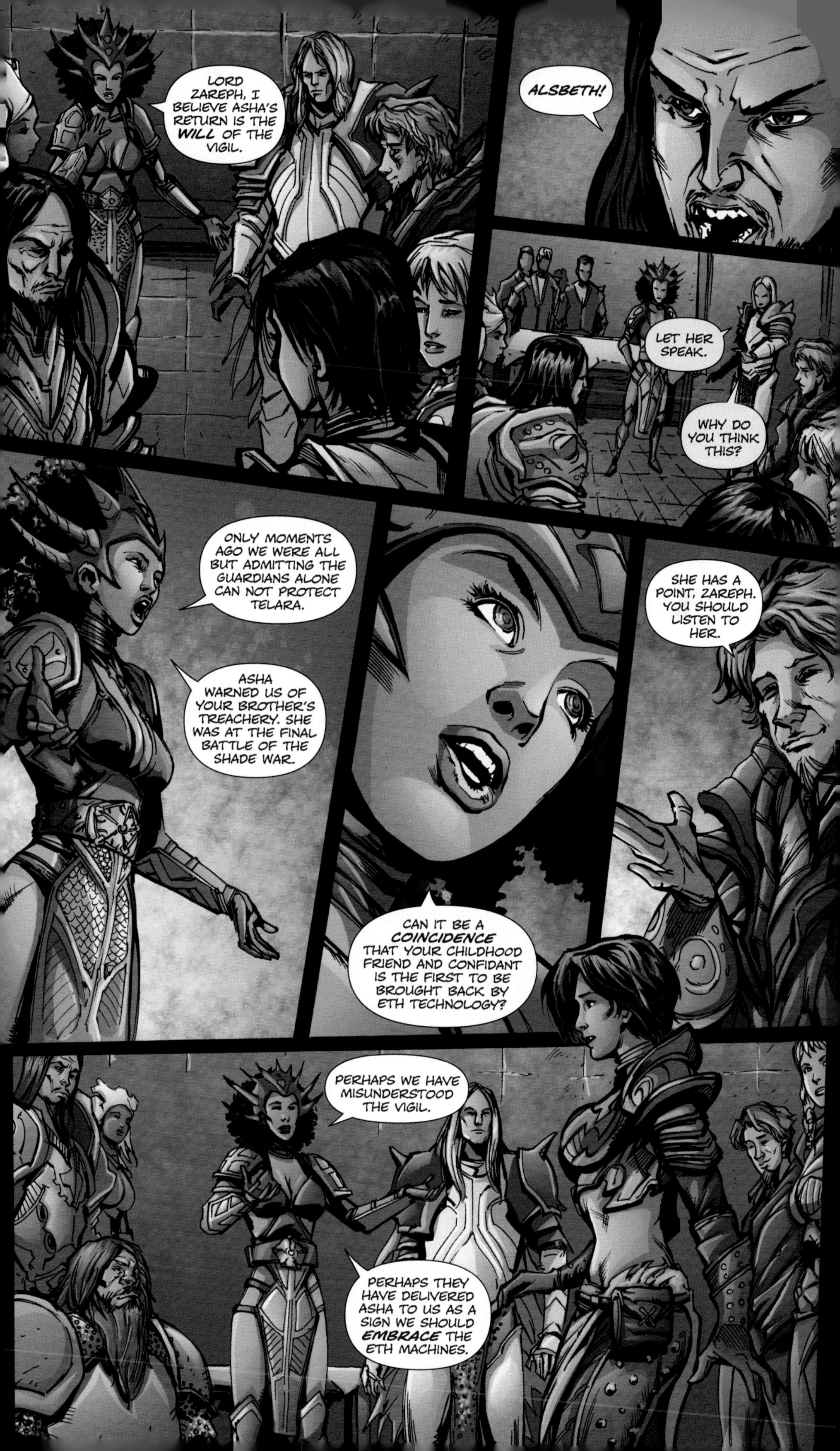
LORD ZAREPH, I BELIEVE ASHA'S RETURN IS THE WILL OF THE VIGIL.
ALSBETH!
LET HER SPEAK.
WHY DO YOU THINK THIS?
ONLY MOMENTS AGO WE WERE ALL BUT ADMITTING THE GUARDIANS ALONE CAN NOT PROTECT TELARA.
ASHA WARNED US OF YOUR BROTHER'S TREACHERY. SHE WAS AT THE FINAL BATTLE OF THE SHADE WAR.
CAN IT BE A COINCIDENCE THAT YOUR CHILDHOOD FRIEND AND CONFIDANT IS THE FIRST TO BE BROUGHT BACK BY ETH TECHNOLOGY?
SHE HAS A POINT, ZAREPH. YOU SHOULD LISTEN TO HER.
PERHAPS WE HAVE MISUNDERSTOOD THE VIGIL.
PERHAPS THEY HAVE DELIVERED ASHA TO US AS A SIGN WE SHOULD EMBRACE THE ETH MACHINES.

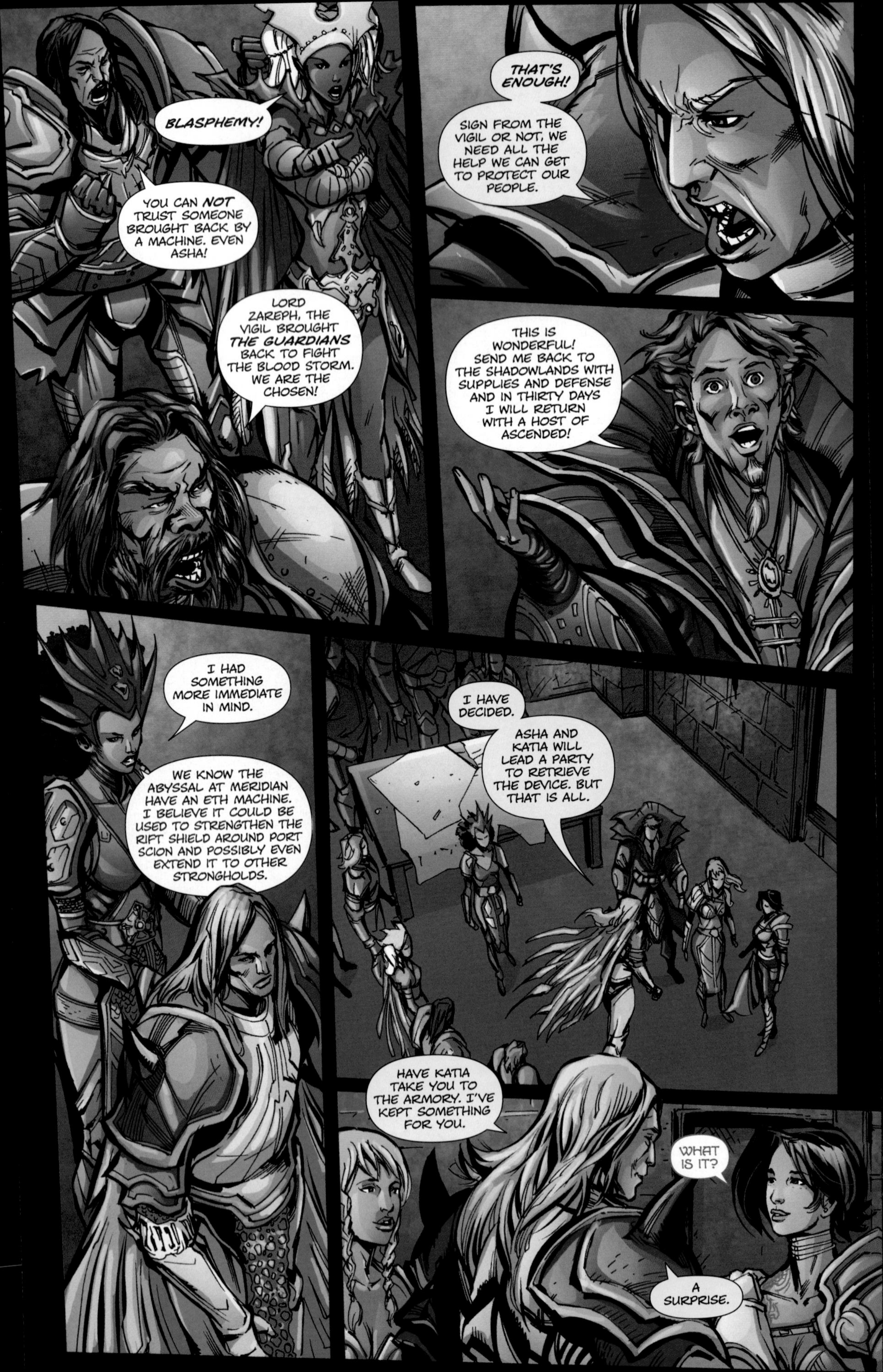
BLASPHEMY!
YOU CAN NOT TRUST SOMEONE BROUGHT BACK BY A MACHINE. EVEN ASHA!
LORD ZAREPH, THE VIGIL BROUGHT THE GUARDIANS BACK TO FIGHT THE BLOOD STORM. WE ARE THE CHOSEN!
THAT'S ENOUGH!
SIGN FROM THE VIGIL OR NOT, WE NEED ALL THE HELP WE CAN GET TO PROTECT OUR PEOPLE.
THIS IS WONDERFUL! SEND ME BACK TO THE SHADOWLANDS WITH SUPPLIES AND DEFENSE AND IN THIRTY DAYS I WILL RETURN WITH A HOST OF ASCENDED!
I HAD SOMETHING MORE IMMEDIATE IN MIND.
WE KNOW THE ABYSSAL AT MERIDIAN HAVE AN ETH MACHINE. I BELIEVE IT COULD BE USED TO STRENGTHEN THE RIFT SHIELD AROUND PORT SCION AND POSSIBLY EVEN EXTEND IT TO OTHER STRONGHOLDS.
I HAVE DECIDED.
ASHA AND KATIA WILL LEAD A PARTY TO RETRIEVE THE DEVICE. BUT THAT IS ALL.
HAVE KATIA TAKE YOU TO THE ARMORY. I'VE KEPT SOMETHING FOR YOU.
WHAT IS IT?
A SURPRISE.

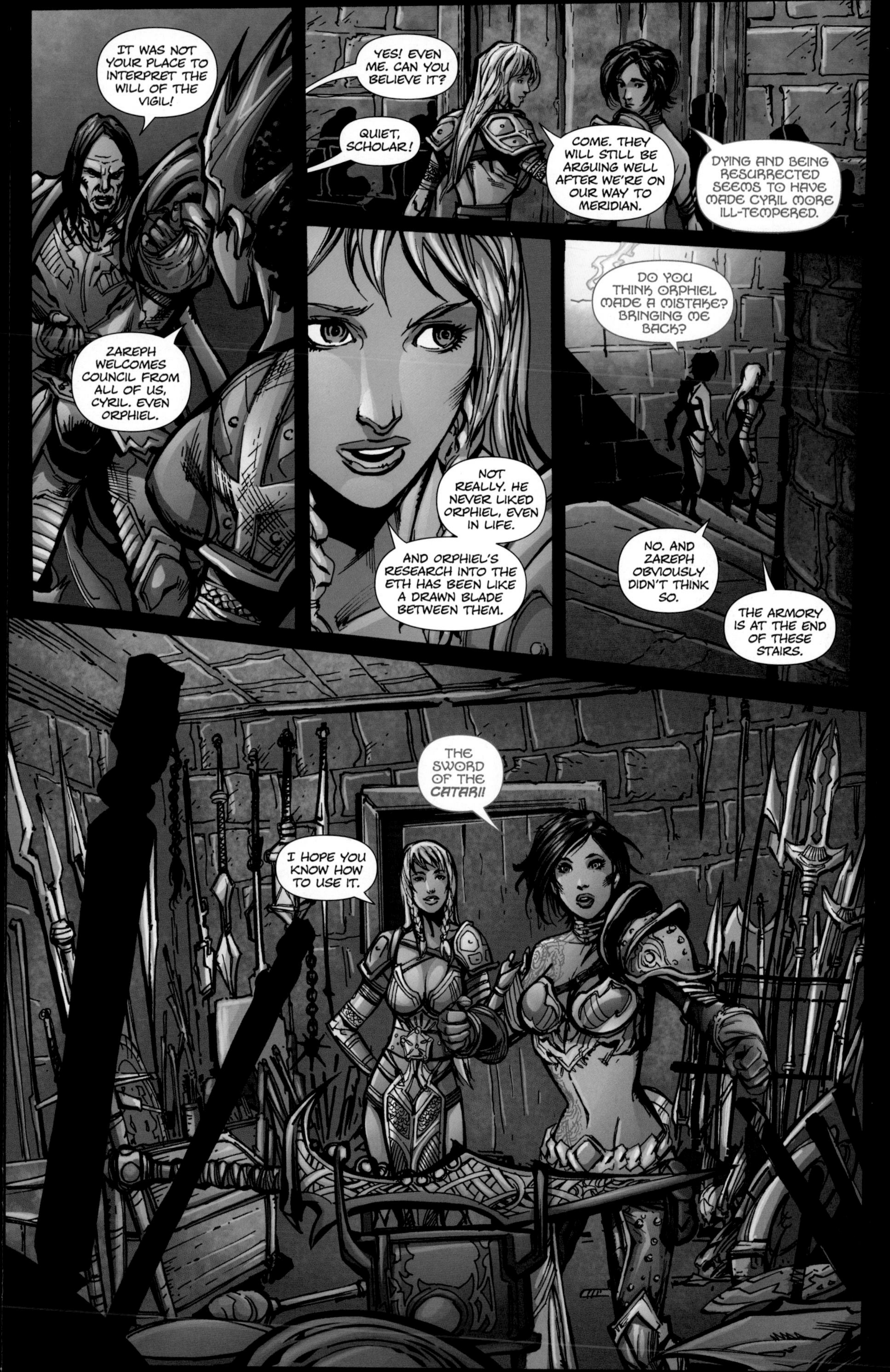
IT WAS NOT YOUR PLACE TO INTERPRET THE WILL OF THE VIGIL!
YES! EVEN ME. CAN YOU BELIEVE IT?
QUIET, SCHOLAR!
COME. THEY WILL STILL BE ARGUING WELL AFTER WE'RE ON OUR WAY TO MERIDIAN.
DYING AND BEING RESURRECTED SEEMS TO HAVE MADE CYRIL MORE ILL-TEMPERED.
ZAREPH WELCOMES COUNCIL FROM ALL OF US, CYRIL. EVEN ORPHIEL.
NOT REALLY. HE NEVER LIKED ORPHIEL, EVEN IN LIFE.
AND ORPHIEL'S RESEARCH INTO THE ETH HAS BEEN LIKE A DRAWN BLADE BETWEEN THEM.
DO YOU THINK ORPHIEL MADE A MISTAKE? BRINGING ME BACK?
NO. AND ZAREPH OBVIOUSLY DIDN'T THINK SO.
THE ARMORY IS AT THE END OF THESE STAIRS.
THE SWORD OF THE CATARI!
I HOPE YOU KNOW HOW TO USE IT.

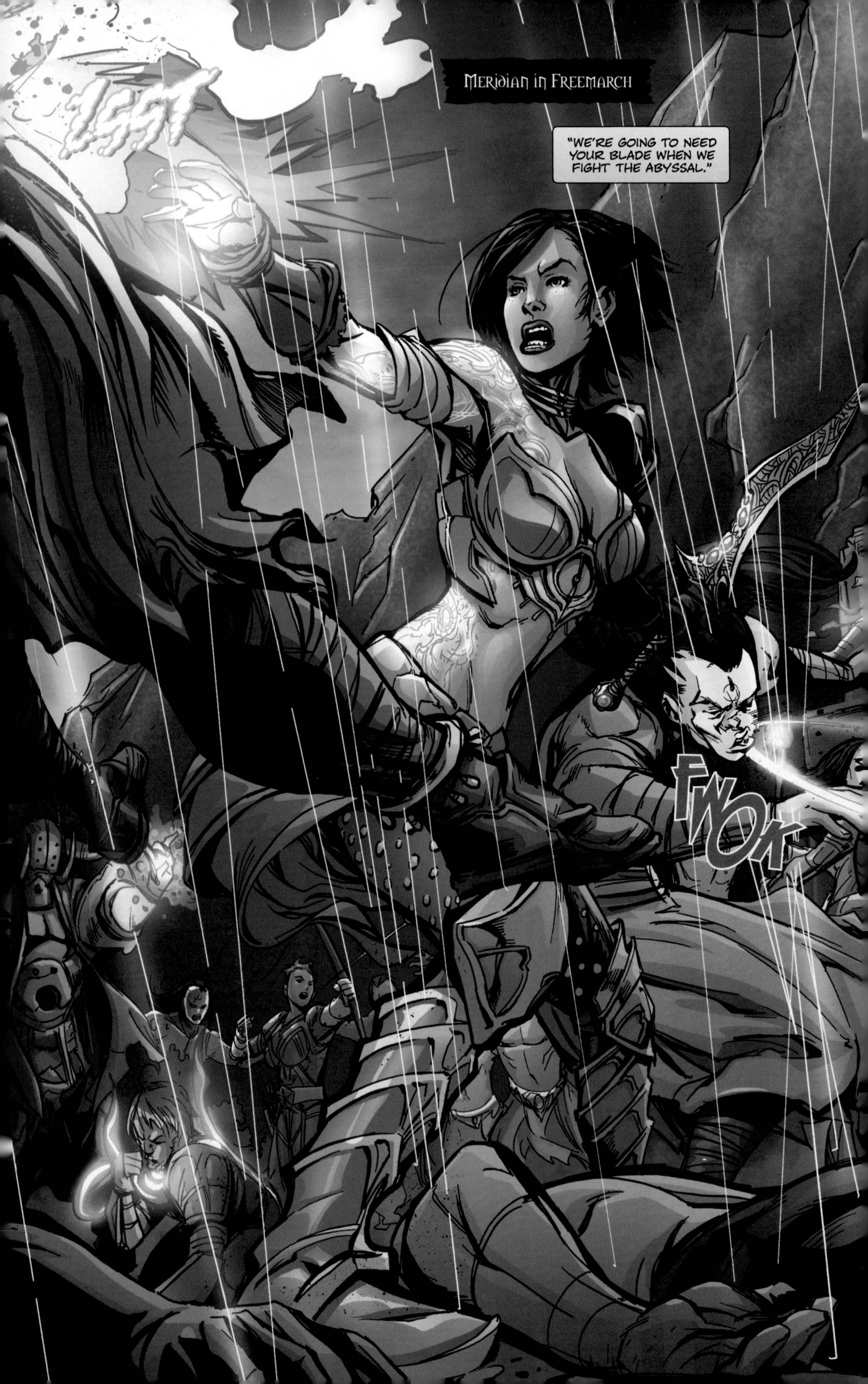

Meridian in Freemarch
"WE'RE GOING TO NEED YOUR BLADE WHEN WE FIGHT THE ABYSSAL."
FWOK

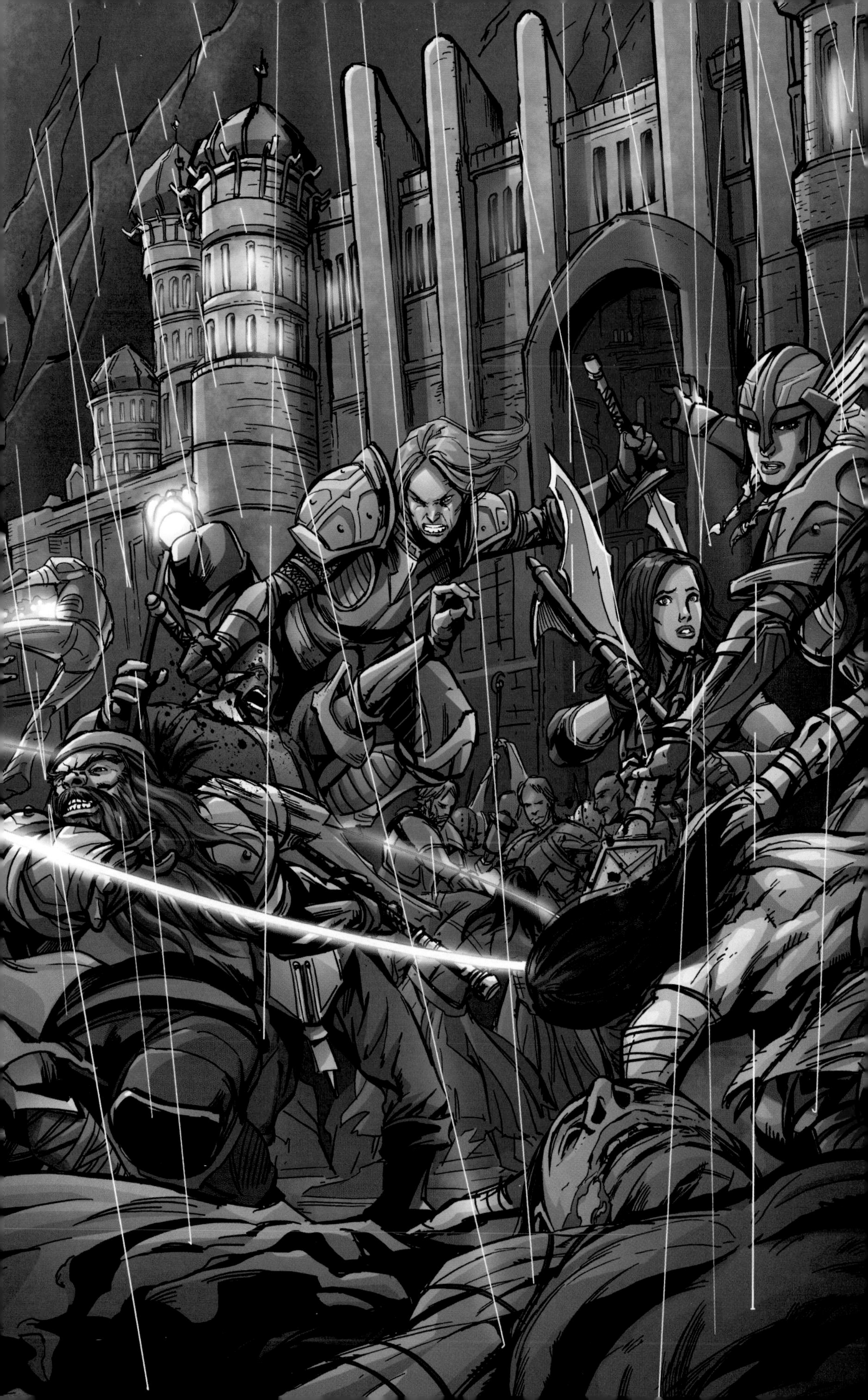

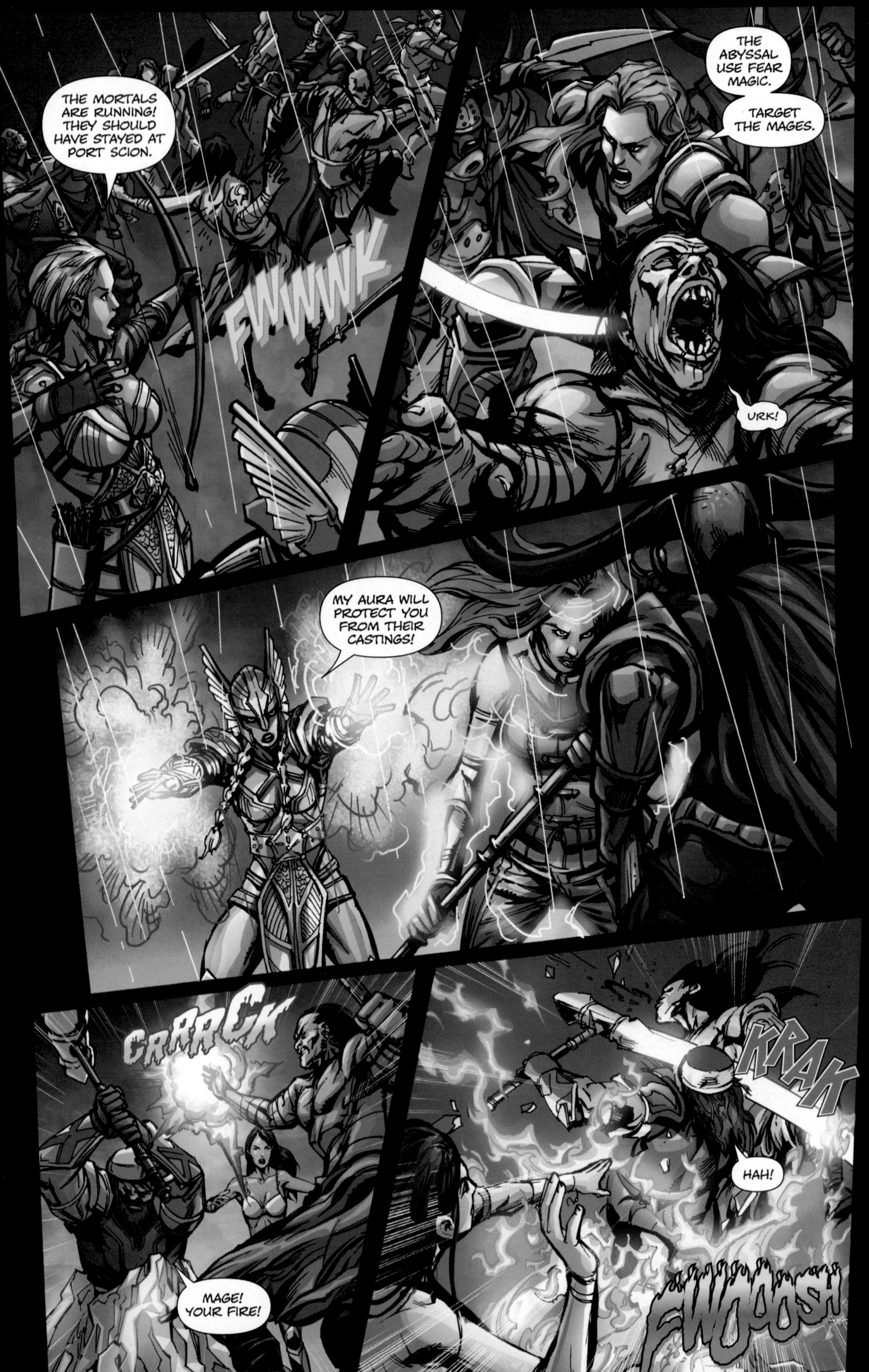
THE MORTALS ARE RUNNING! THEY SHOULD HAVE STAYED AT PORT SCION.
FWWWK
THE ABYSSAL USE FEAR MAGIC.
TARGET THE MAGES.
URK!
MY AURA WILL PROTECT YOU FROM THEIR CASTINGS!
CRRRCK
MAGE! YOUR FIRE!
KRAK
HAH!
FWOOOSH

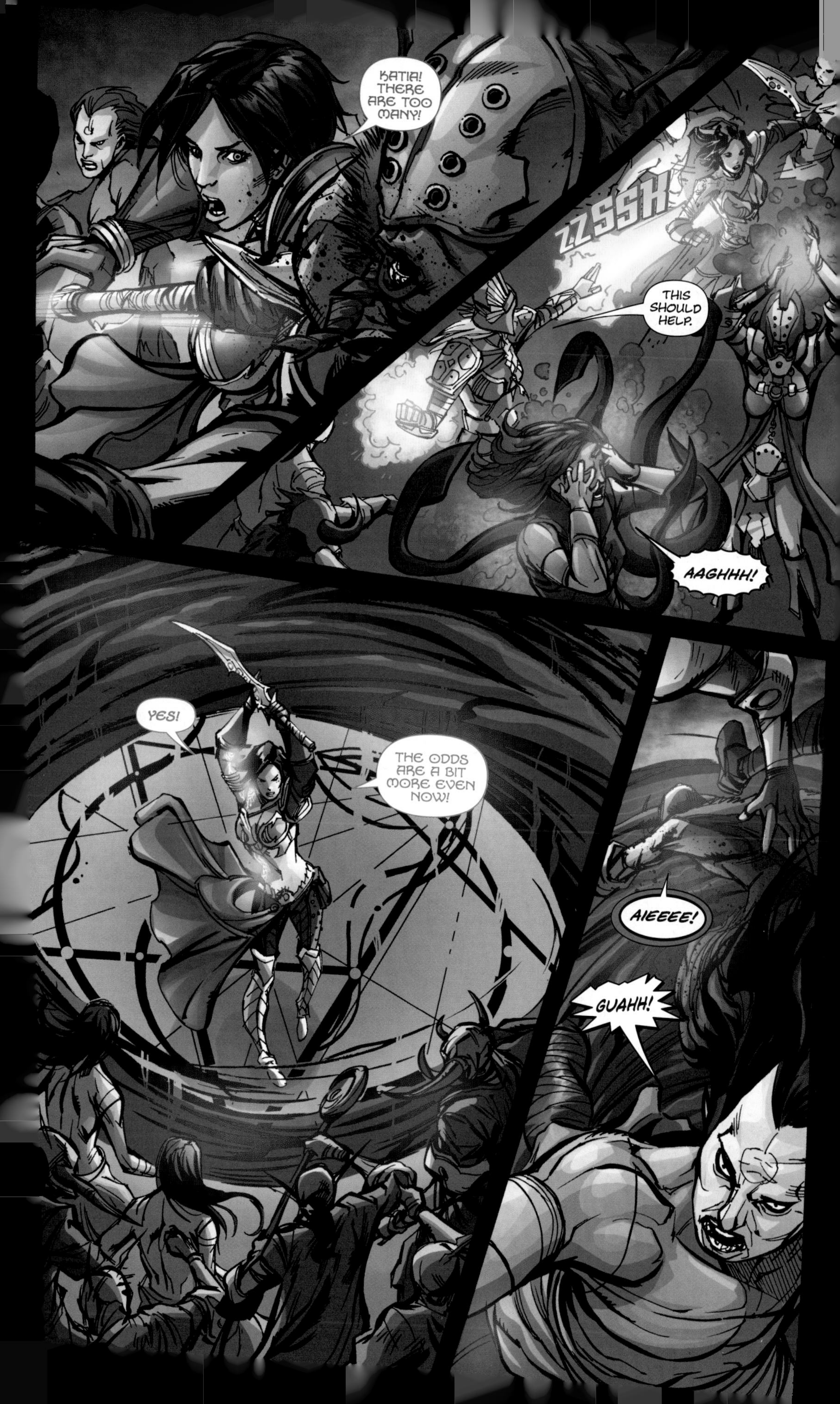
KATIA! THERE ARE TOO MANY!
ZZSSH
THIS SHOULD HELP.
AAGHHH!
YES!
THE ODDS ARE A BIT MORE EVEN NOW!
AIEEEE!
GUAHH!

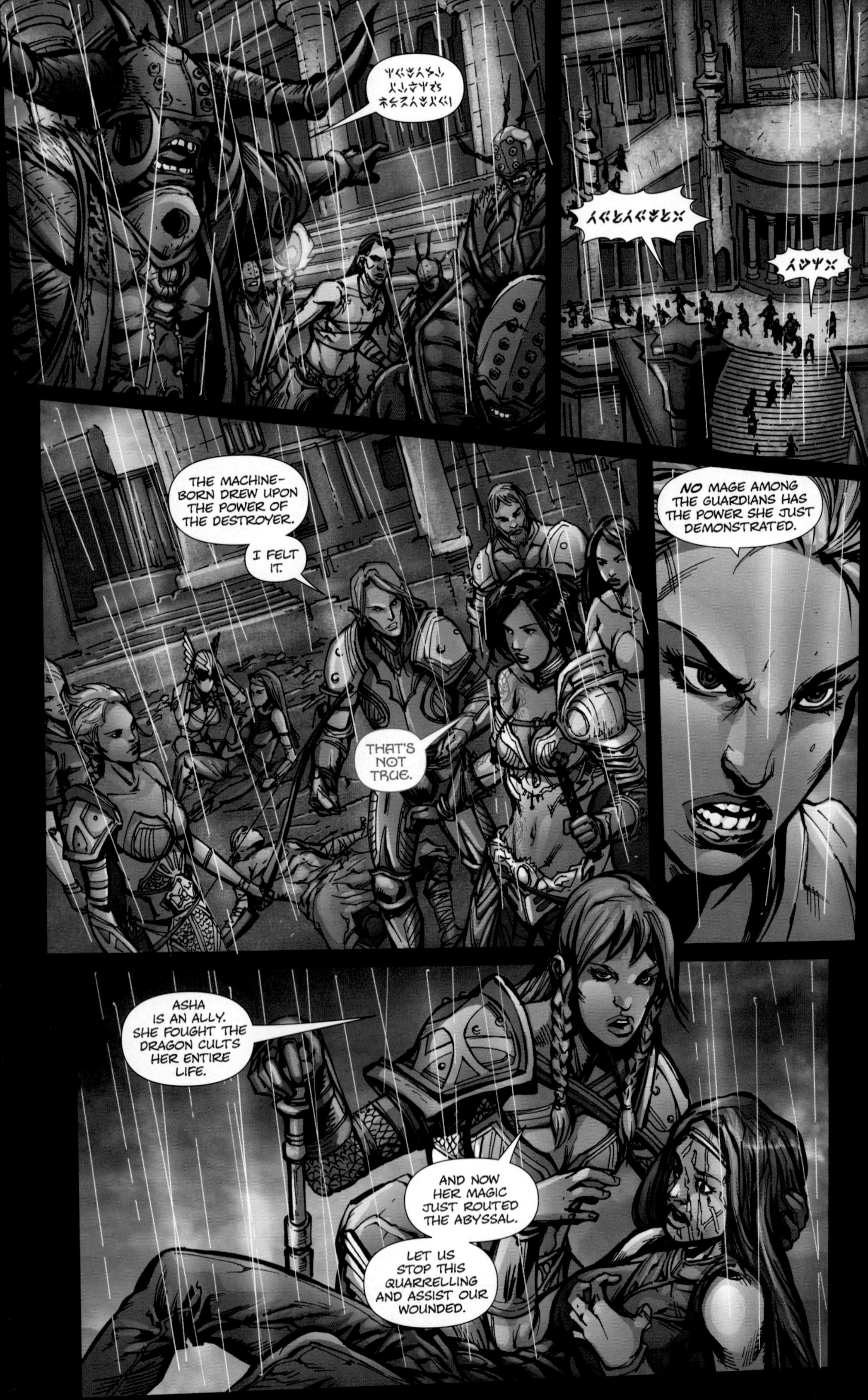
THE MACHINE-BORN DREW UPON THE POWER OF THE DESTROYER.
I FELT IT.
THAT'S NOT TRUE.
NO MAGE AMONG THE GUARDIANS HAS THE POWER SHE JUST DEMONSTRATED.
ASHA IS AN ALLY. SHE FOUGHT THE DRAGON CULTS HER ENTIRE LIFE.
AND NOW HER MAGIC JUST ROUTED THE ABYSSAL.
LET US STOP THIS QUARRELLING AND ASSIST OUR WOUNDED.

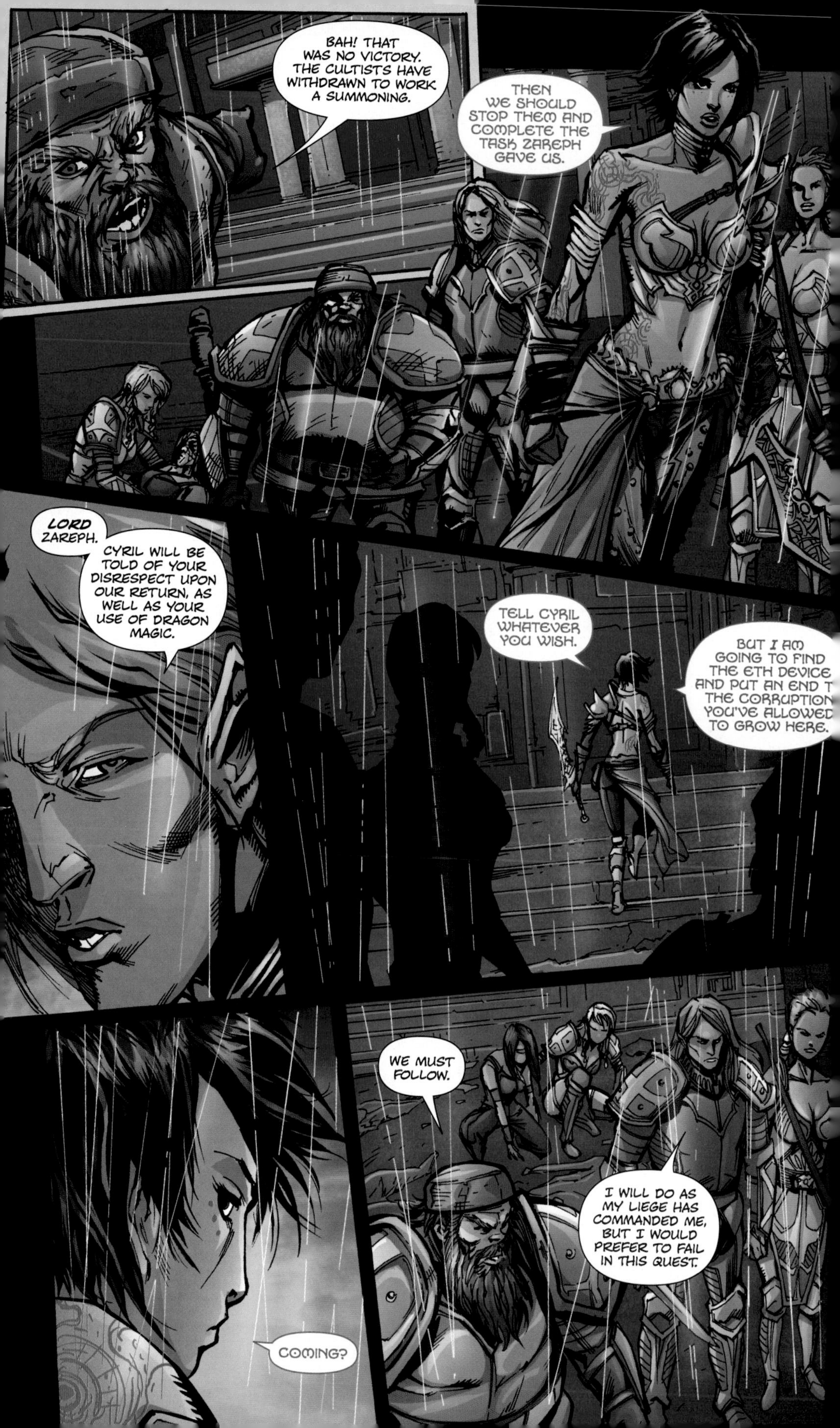
BAH! THAT WAS NO VICTORY. THE CULTISTS HAVE WITHDRAWN TO WORK A SUMMONING.
THEN WE SHOULD STOP THEM AND COMPLETE THE TASK ZAREPH GAVE US.
LORD ZAREPH.
CYRIL WILL BE TOLD OF YOUR DISRESPECT UPON OUR RETURN, AS WELL AS YOUR USE OF DRAGON MAGIC.
TELL CYRIL WHATEVER YOU WISH.
BUT I AM GOING TO FIND THE ETH DEVICE AND PUT AN END T THE CORRUPTION YOU'VE ALLOWED TO GROW HERE.
WE MUST FOLLOW.
I WILL DO AS MY LIEGE HAS COMMANDED ME, BUT I WOULD PREFER TO FAIL IN THIS QUEST.
COMING?

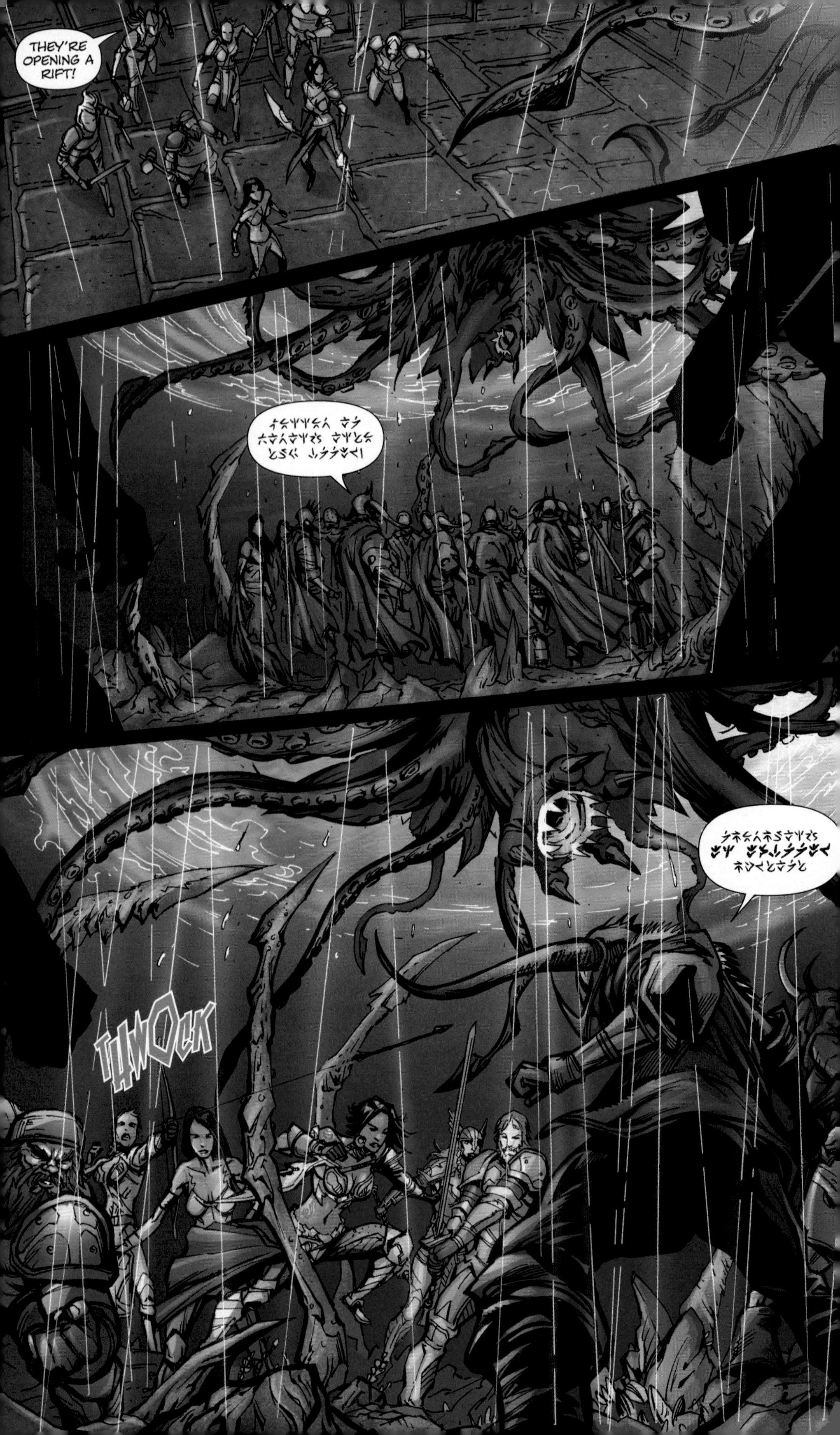
THEY'RE OPENING A RIFT!
THWOCK

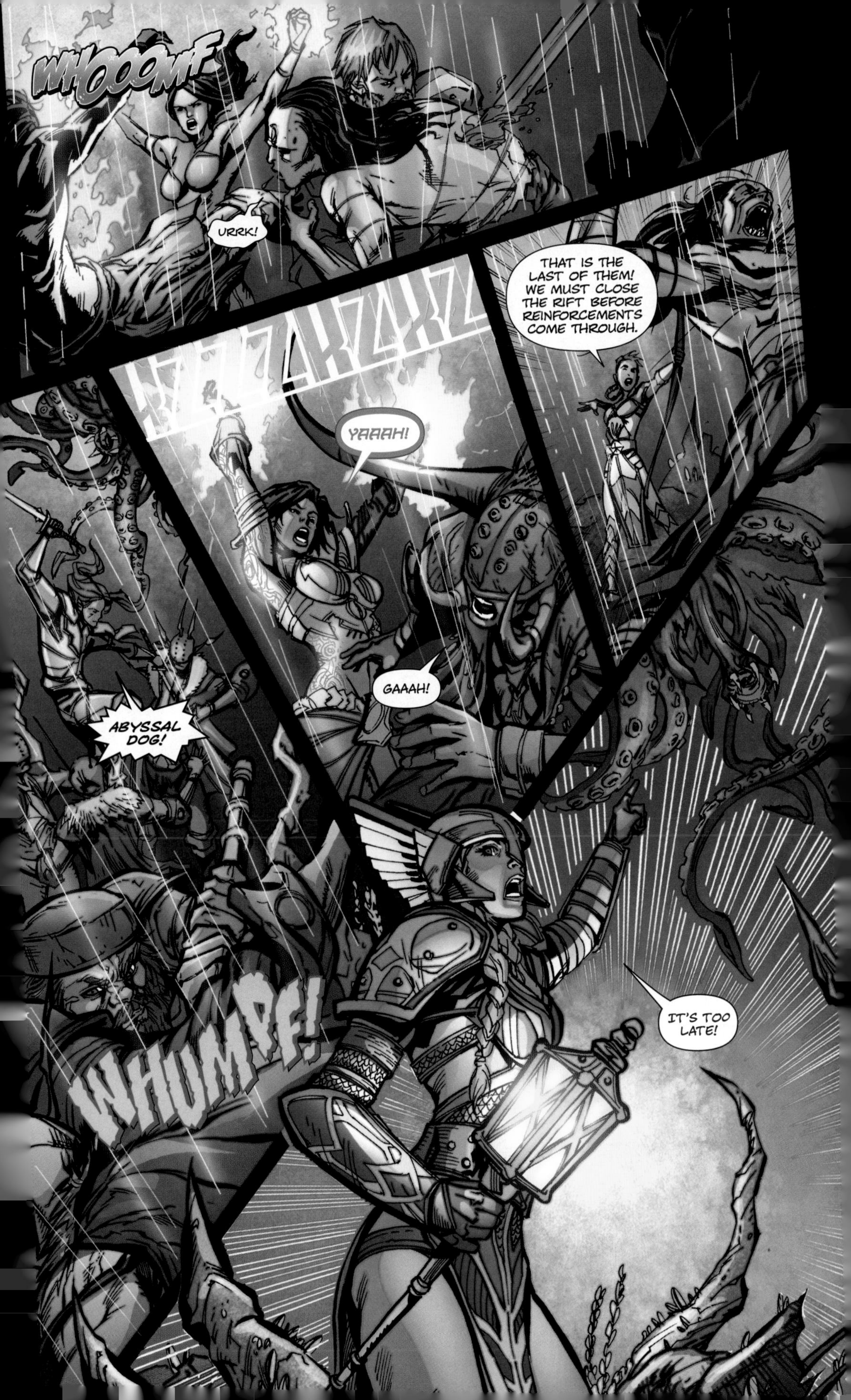
WHOOOMF
URRK!
THAT IS THE LAST OF THEM! WE MUST CLOSE THE RIFT BEFORE REINFORCEMENTS COME THROUGH.
YAAAH!
GAAAH!
ABYSSAL DOG!
IT'S TOO LATE!
WHUMPF!

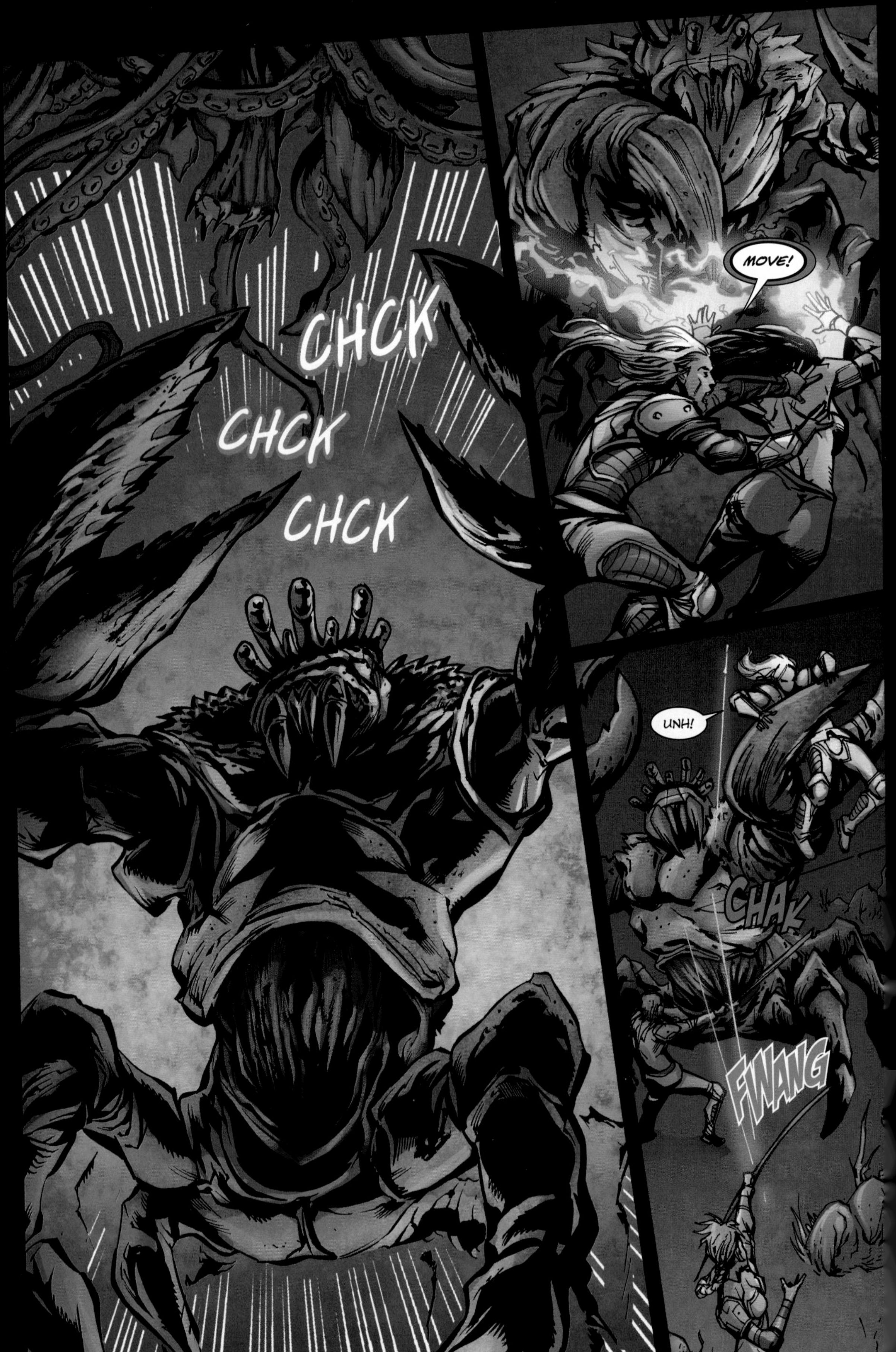
CHCK
CHCK
CHCK
MOVE!
UNH!
CHAK
FWANG

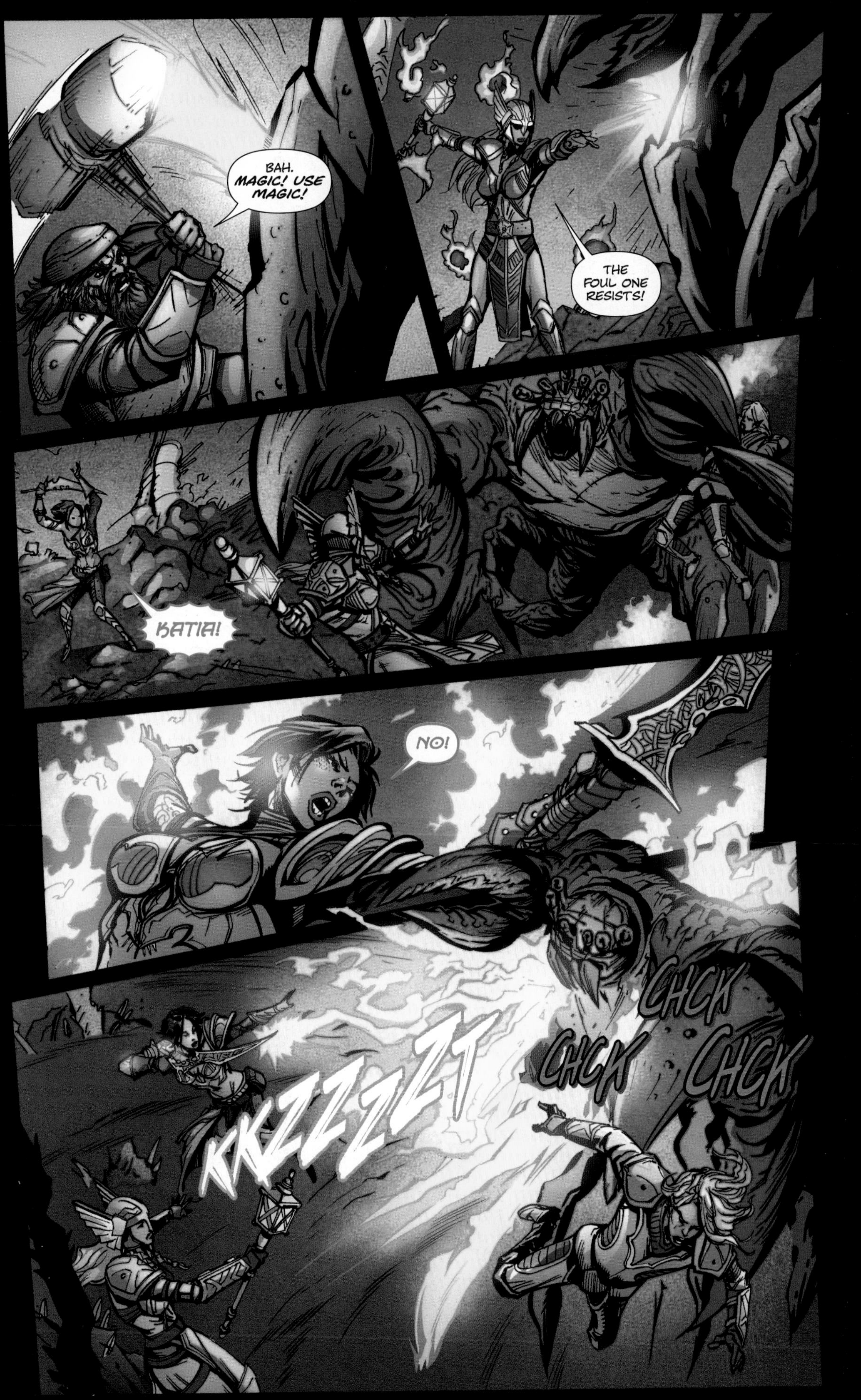
BAH. MAGIC! USE MAGIC!
THE FOUL ONE RESISTS!
KATIA!
NO!
CHCK CHCK CHCK
KKZZZZZZT

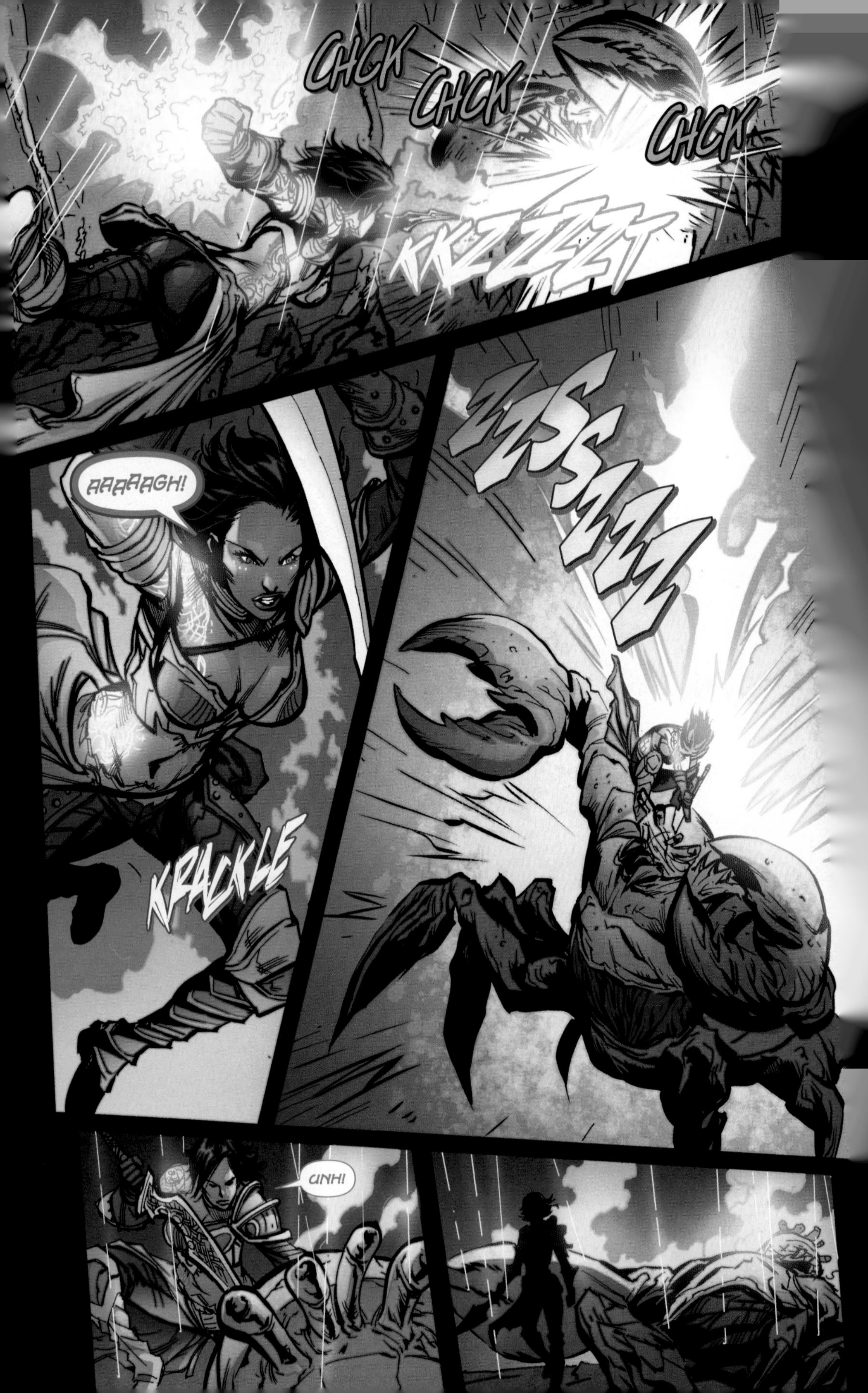
CHCK
CHCK
CHCK
KKZZZZT
AAAAAGH!
KRACKLE
ZZSSMMM
UNH!

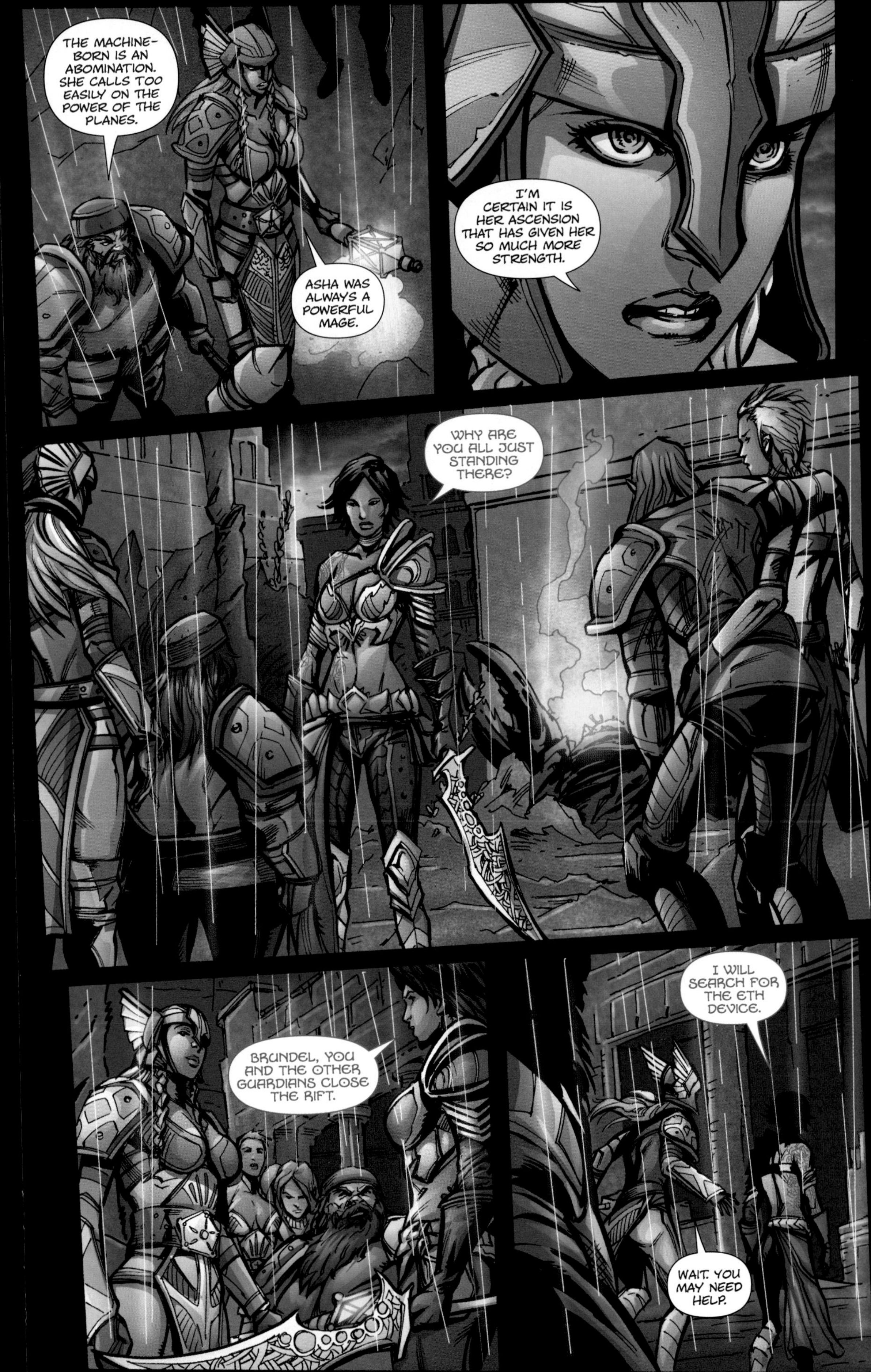
THE MACHINE-BORN IS AN ABOMINATION. SHE CALLS TOO EASILY ON THE POWER OF THE PLANES.
ASHA WAS ALWAYS A POWERFUL MAGE.
I'M CERTAIN IT IS HER ASCENSION THAT HAS GIVEN HER SO MUCH MORE STRENGTH.
WHY ARE YOU ALL JUST STANDING THERE?
BRUNDEL, YOU AND THE OTHER GUARDIANS CLOSE THE RIFT.
I WILL SEARCH FOR THE ETH DEVICE.
WAIT. YOU MAY NEED HELP.

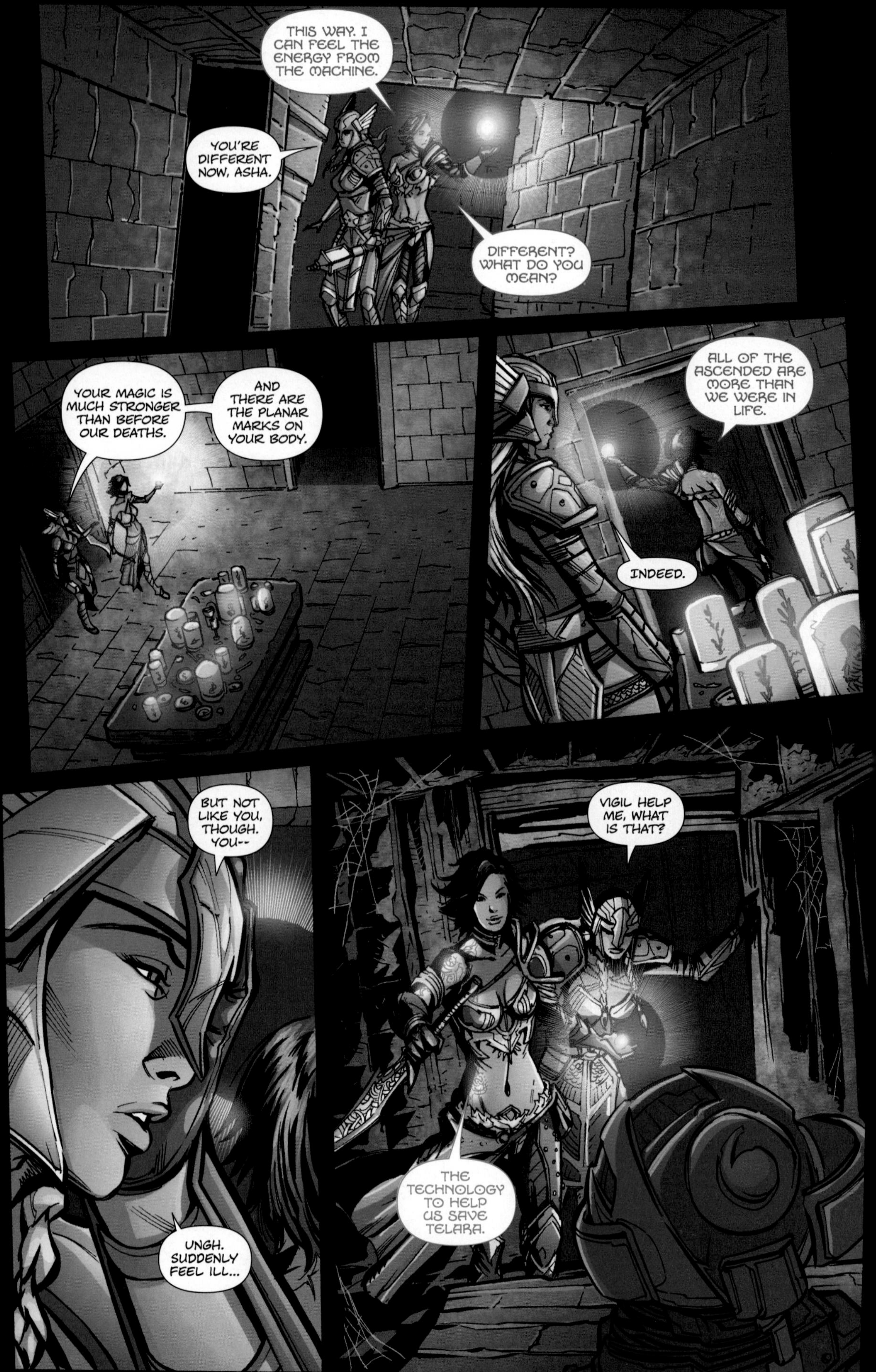

THIS WAY. I CAN FEEL THE ENERGY FROM THE MACHINE.
YOU'RE DIFFERENT NOW, ASHA.
DIFFERENT? WHAT DO YOU MEAN?
YOUR MAGIC IS MUCH STRONGER THAN BEFORE OUR DEATHS.
AND THERE ARE THE PLANAR MARKS ON YOUR BODY.
ALL OF THE ASCENDED ARE MORE THAN WE WERE IN LIFE.
INDEED.
BUT NOT LIKE YOU, THOUGH. YOU--
UNGH. SUDDENLY FEEL ILL...
VIGIL HELP ME, WHAT IS THAT?
THE TECHNOLOGY TO HELP US SAVE TELARA.

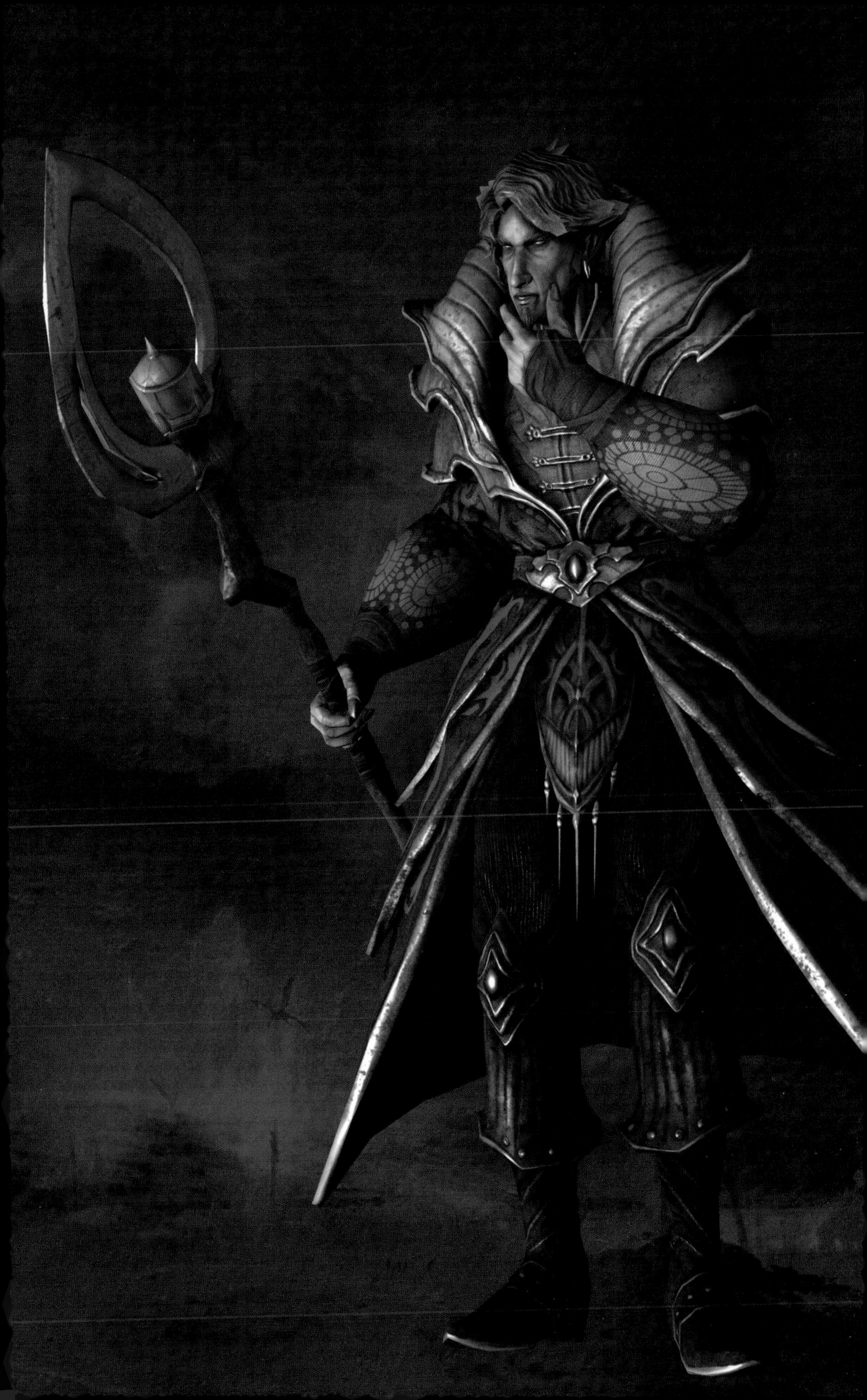

Chapter Four

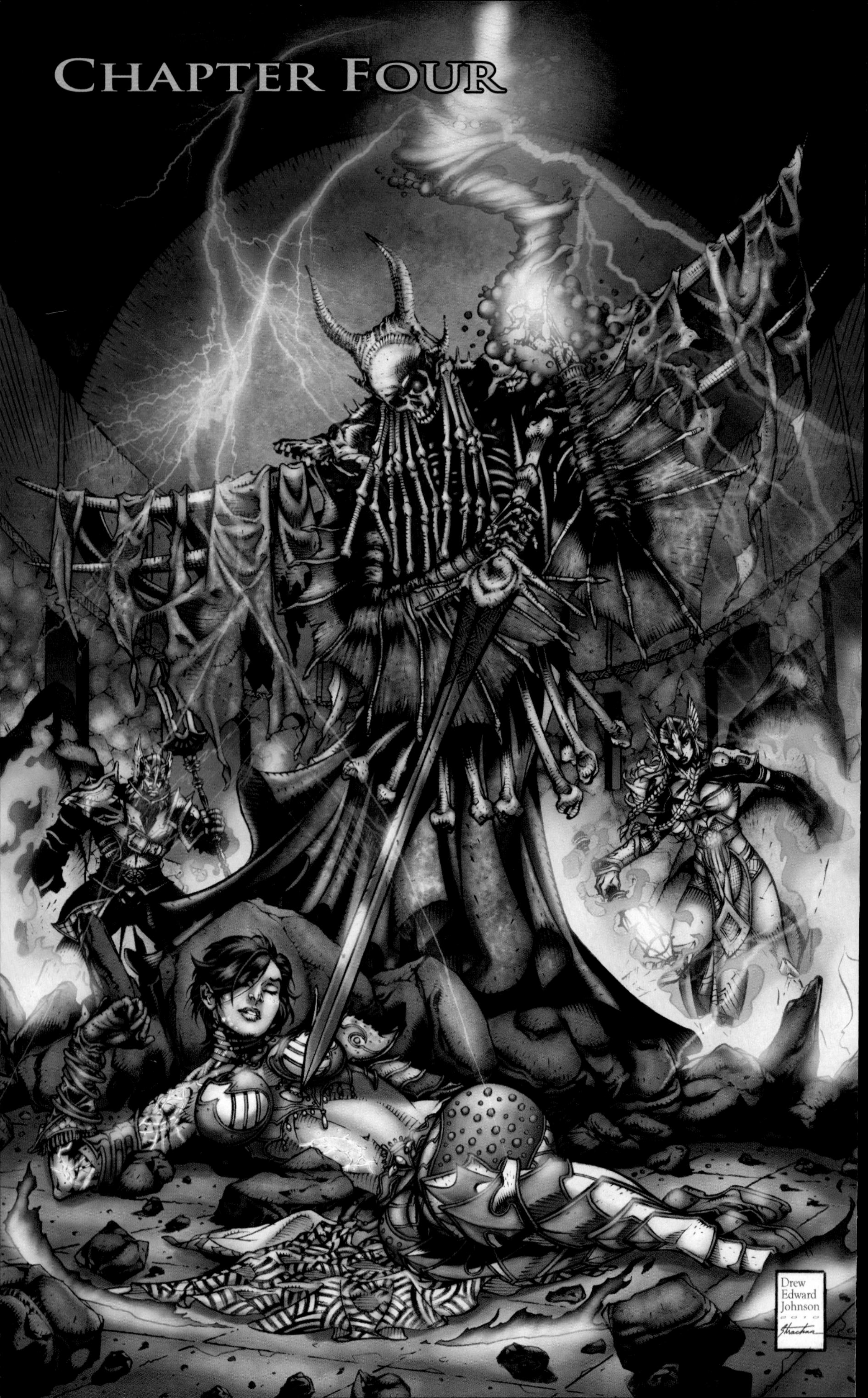
Drew
Edward
Johnson
2010

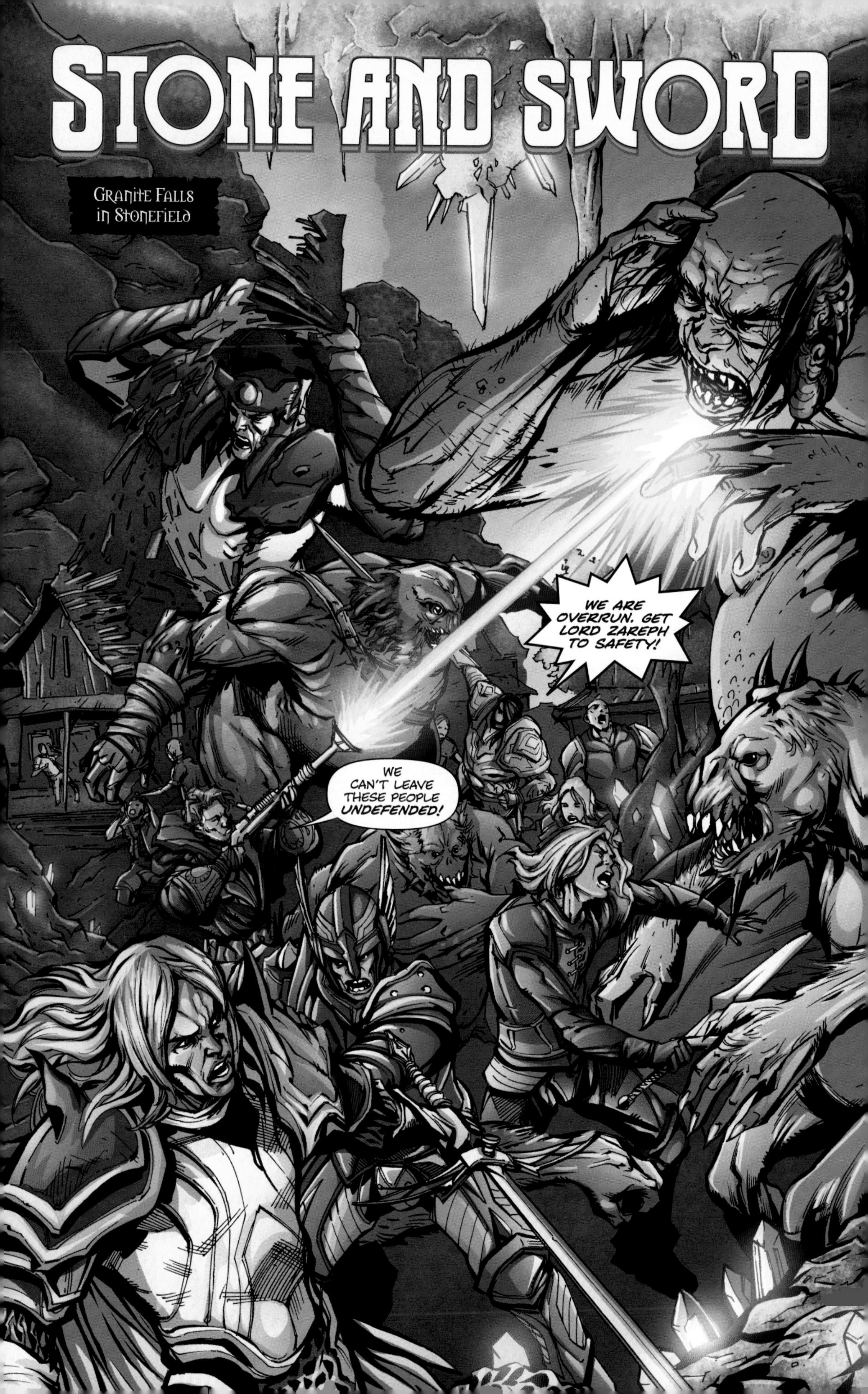
STONE AND SWORD
Granite Falls in Stonefield
WE ARE OVERRUN. GET LORD ZAREPH TO SAFETY!
WE CAN'T LEAVE THESE PEOPLE UNDEFENDED!

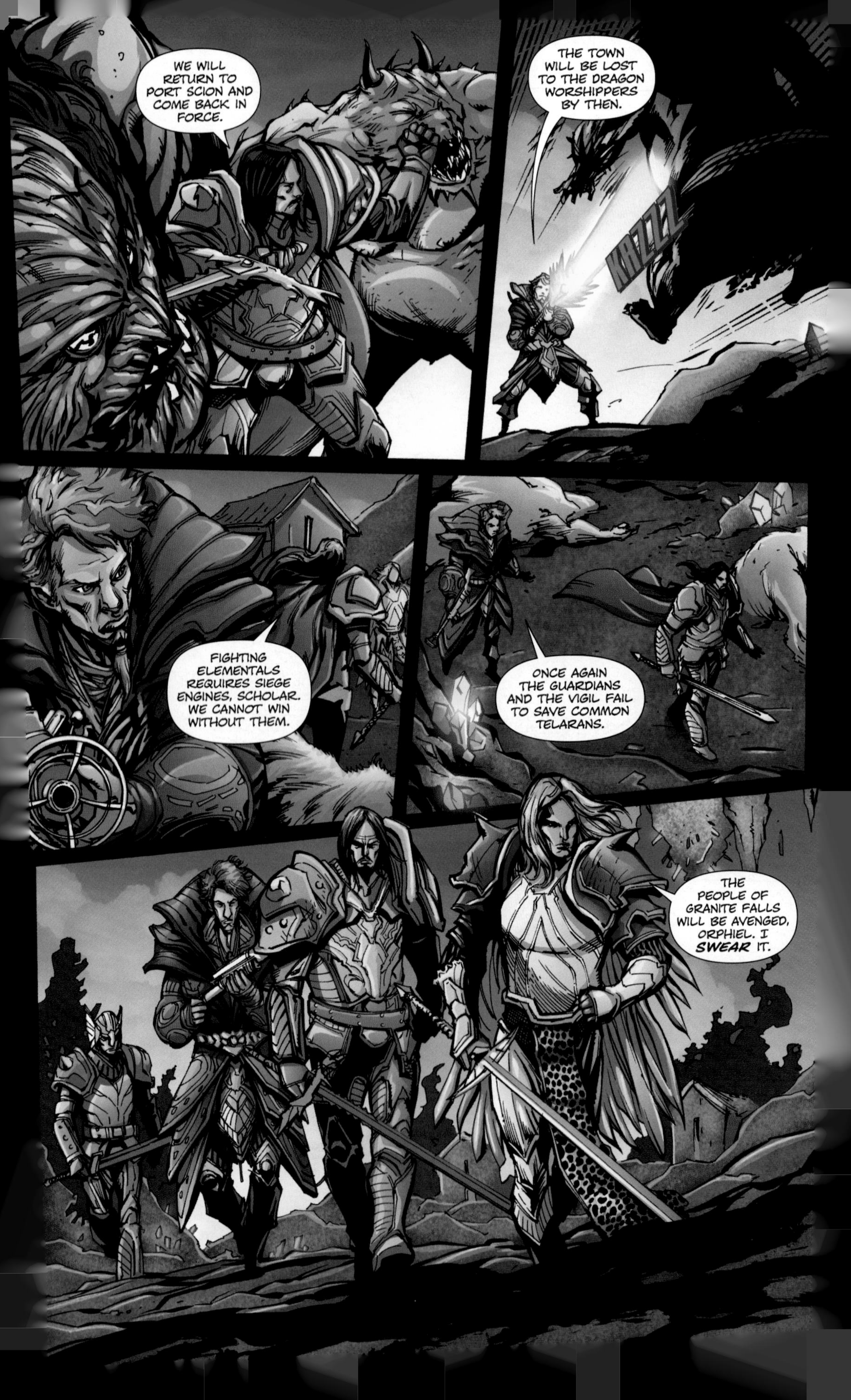
WE WILL RETURN TO PORT SCION AND COME BACK IN FORCE.
THE TOWN WILL BE LOST TO THE DRAGON WORSHIPPERS BY THEN.
KRZZZL
FIGHTING ELEMENTALS REQUIRES SIEGE ENGINES, SCHOLAR. WE CANNOT WIN WITHOUT THEM.
ONCE AGAIN THE GUARDIANS AND THE VIGIL FAIL TO SAVE COMMON TELARANS.
THE PEOPLE OF GRANITE FALLS WILL BE AVENGED, ORPHIEL. I SWEAR IT.

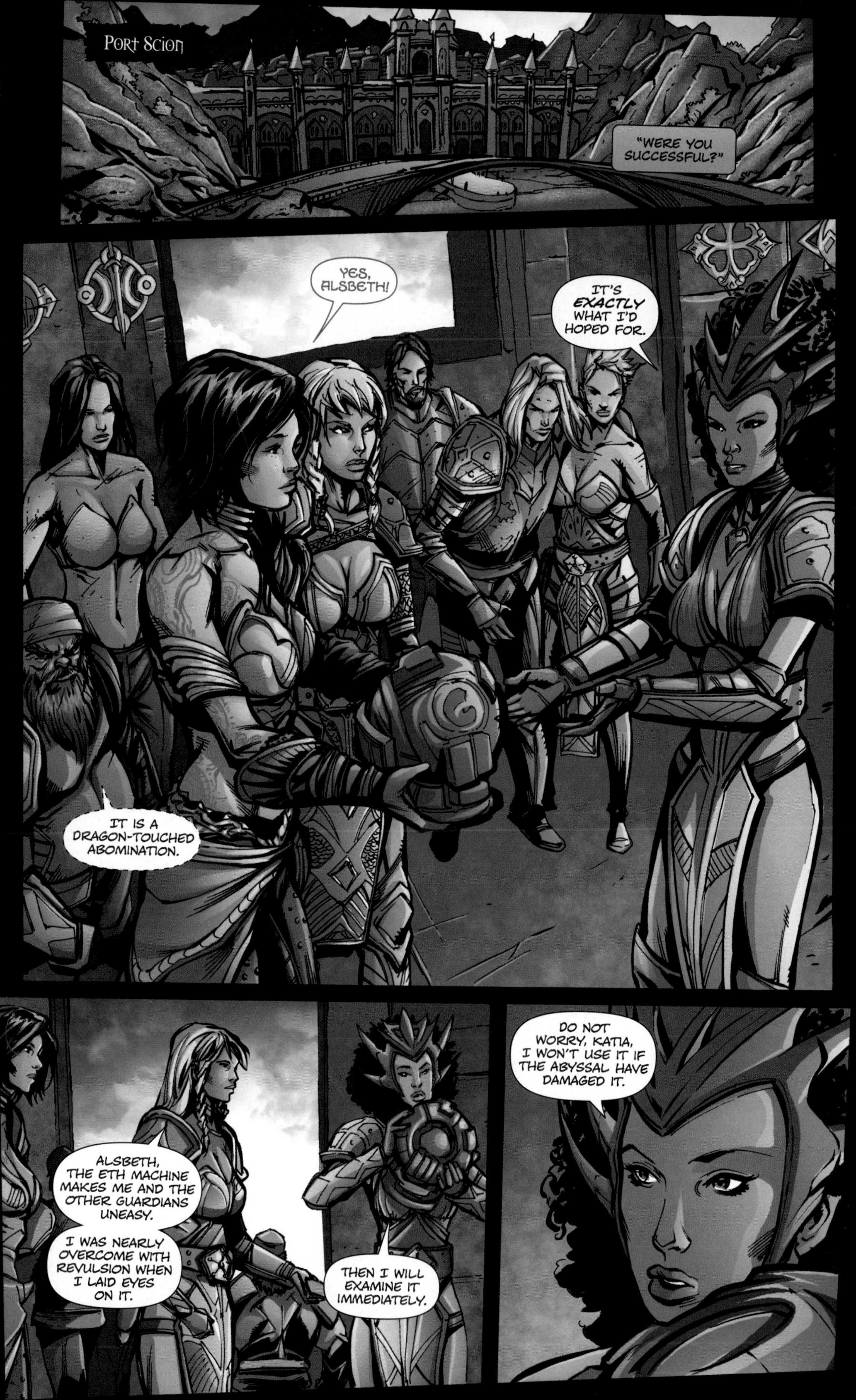
Port Scion
"WERE YOU SUCCESSFUL?"
YES, ALSBETH!
IT'S EXACTLY WHAT I'D HOPED FOR.
IT IS A DRAGON-TOUCHED ABOMINATION.
ALSBETH, THE ETH MACHINE MAKES ME AND THE OTHER GUARDIANS UNEASY.
I WAS NEARLY OVERCOME WITH REVULSION WHEN I LAID EYES ON IT.
THEN I WILL EXAMINE IT IMMEDIATELY.
DO NOT WORRY, KATIA, I WON'T USE IT IF THE ABYSSAL HAVE DAMAGED IT.

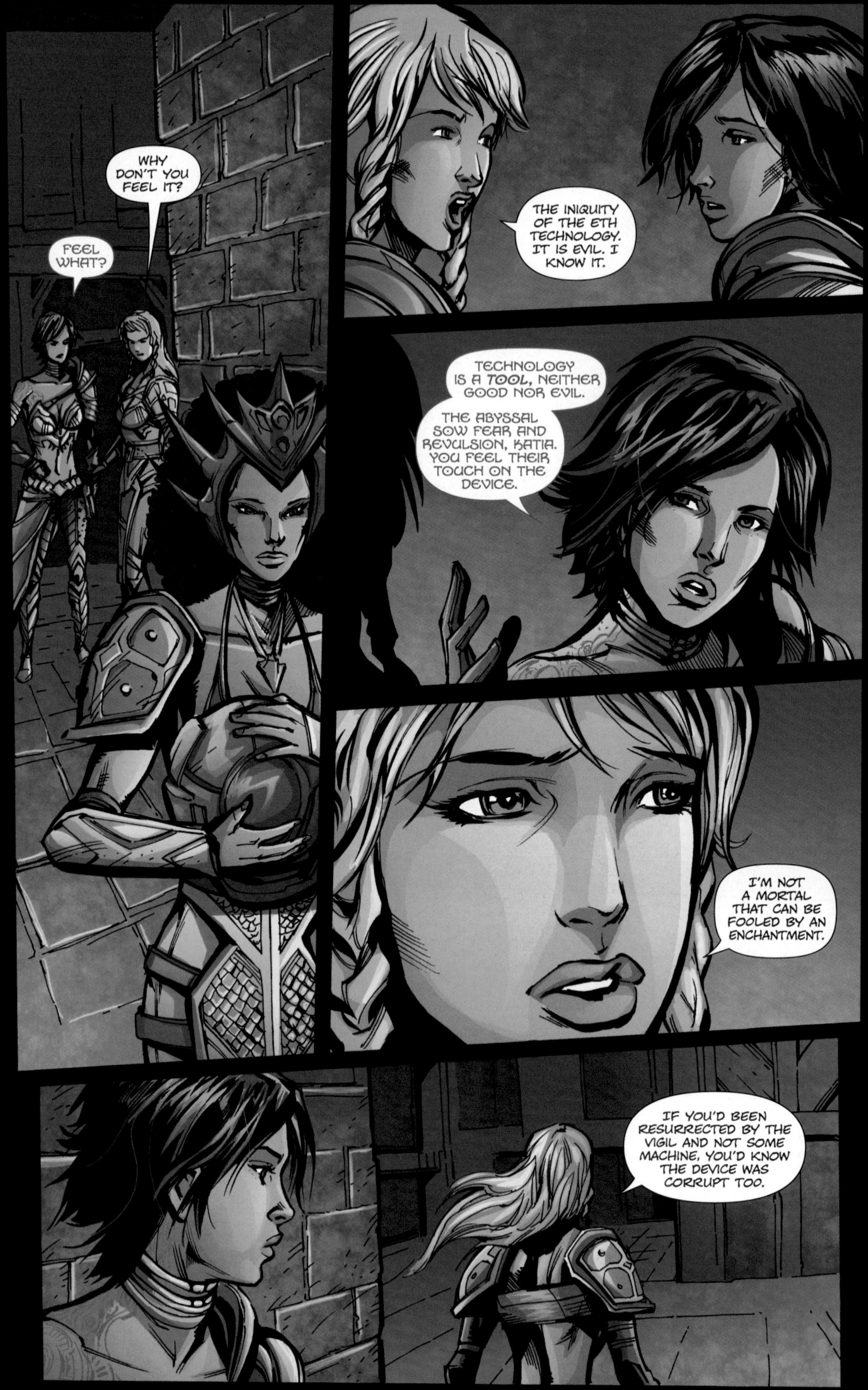
WHY DON'T YOU FEEL IT?
FEEL WHAT?
THE INIQUITY OF THE ETH TECHNOLOGY. IT IS EVIL. I KNOW IT.
TECHNOLOGY IS A TOOL, NEITHER GOOD NOR EVIL.
THE ABYSSAL SOW FEAR AND REVULSION, KATIA. YOU FEEL THEIR TOUCH ON THE DEVICE.
I'M NOT A MORTAL THAT CAN BE FOOLED BY AN ENCHANTMENT.
IF YOU'D BEEN RESURRECTED BY THE VIGIL AND NOT SOME MACHINE, YOU'D KNOW THE DEVICE WAS CORRUPT TOO.

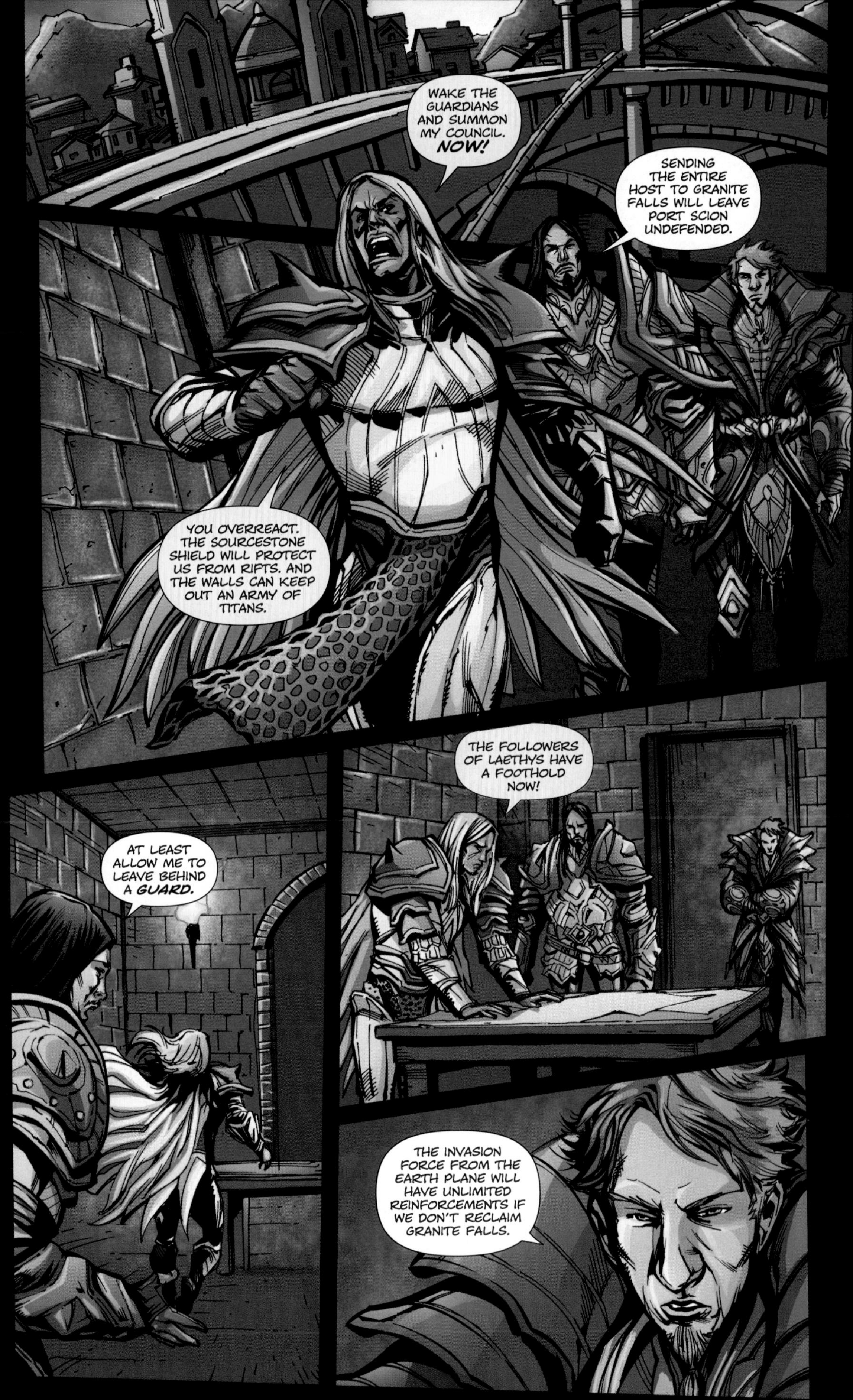
WAKE THE GUARDIANS AND SUMMON MY COUNCIL. NOW!
SENDING THE ENTIRE HOST TO GRANITE FALLS WILL LEAVE PORT SCION UNDEFENDED.
YOU OVERREACT. THE SOURCESTONE SHIELD WILL PROTECT US FROM RIFTS. AND THE WALLS CAN KEEP OUT AN ARMY OF TITANS.
AT LEAST ALLOW ME TO LEAVE BEHIND A GUARD.
THE FOLLOWERS OF LAETHYS HAVE A FOOTHOLD NOW!
THE INVASION FORCE FROM THE EARTH PLANE WILL HAVE UNLIMITED REINFORCEMENTS IF WE DON'T RECLAIM GRANITE FALLS.

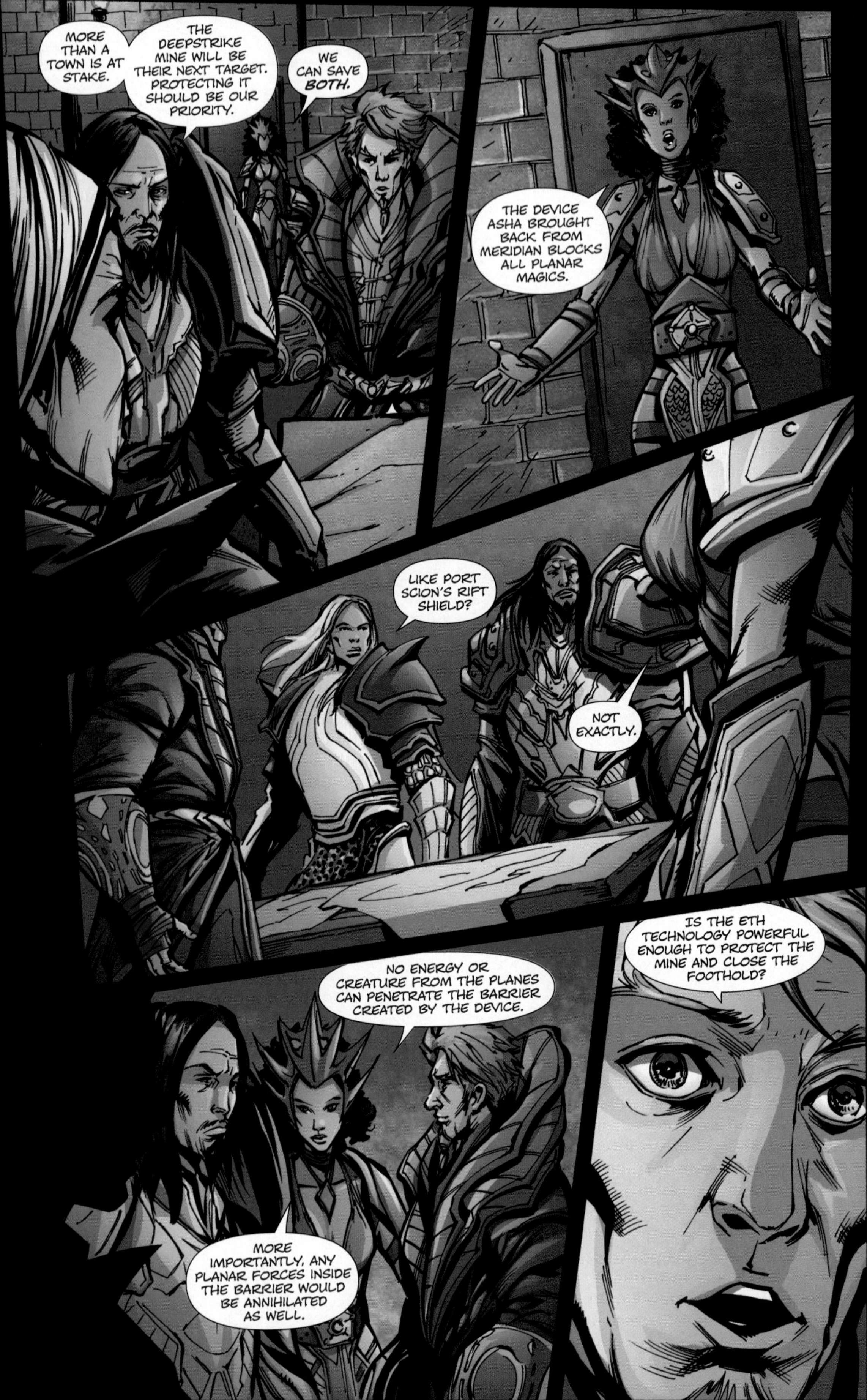
MORE THAN A TOWN IS AT STAKE.
THE DEEPSTRIKE MINE WILL BE THEIR NEXT TARGET. PROTECTING IT SHOULD BE OUR PRIORITY.
WE CAN SAVE *BOTH.*
THE DEVICE ASHA BROUGHT BACK FROM MERIDIAN BLOCKS ALL PLANAR MAGICS.
LIKE PORT SCION'S RIFT SHIELD?
NOT EXACTLY.
IS THE ETH TECHNOLOGY POWERFUL ENOUGH TO PROTECT THE MINE AND CLOSE THE FOOTHOLD?
NO ENERGY OR CREATURE FROM THE PLANES CAN PENETRATE THE BARRIER CREATED BY THE DEVICE.
MORE IMPORTANTLY, ANY PLANAR FORCES INSIDE THE BARRIER WOULD BE ANNIHILATED AS WELL.

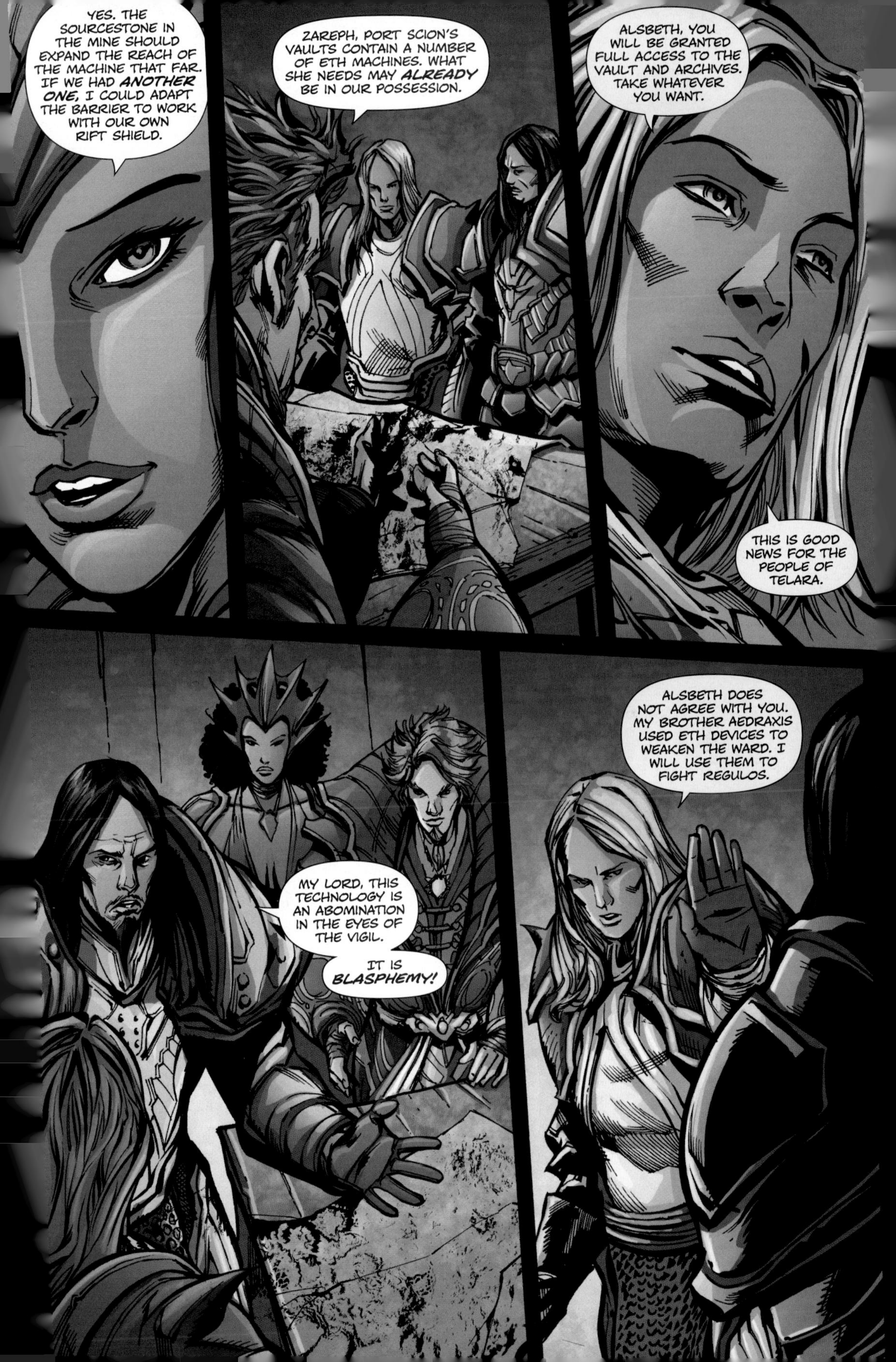
YES. THE SOURCESTONE IN THE MINE SHOULD EXPAND THE REACH OF THE MACHINE THAT FAR. IF WE HAD ANOTHER ONE, I COULD ADAPT THE BARRIER TO WORK WITH OUR OWN RIFT SHIELD.
ZAREPH, PORT SCION'S VAULTS CONTAIN A NUMBER OF ETH MACHINES. WHAT SHE NEEDS MAY ALREADY BE IN OUR POSSESSION.
ALSBETH, YOU WILL BE GRANTED FULL ACCESS TO THE VAULT AND ARCHIVES. TAKE WHATEVER YOU WANT.
THIS IS GOOD NEWS FOR THE PEOPLE OF TELARA.
MY LORD, THIS TECHNOLOGY IS AN ABOMINATION IN THE EYES OF THE VIGIL.
IT IS BLASPHEMY!
ALSBETH DOES NOT AGREE WITH YOU. MY BROTHER AEDRAXIS USED ETH DEVICES TO WEAKEN THE WARD. I WILL USE THEM TO FIGHT REGULOS.

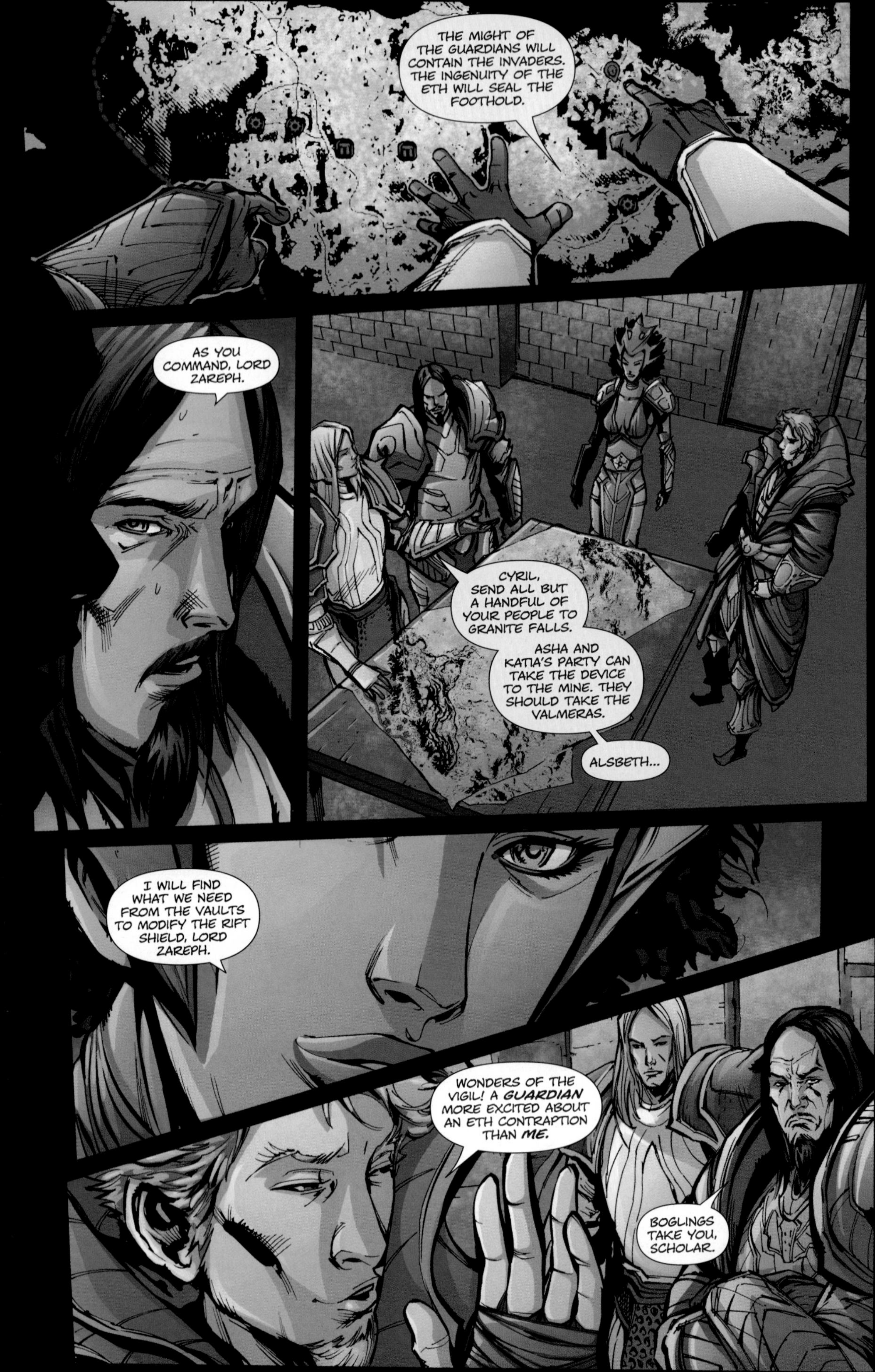
THE MIGHT OF THE GUARDIANS WILL CONTAIN THE INVADERS. THE INGENUITY OF THE ETH WILL SEAL THE FOOTHOLD.
AS YOU COMMAND, LORD ZAREPH.
CYRIL, SEND ALL BUT A HANDFUL OF YOUR PEOPLE TO GRANITE FALLS.
ASHA AND KATIA'S PARTY CAN TAKE THE DEVICE TO THE MINE. THEY SHOULD TAKE THE VALMERAS.
ALSBETH...
I WILL FIND WHAT WE NEED FROM THE VAULTS TO MODIFY THE RIFT SHIELD, LORD ZAREPH.
WONDERS OF THE VIGIL! A *GUARDIAN* MORE EXCITED ABOUT AN ETH CONTRAPTION THAN *ME.*
BOGLINGS TAKE YOU, SCHOLAR.

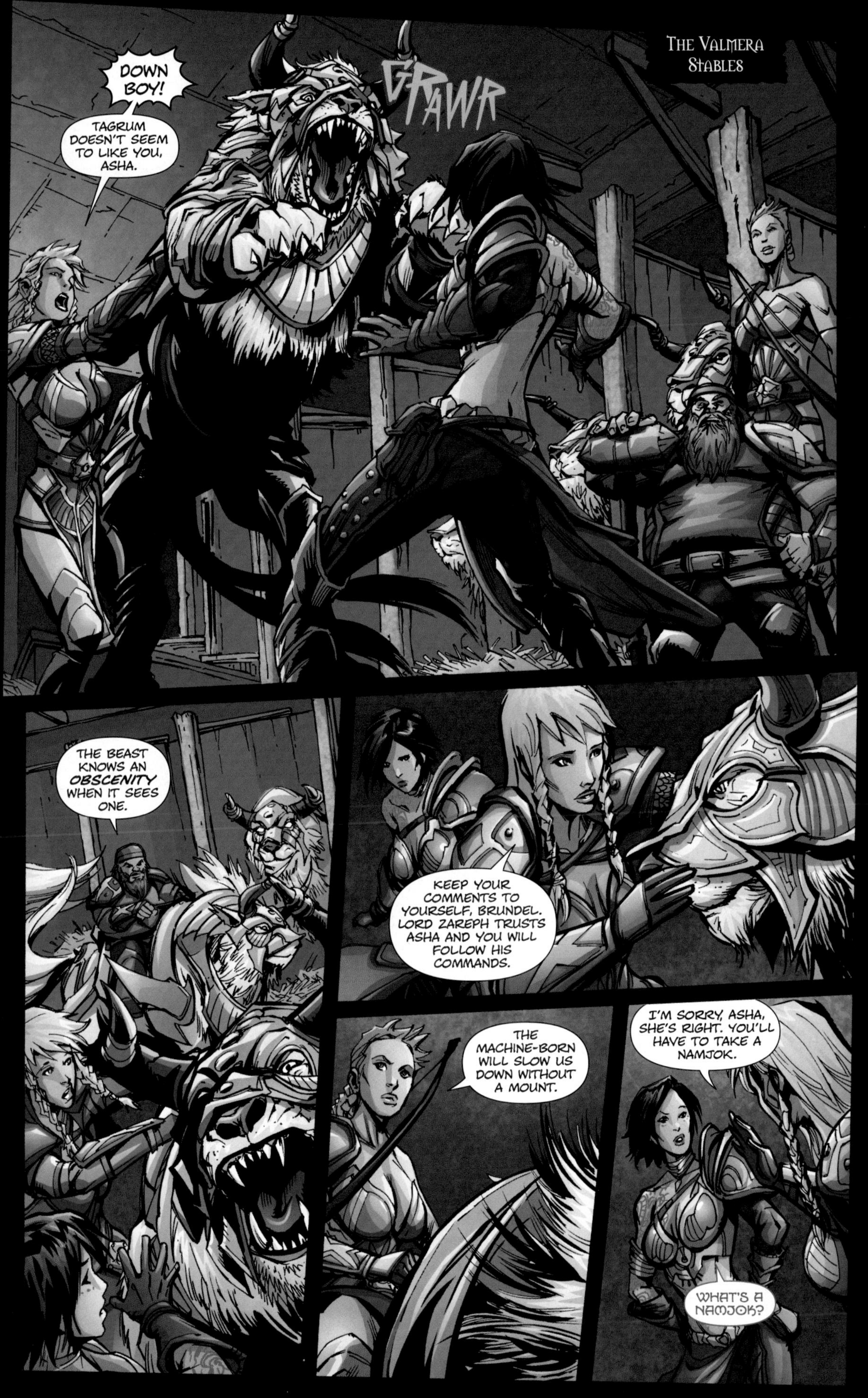

The Valmera Stables
DOWN BOY!
TAGRUM DOESN'T SEEM TO LIKE YOU, ASHA.
GRAWR
THE BEAST KNOWS AN *OBSCENITY* WHEN IT SEES ONE.
KEEP YOUR COMMENTS TO YOURSELF, BRUNDEL. LORD ZAREPH TRUSTS ASHA AND YOU WILL FOLLOW HIS COMMANDS.
THE MACHINE-BORN WILL SLOW US DOWN WITHOUT A MOUNT.
I'M SORRY, ASHA, SHE'S RIGHT. YOU'LL HAVE TO TAKE A NAMJOK.
WHAT'S A NAMJOK?

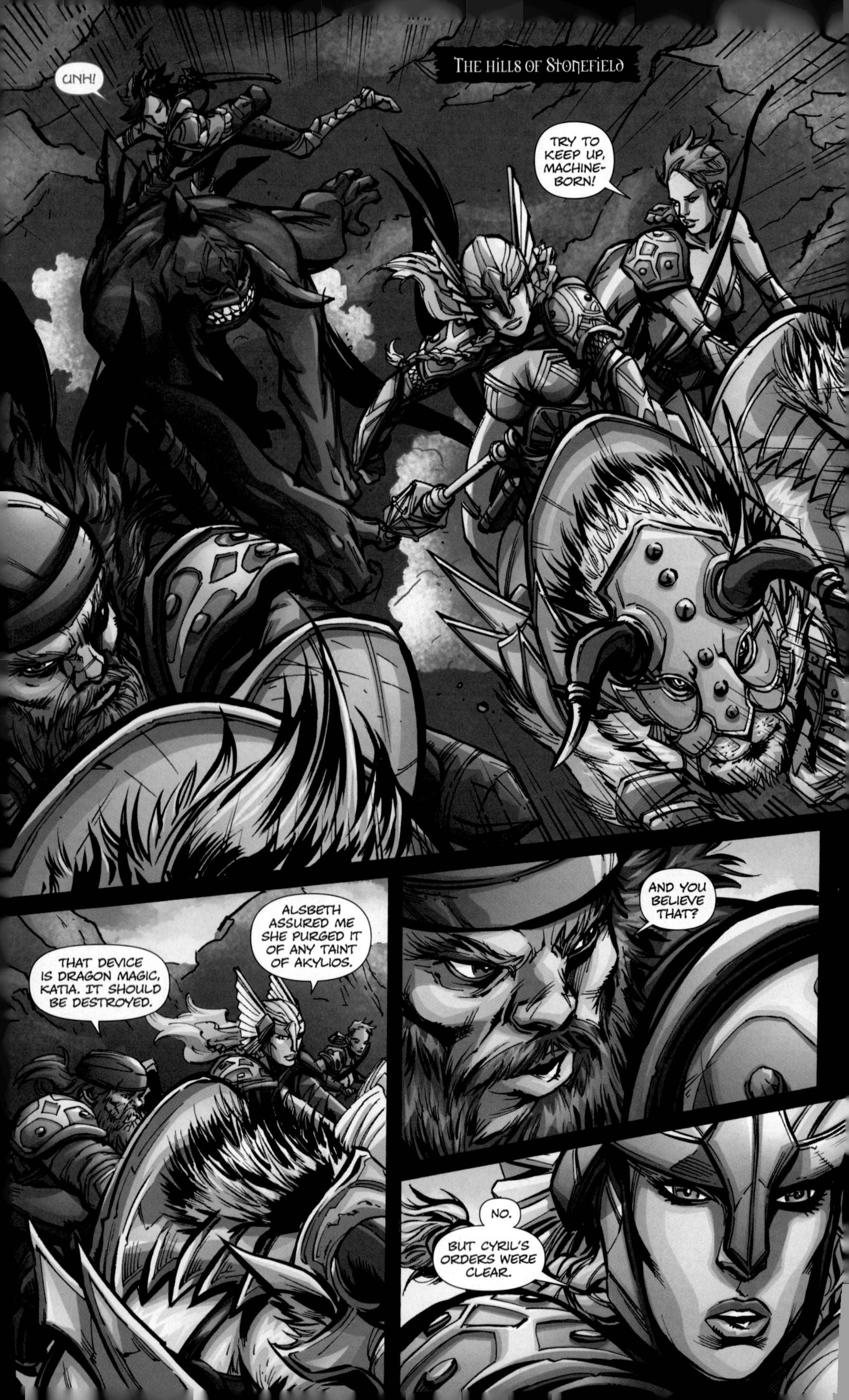
The hills of Stonefield
UNH!
TRY TO KEEP UP, MACHINE-BORN!
THAT DEVICE IS DRAGON MAGIC, KATIA. IT SHOULD BE DESTROYED.
ALSBETH ASSURED ME SHE PURGED IT OF ANY TAINT OF AKYLIOS.
AND YOU BELIEVE THAT?
NO.
BUT CYRIL'S ORDERS WERE CLEAR.

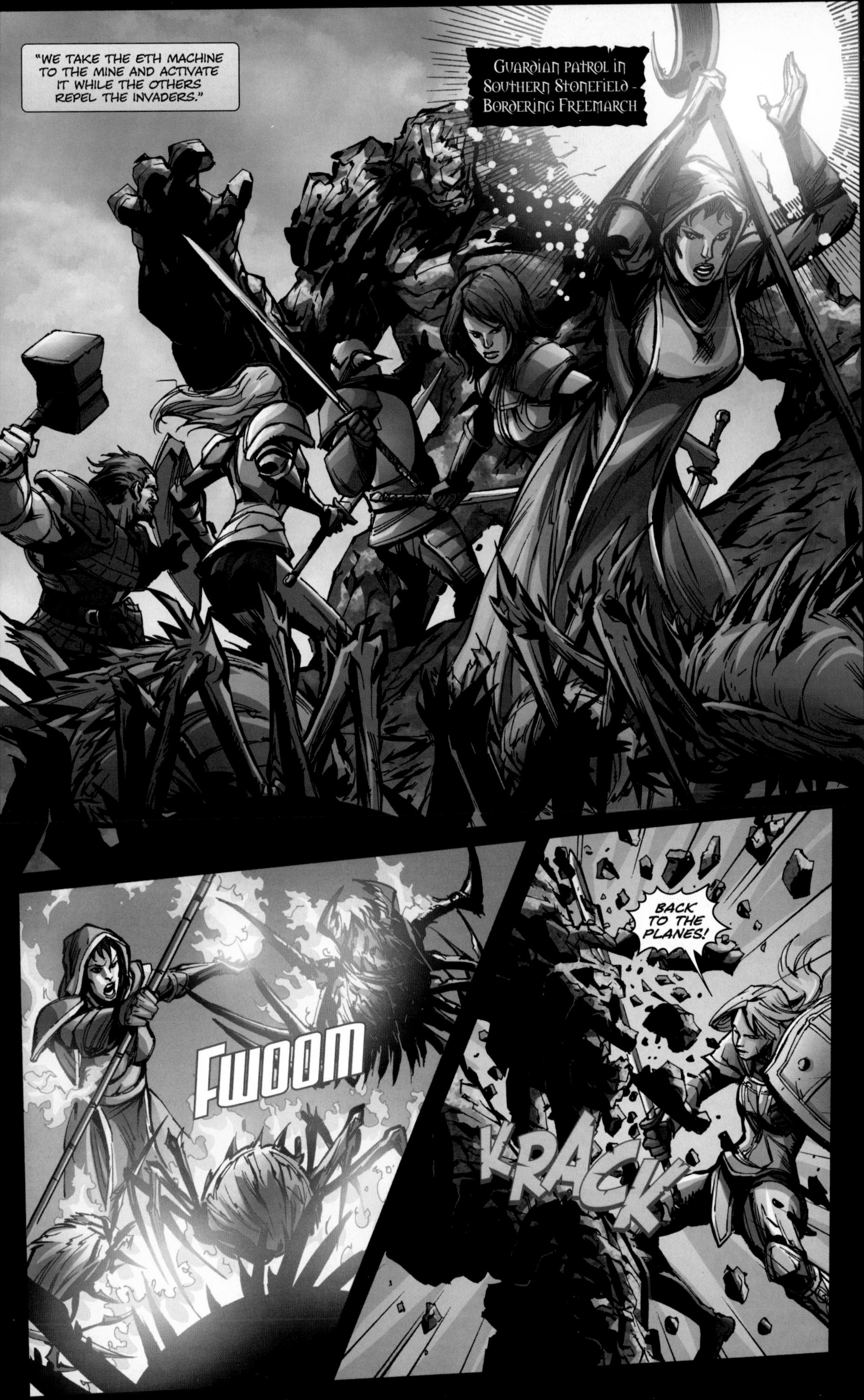
"WE TAKE THE ETH MACHINE TO THE MINE AND ACTIVATE IT WHILE THE OTHERS REPEL THE INVADERS."
Guardian patrol in Southern Stonefield - Bordering Freemarch
FWOOM
BACK TO THE PLANES!
KRACK

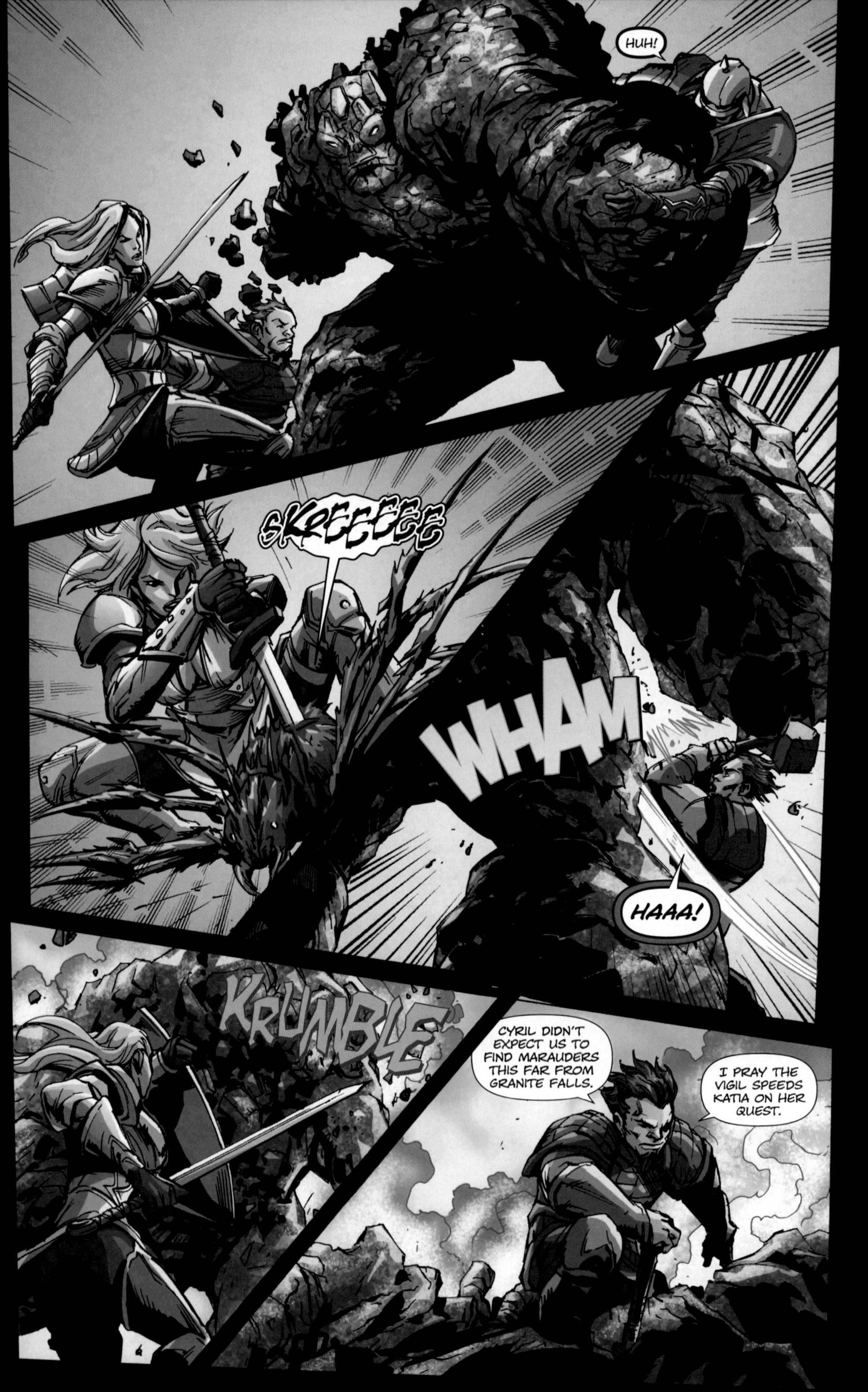
HUH!
SKREEEEEE
WHAM
HAAA!
KRUMBLE
CYRIL DIDN'T EXPECT US TO FIND MARAUDERS THIS FAR FROM GRANITE FALLS.
I PRAY THE VIGIL SPEEDS KATIA ON HER QUEST.

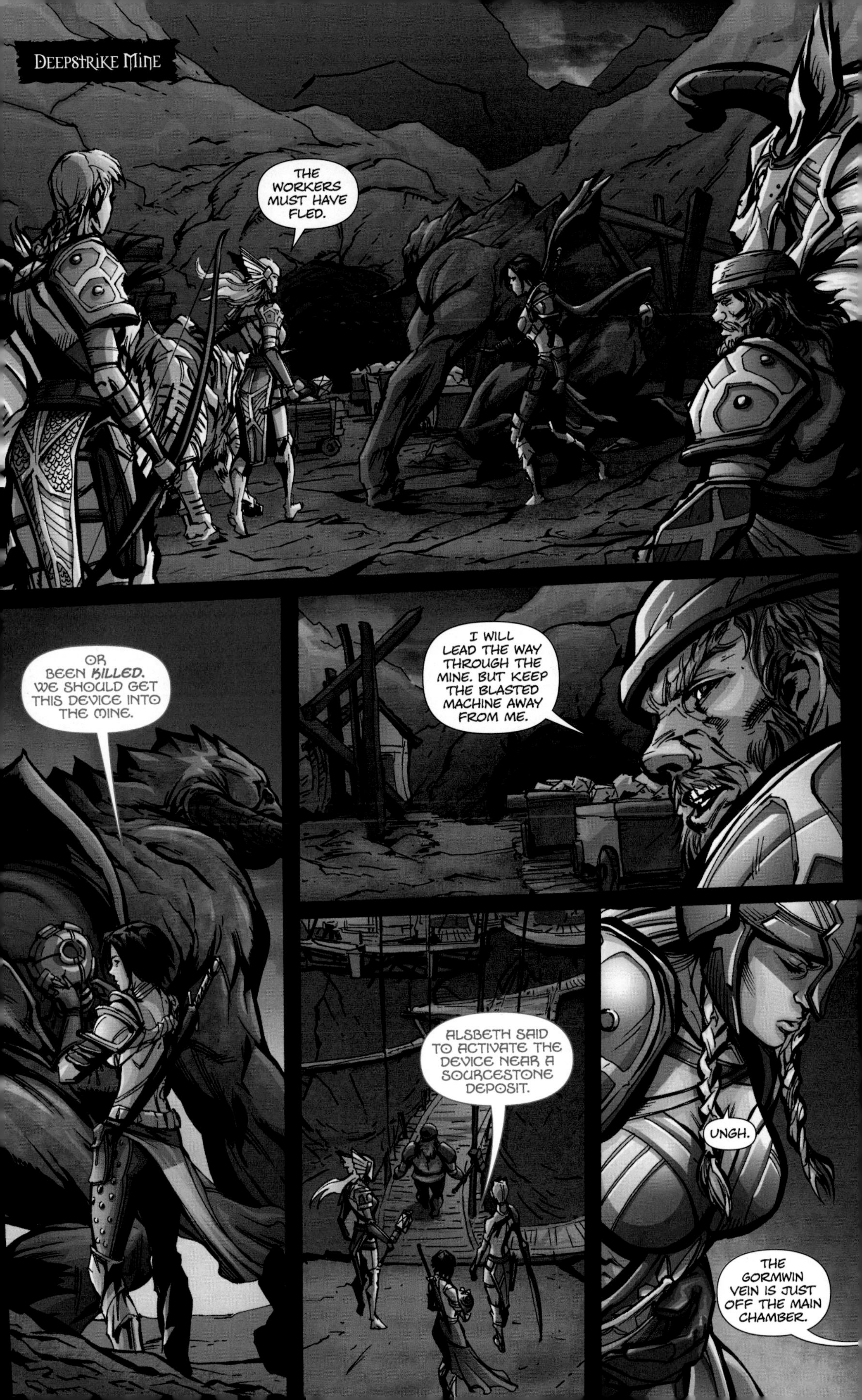
DEEPSTRIKE MINE
THE WORKERS MUST HAVE FLED.
OR BEEN KILLED. WE SHOULD GET THIS DEVICE INTO THE MINE.
I WILL LEAD THE WAY THROUGH THE MINE. BUT KEEP THE BLASTED MACHINE AWAY FROM ME.
ALSBETH SAID TO ACTIVATE THE DEVICE NEAR A SOURCESTONE DEPOSIT.
UNGH.
THE GORMWIN VEIN IS JUST OFF THE MAIN CHAMBER.

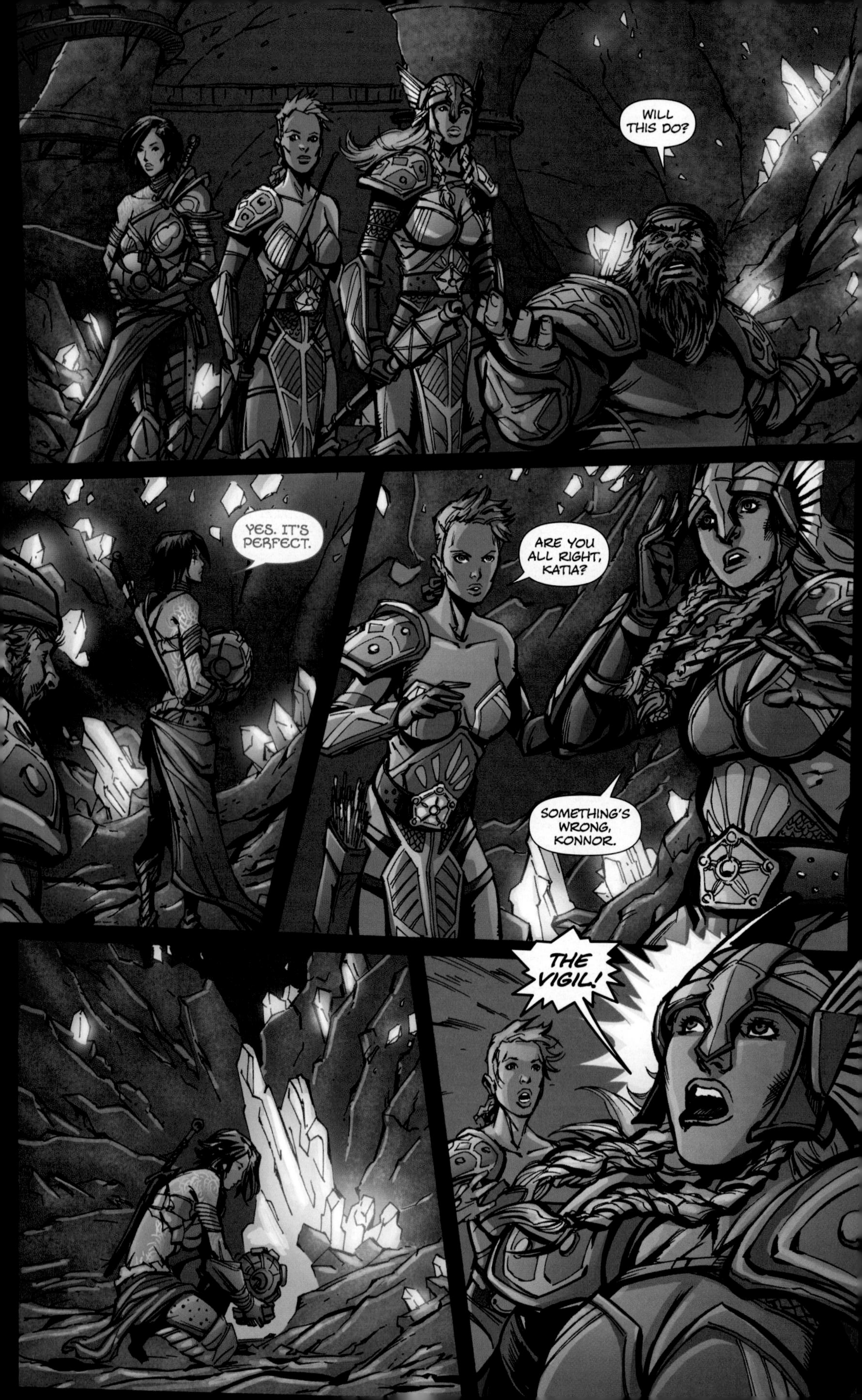
WILL THIS DO?
YES. IT'S PERFECT.
ARE YOU ALL RIGHT, KATIA?
SOMETHING'S WRONG, KONNOR.
THE VIGIL!

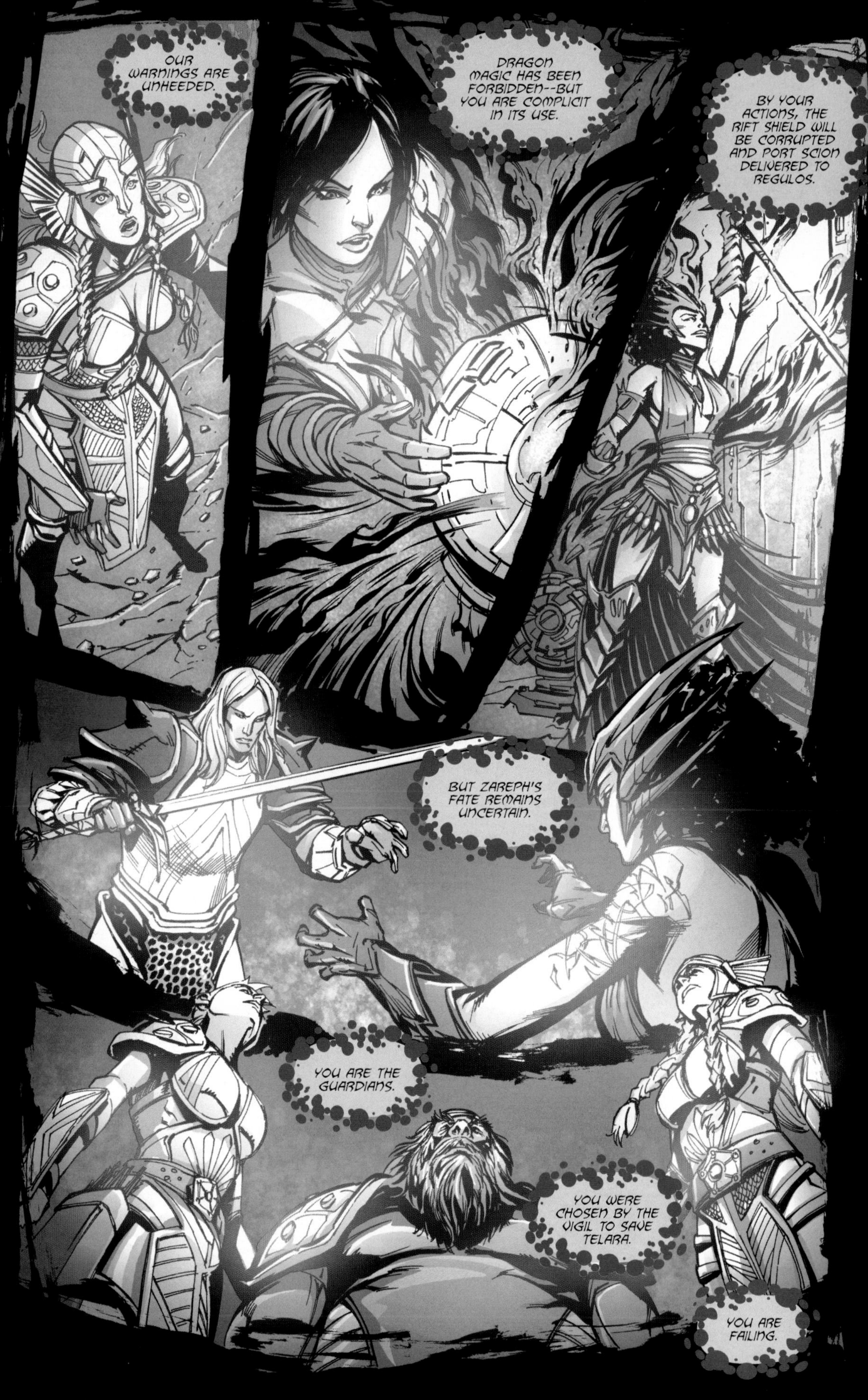
OUR WARNINGS ARE UNHEEDED.
DRAGON MAGIC HAS BEEN FORBIDDEN--BUT YOU ARE COMPLICIT IN ITS USE.
BY YOUR ACTIONS, THE RIFT SHIELD WILL BE CORRUPTED AND PORT SCION DELIVERED TO REGULOS.
BUT ZAREPH'S FATE REMAINS UNCERTAIN.
YOU ARE THE GUARDIANS.
YOU WERE CHOSEN BY THE VIGIL TO SAVE TELARA.
YOU ARE FAILING.

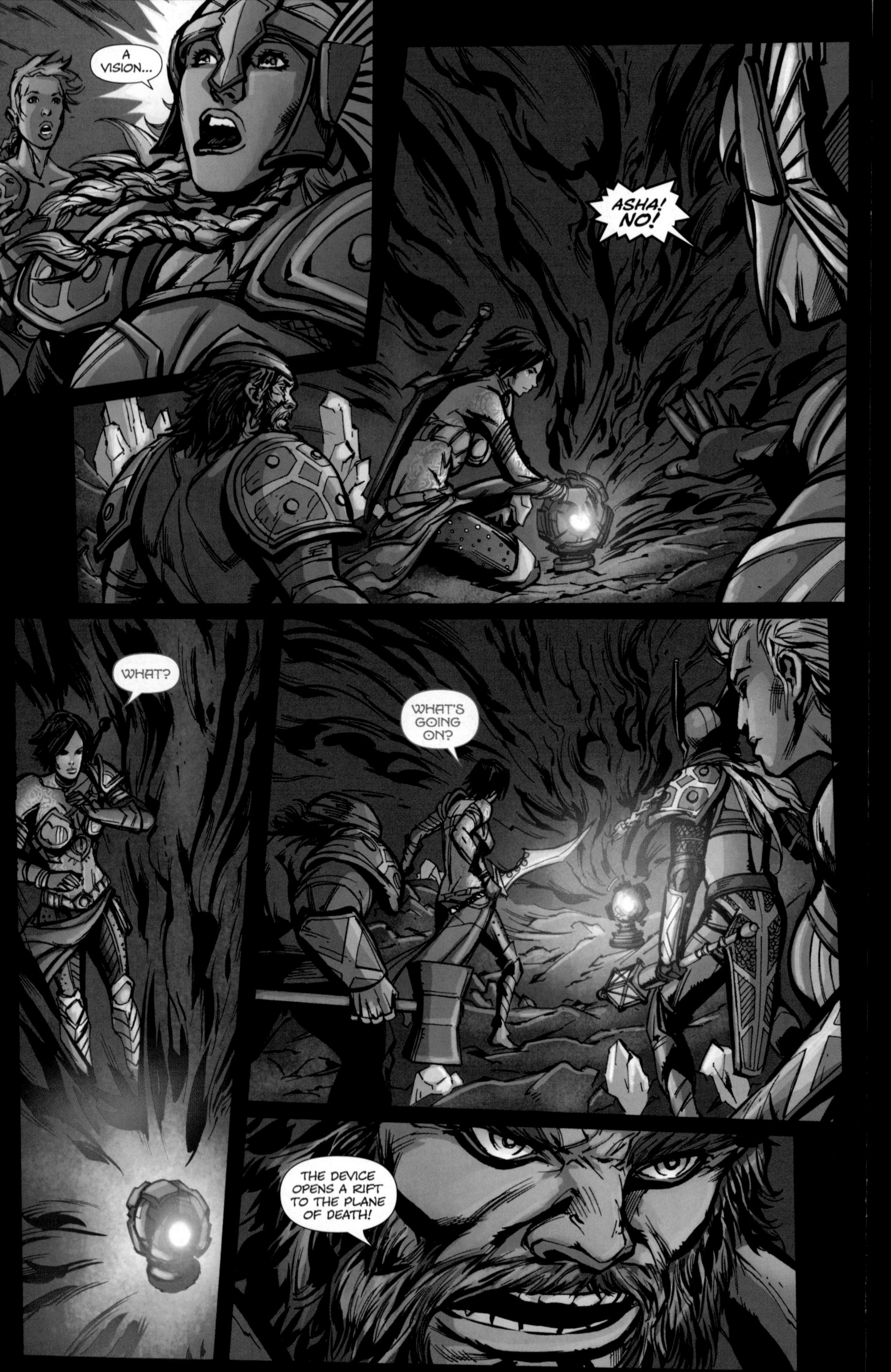
A VISION...
ASHA! NO!
WHAT?
WHAT'S GOING ON?
THE DEVICE OPENS A RIFT TO THE PLANE OF DEATH!

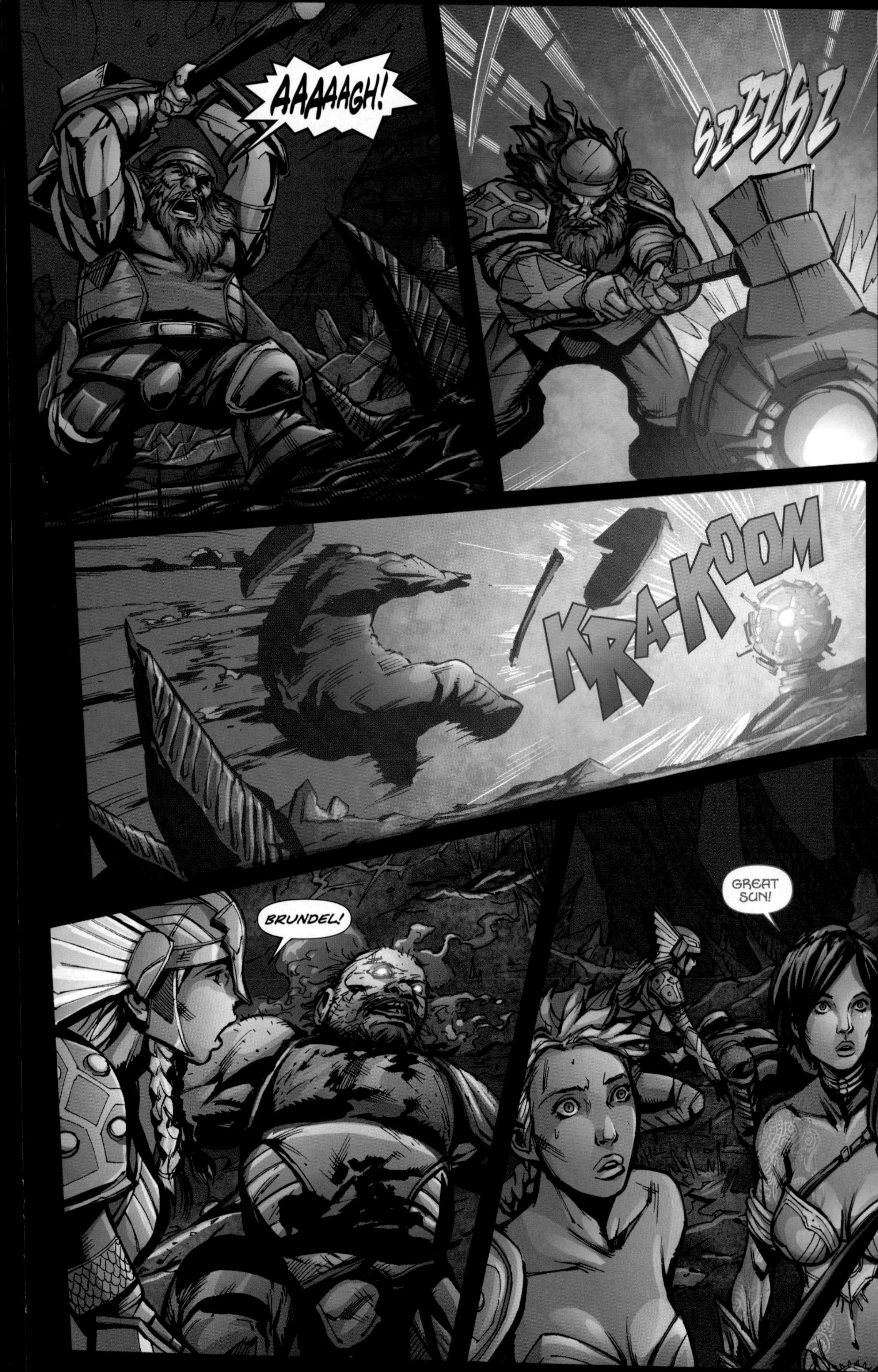
AAAAAGH!
SZZZSZ
KRA-KOOM
BRUNDEL!
GREAT SUN!

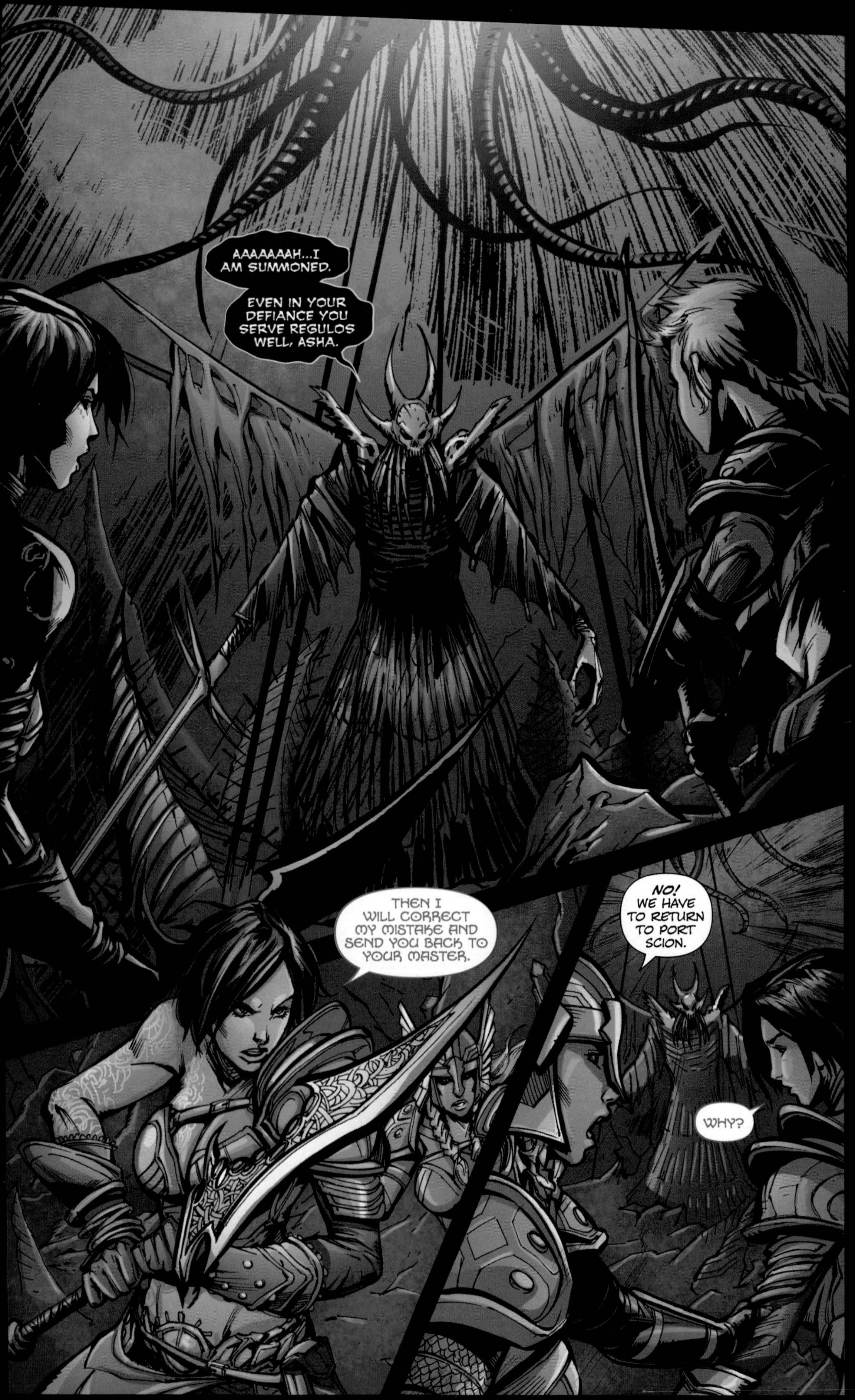
AAAAAAAH...I AM SUMMONED.
EVEN IN YOUR DEFIANCE YOU SERVE REGULOS WELL, ASHA.
THEN I WILL CORRECT MY MISTAKE AND SEND YOU BACK TO YOUR MASTER.
NO! WE HAVE TO RETURN TO PORT SCION.
WHY?

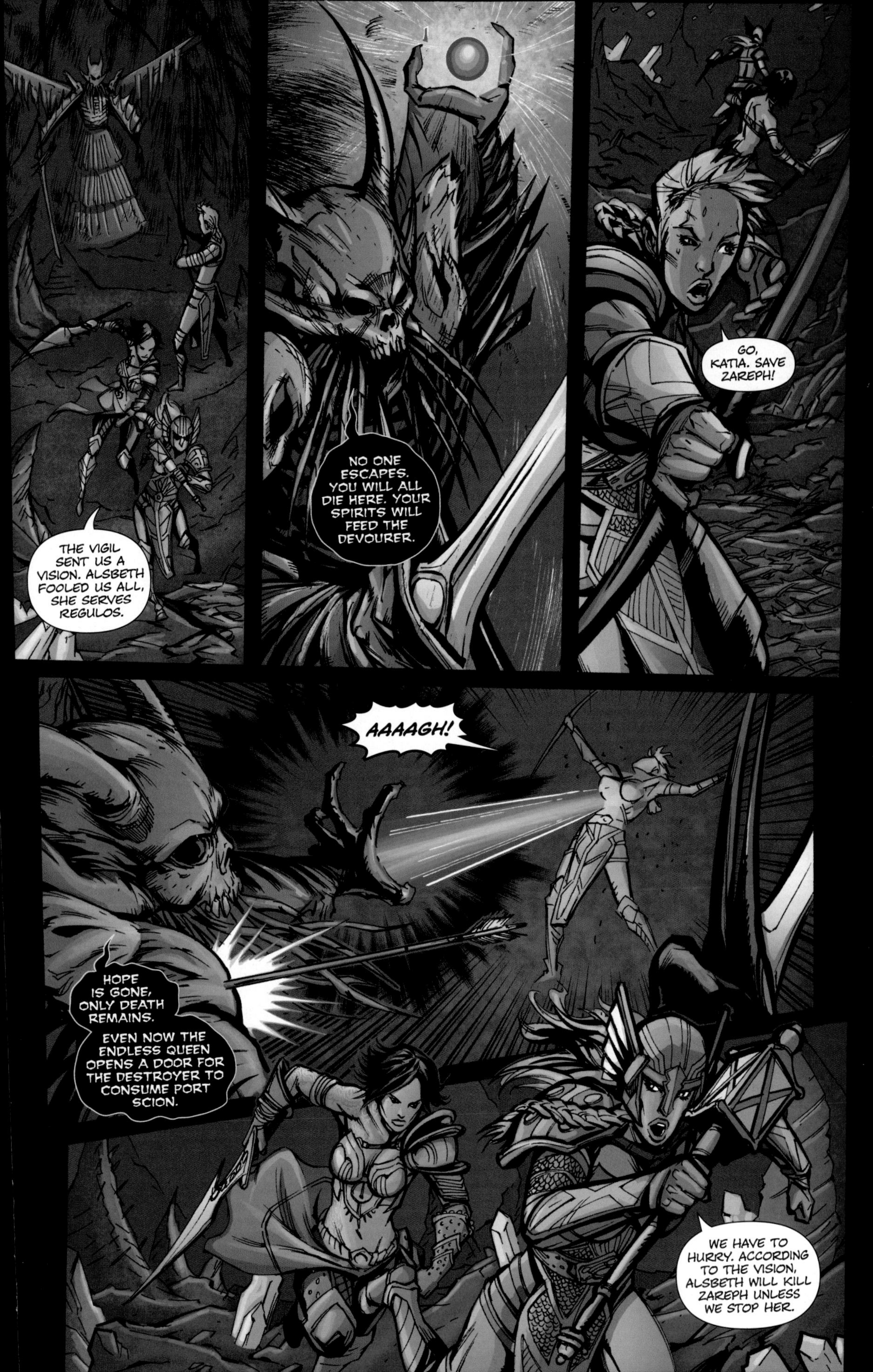
THE VIGIL SENT US A VISION. ALSBETH FOOLED US ALL, SHE SERVES REGULOS.
NO ONE ESCAPES. YOU WILL ALL DIE HERE. YOUR SPIRITS WILL FEED THE DEVOURER.
GO, KATIA. SAVE ZAREPH!
AAAAGH!
HOPE IS GONE, ONLY DEATH REMAINS.
EVEN NOW THE ENDLESS QUEEN OPENS A DOOR FOR THE DESTROYER TO CONSUME PORT SCION.
WE HAVE TO HURRY. ACCORDING TO THE VISION, ALSBETH WILL KILL ZAREPH UNLESS WE STOP HER.

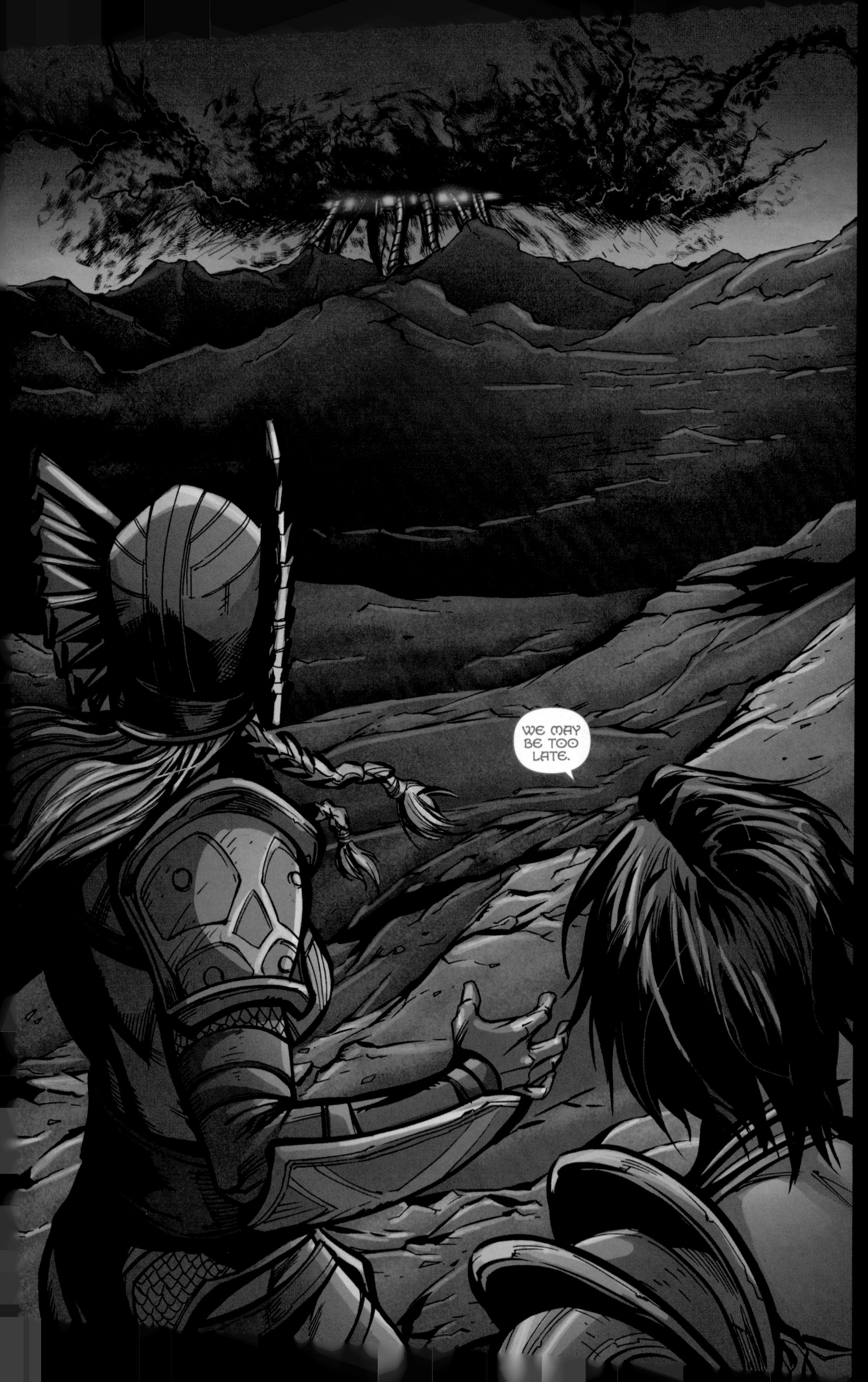
WE MAY BE TOO LATE.

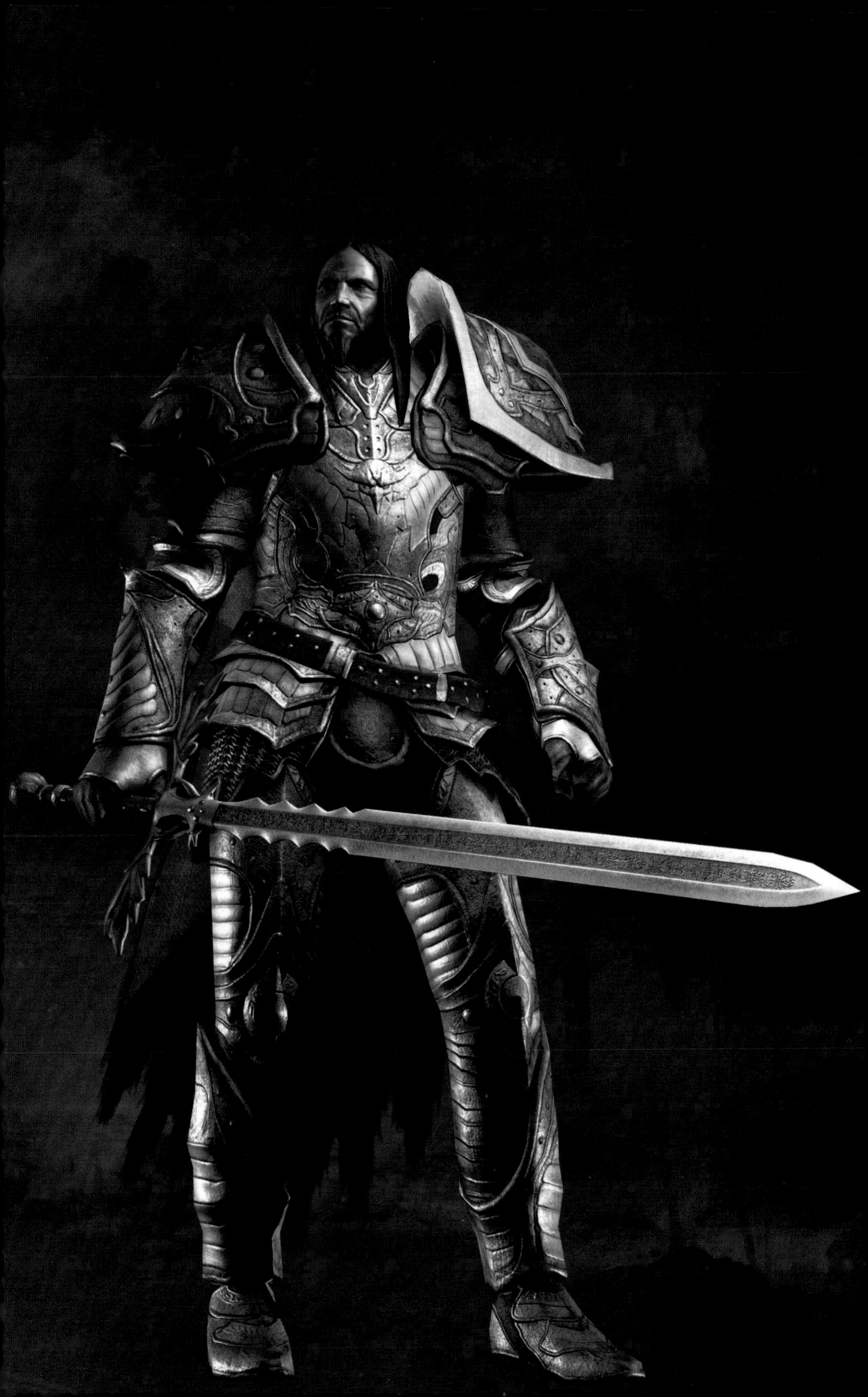

Chapter Five

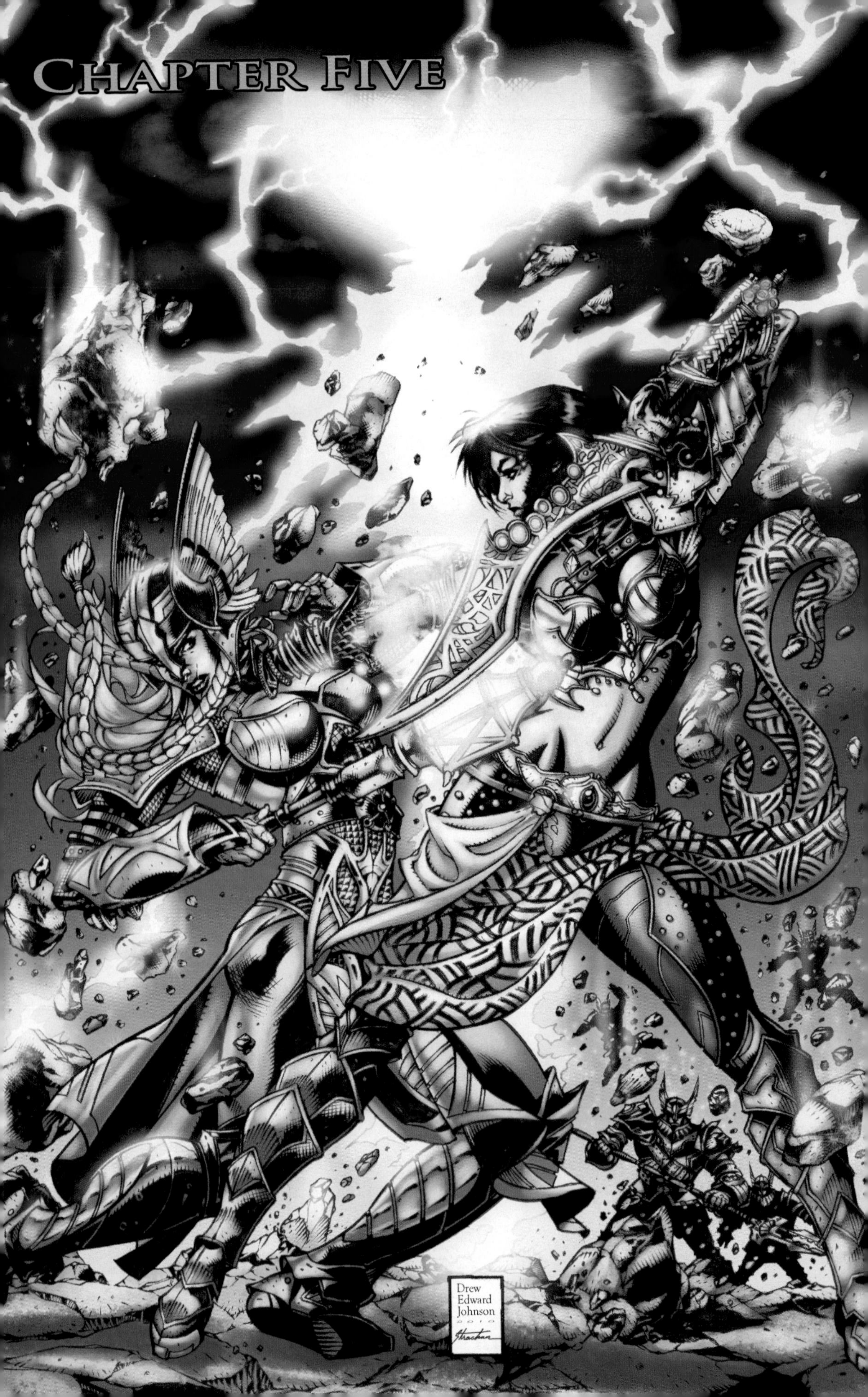
Drew
Edward
Johnson
2010
Strachan

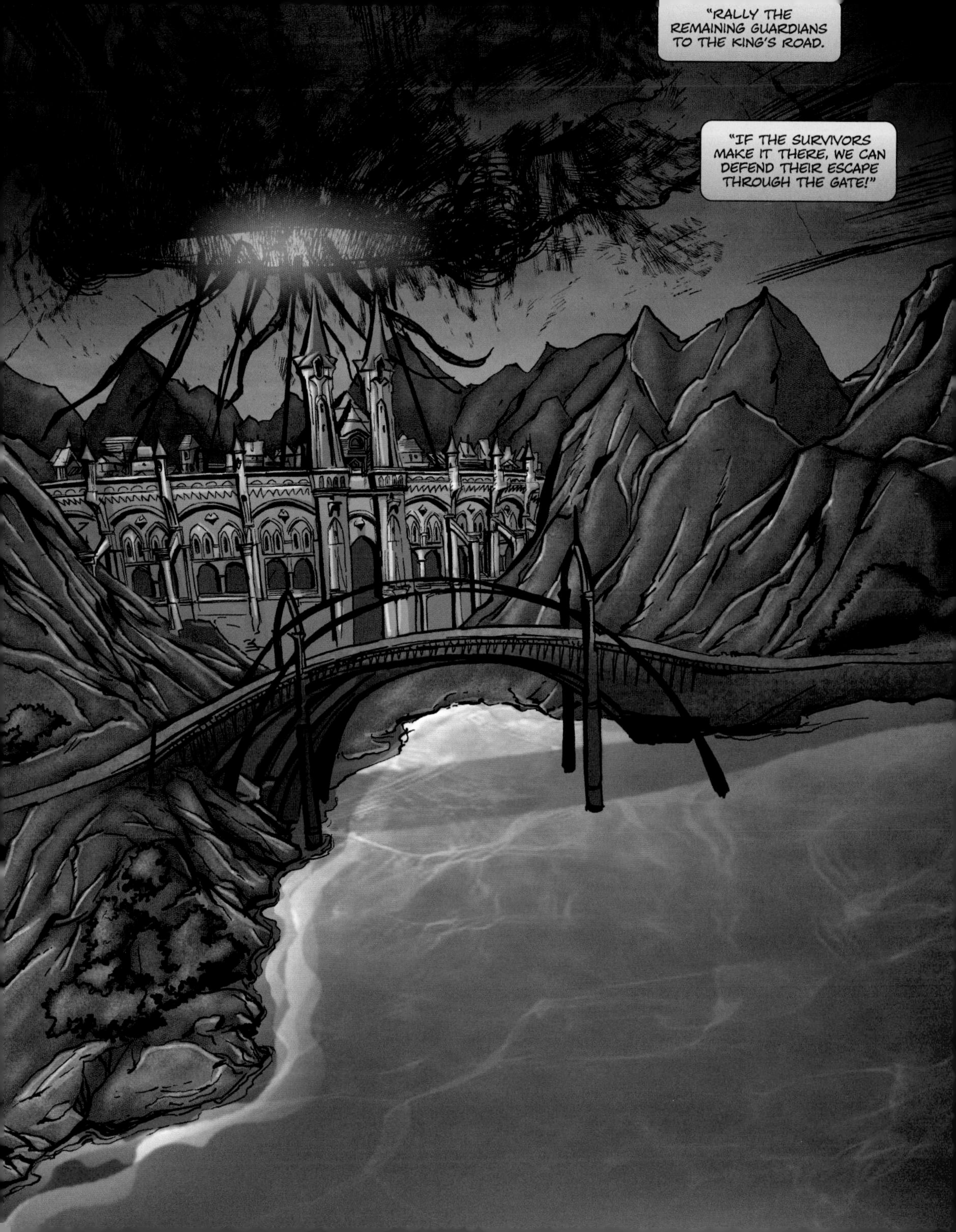
"RALLY THE REMAINING GUARDIANS TO THE KING'S ROAD.
"IF THE SURVIVORS MAKE IT THERE, WE CAN DEFEND THEIR ESCAPE THROUGH THE GATE!"

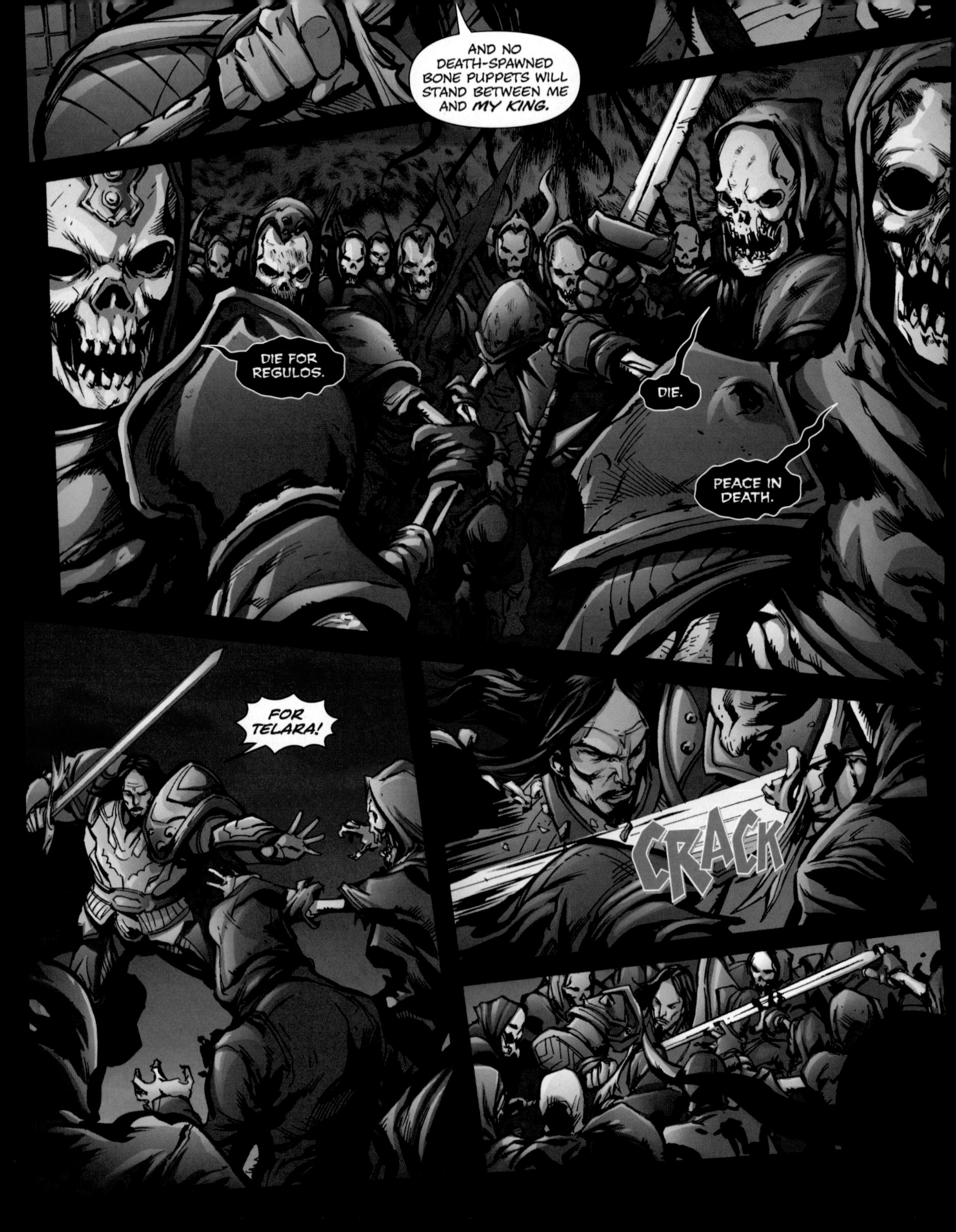
AND NO DEATH-SPAWNED BONE PUPPETS WILL STAND BETWEEN ME AND MY KING.
DIE FOR REGULOS.
DIE.
PEACE IN DEATH.
FOR TELARA!
CRACK

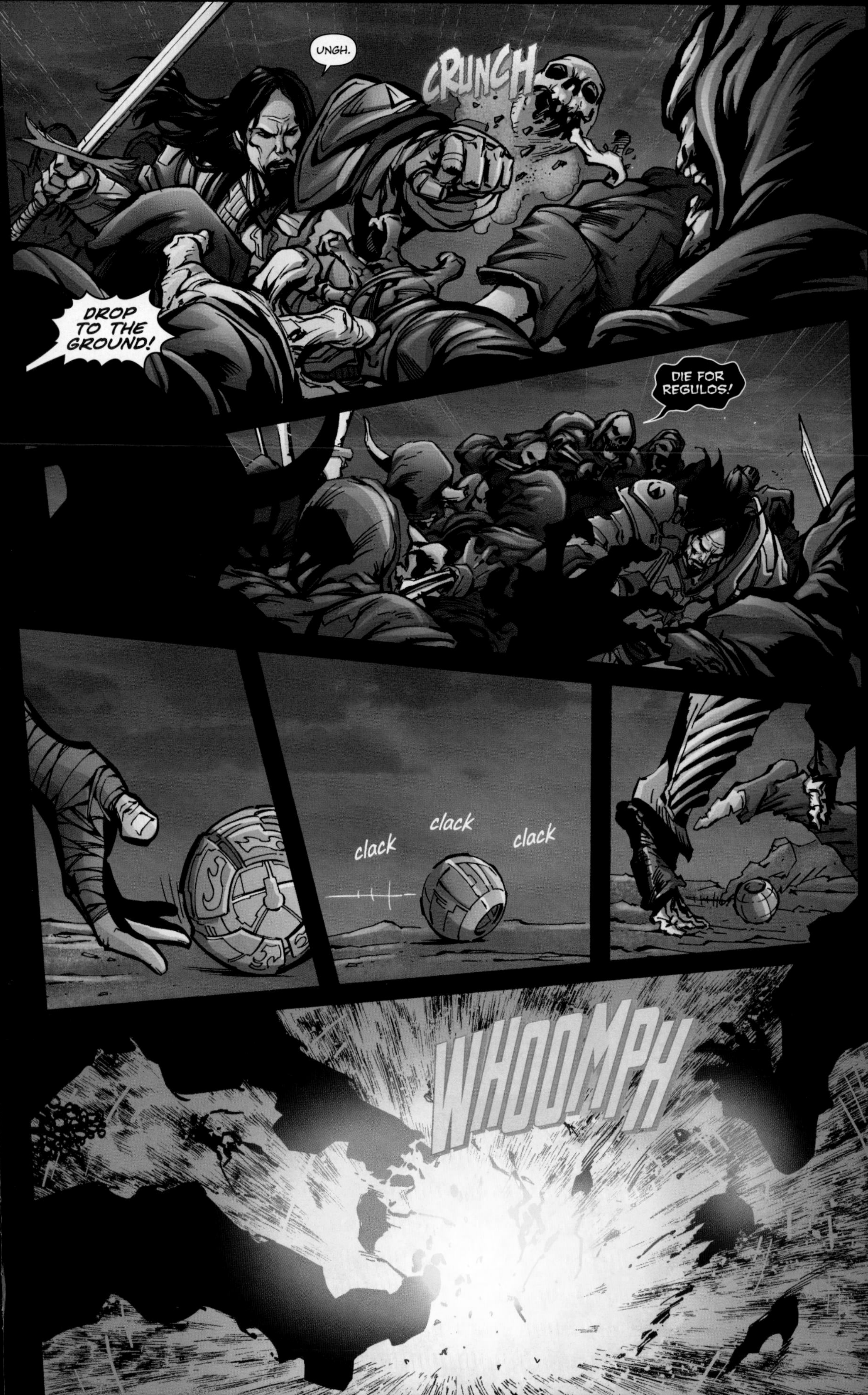
UNGH.
CRUNCH
DROP TO THE GROUND!
DIE FOR REGULOS!
clack
clack
clack
WHOOMPH

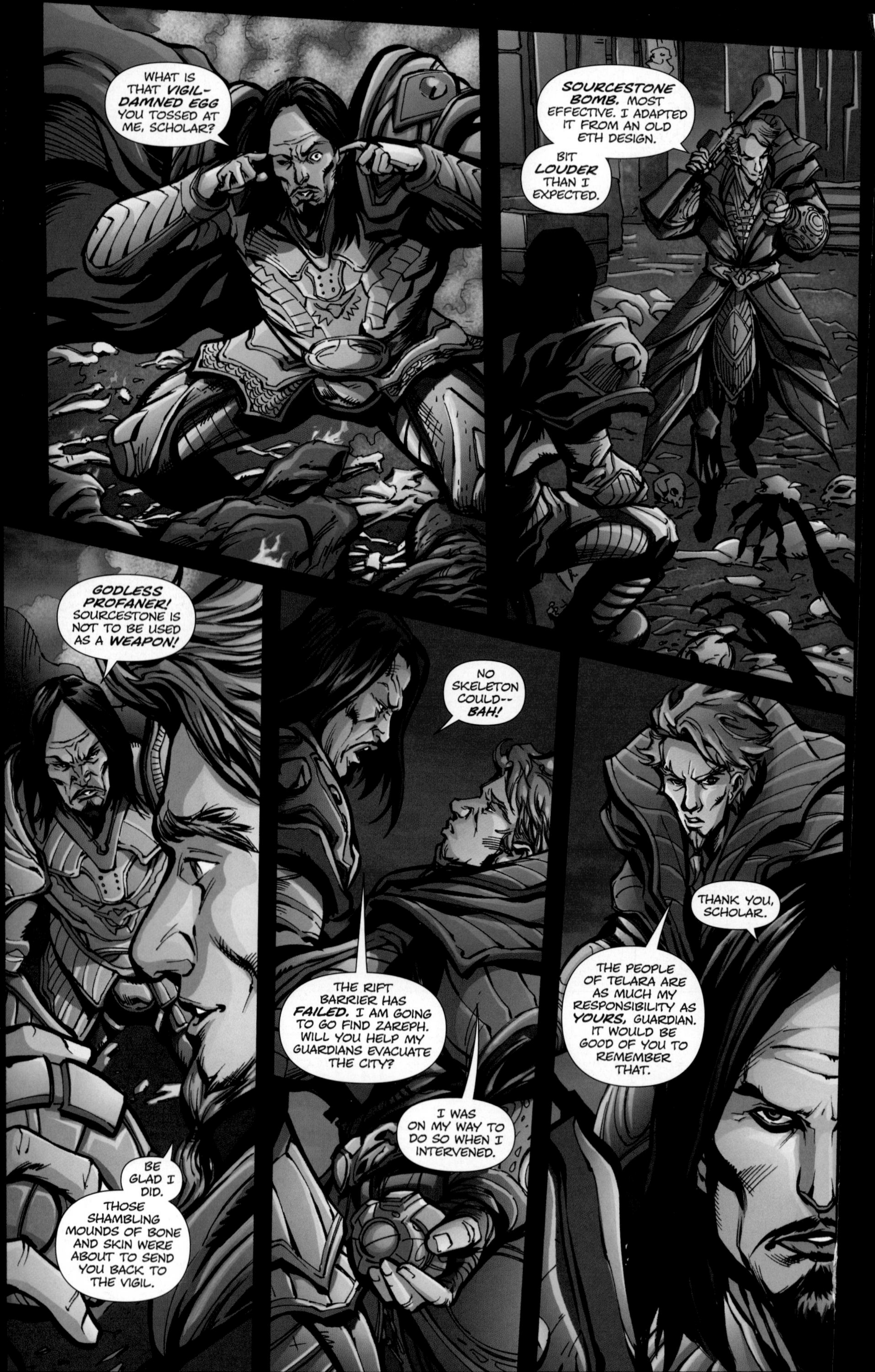
WHAT IS THAT VIGIL-DAMNED EGG YOU TOSSED AT ME, SCHOLAR?
SOURCESTONE BOMB. MOST EFFECTIVE. I ADAPTED IT FROM AN OLD ETH DESIGN.
BIT LOUDER THAN I EXPECTED.
GODLESS PROFANER! SOURCESTONE IS NOT TO BE USED AS A WEAPON!
BE GLAD I DID.
THOSE SHAMBLING MOUNDS OF BONE AND SKIN WERE ABOUT TO SEND YOU BACK TO THE VIGIL.
NO SKELETON COULD-- BAH!
THE RIFT BARRIER HAS FAILED. I AM GOING TO GO FIND ZAREPH. WILL YOU HELP MY GUARDIANS EVACUATE THE CITY?
I WAS ON MY WAY TO DO SO WHEN I INTERVENED.
THANK YOU, SCHOLAR.
THE PEOPLE OF TELARA ARE AS MUCH MY RESPONSIBILITY AS YOURS, GUARDIAN. IT WOULD BE GOOD OF YOU TO REMEMBER THAT.

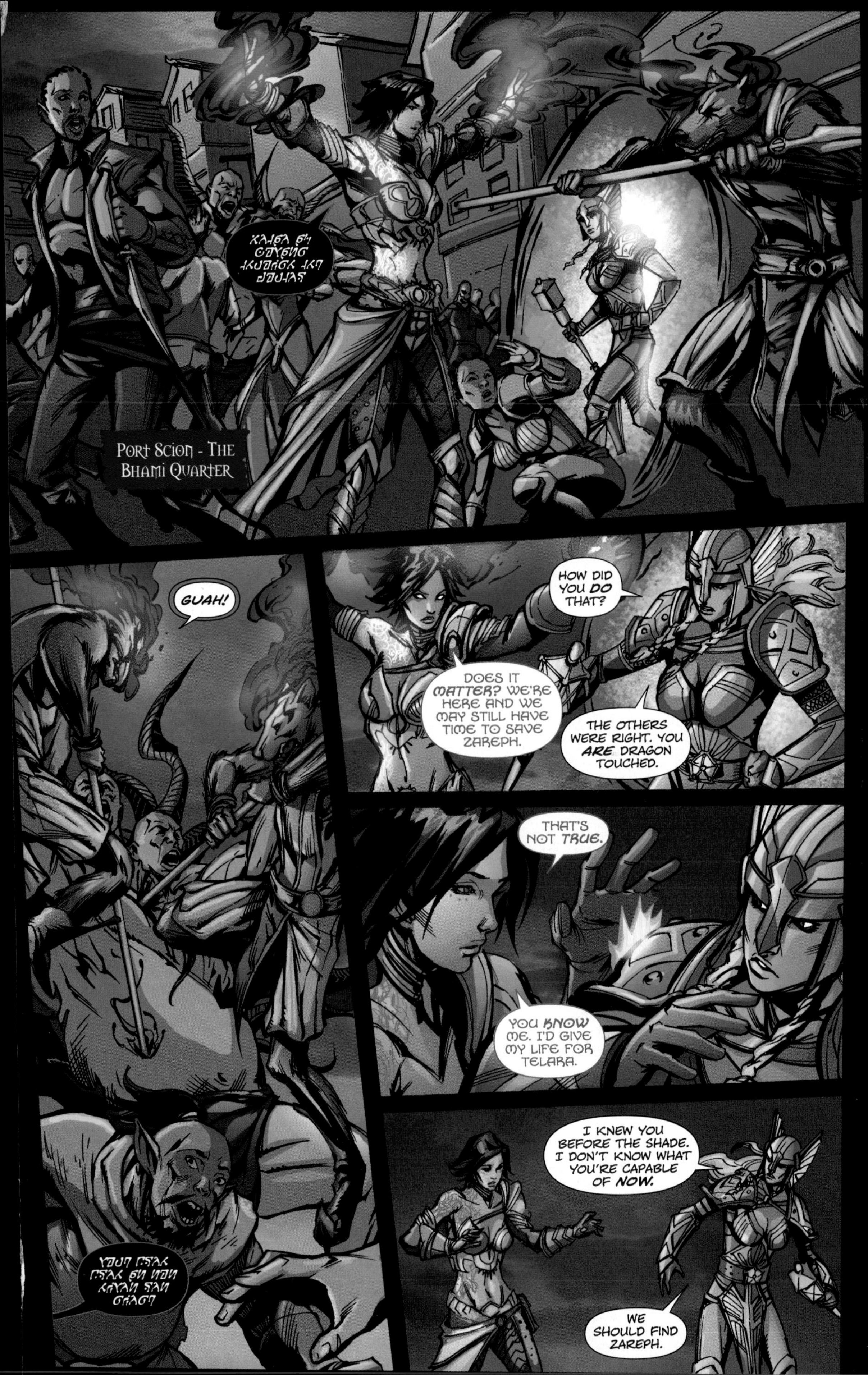
Port Scion - The Bhami Quarter
GUAH!
HOW DID YOU DO THAT?
DOES IT MATTER? WE'RE HERE AND WE MAY STILL HAVE TIME TO SAVE ZAREPH.
THE OTHERS WERE RIGHT. YOU ARE DRAGON TOUCHED.
THAT'S NOT TRUE.
YOU KNOW ME. I'D GIVE MY LIFE FOR TELARA.
I KNEW YOU BEFORE THE SHADE. I DON'T KNOW WHAT YOU'RE CAPABLE OF NOW.
WE SHOULD FIND ZAREPH.

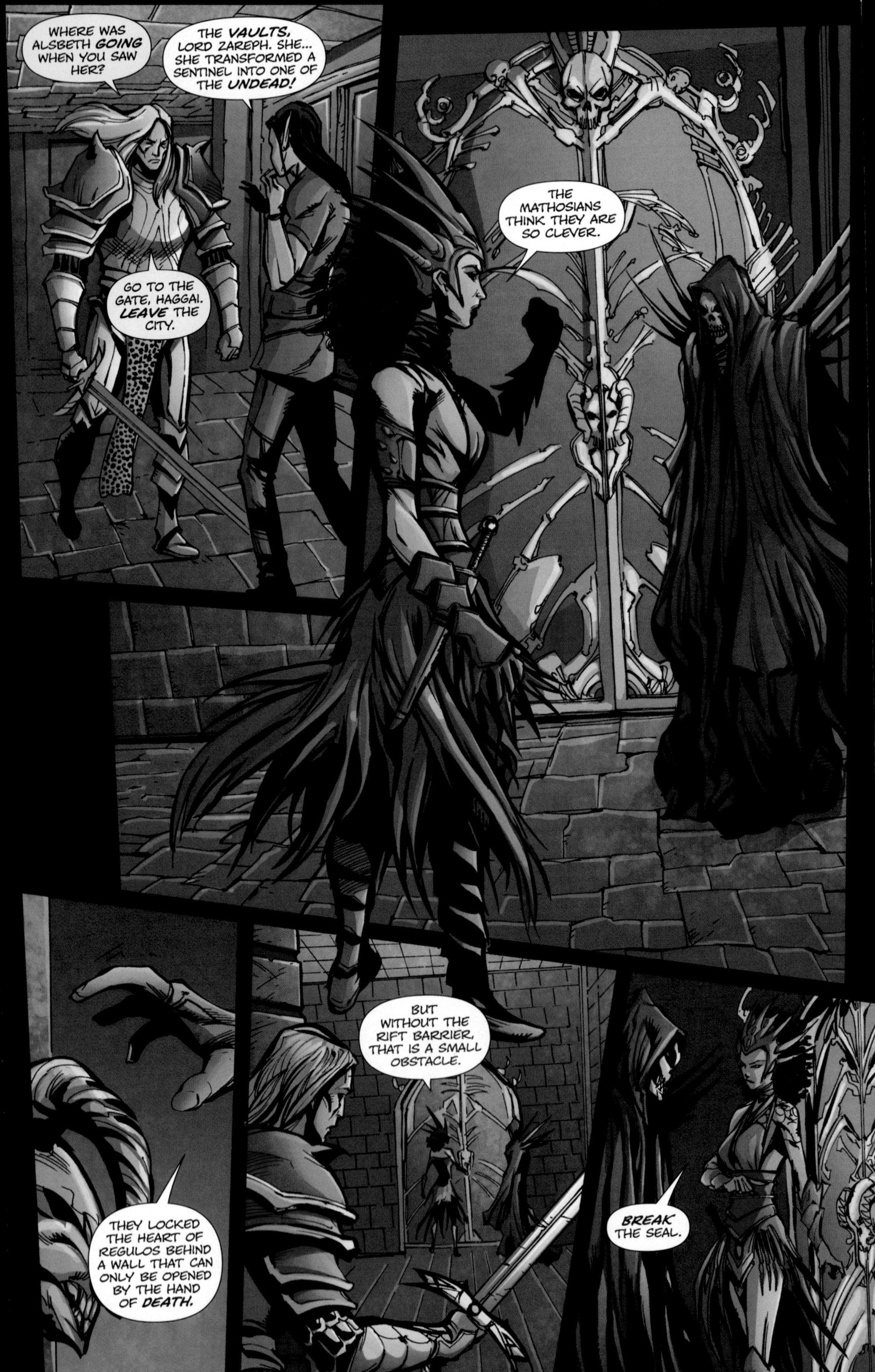

WHERE WAS ALSBETH GOING WHEN YOU SAW HER?
THE VAULTS, LORD ZAREPH. SHE... SHE TRANSFORMED A SENTINEL INTO ONE OF THE UNDEAD!
GO TO THE GATE, HAGGAI. LEAVE THE CITY.
THE MATHOSIANS THINK THEY ARE SO CLEVER.
THEY LOCKED THE HEART OF REGULOS BEHIND A WALL THAT CAN ONLY BE OPENED BY THE HAND OF DEATH.
BUT WITHOUT THE RIFT BARRIER, THAT IS A SMALL OBSTACLE.
BREAK THE SEAL.

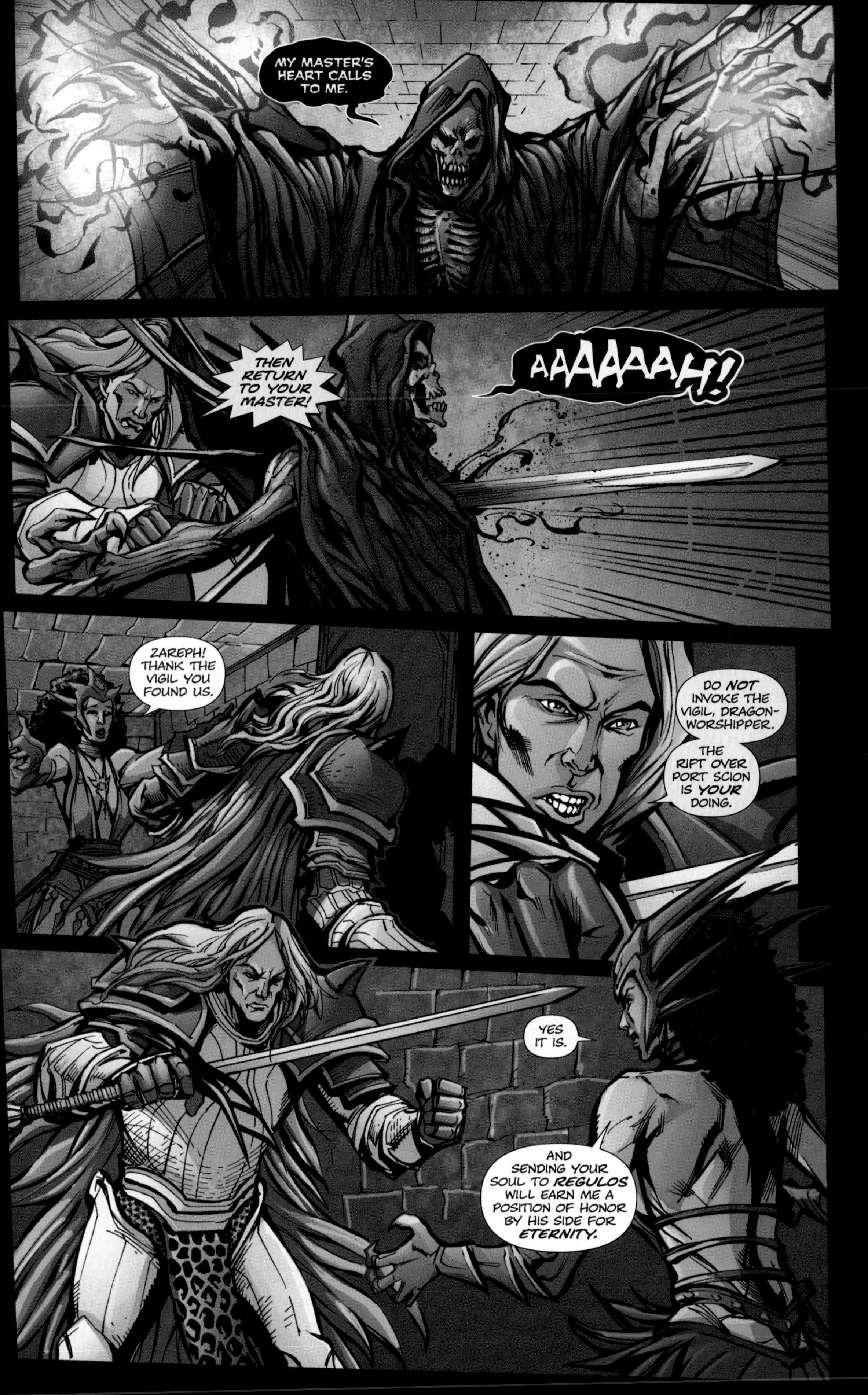
MY MASTER'S HEART CALLS TO ME.
THEN RETURN TO YOUR MASTER!
AAAAAAH!
ZAREPH! THANK THE VIGIL YOU FOUND US.
DO NOT INVOKE THE VIGIL, DRAGON-WORSHIPPER.
THE RIFT OVER PORT SCION IS YOUR DOING.
YES IT IS.
AND SENDING YOUR SOUL TO REGULOS WILL EARN ME A POSITION OF HONOR BY HIS SIDE FOR ETERNITY.

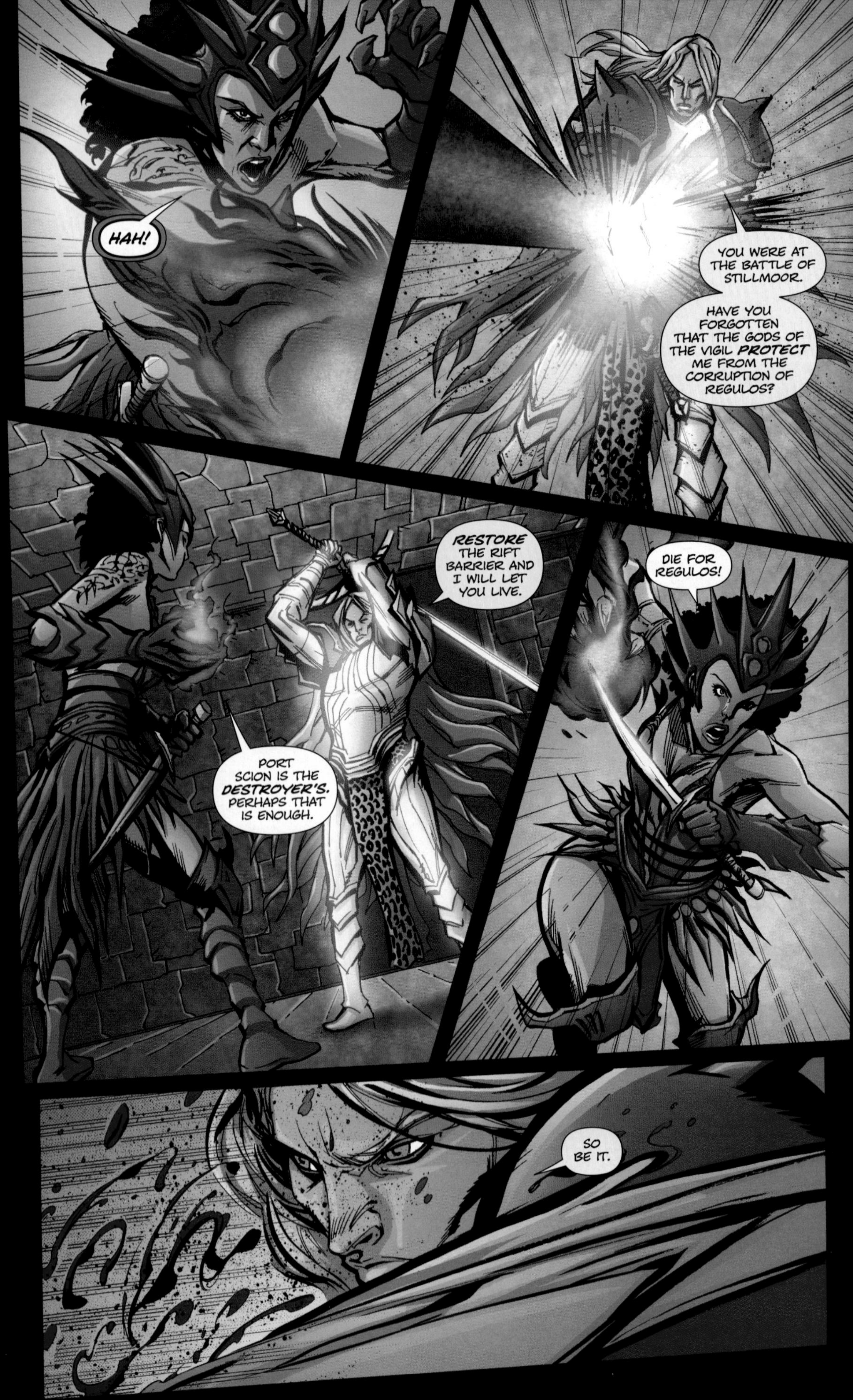
HAH!
YOU WERE AT THE BATTLE OF STILLMOOR.
HAVE YOU FORGOTTEN THAT THE GODS OF THE VIGIL PROTECT ME FROM THE CORRUPTION OF REGULOS?
RESTORE THE RIFT BARRIER AND I WILL LET YOU LIVE.
PORT SCION IS THE DESTROYER'S. PERHAPS THAT IS ENOUGH.
DIE FOR REGULOS!
SO BE IT.

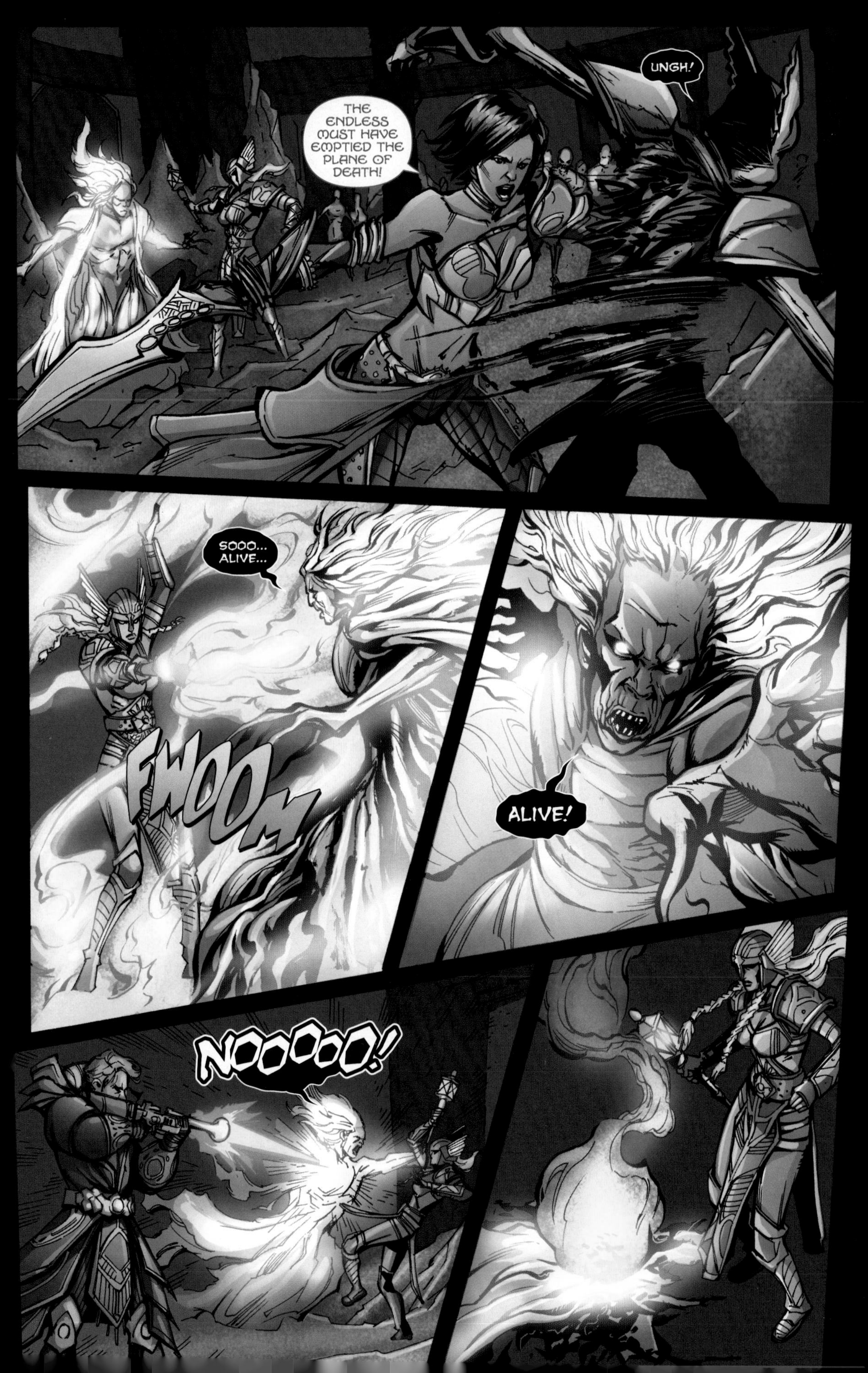
THE ENDLESS MUST HAVE EMPTIED THE PLANE OF DEATH!
UNGH!
SOOO... ALIVE...
FWOOM
ALIVE!
NOOOOO!

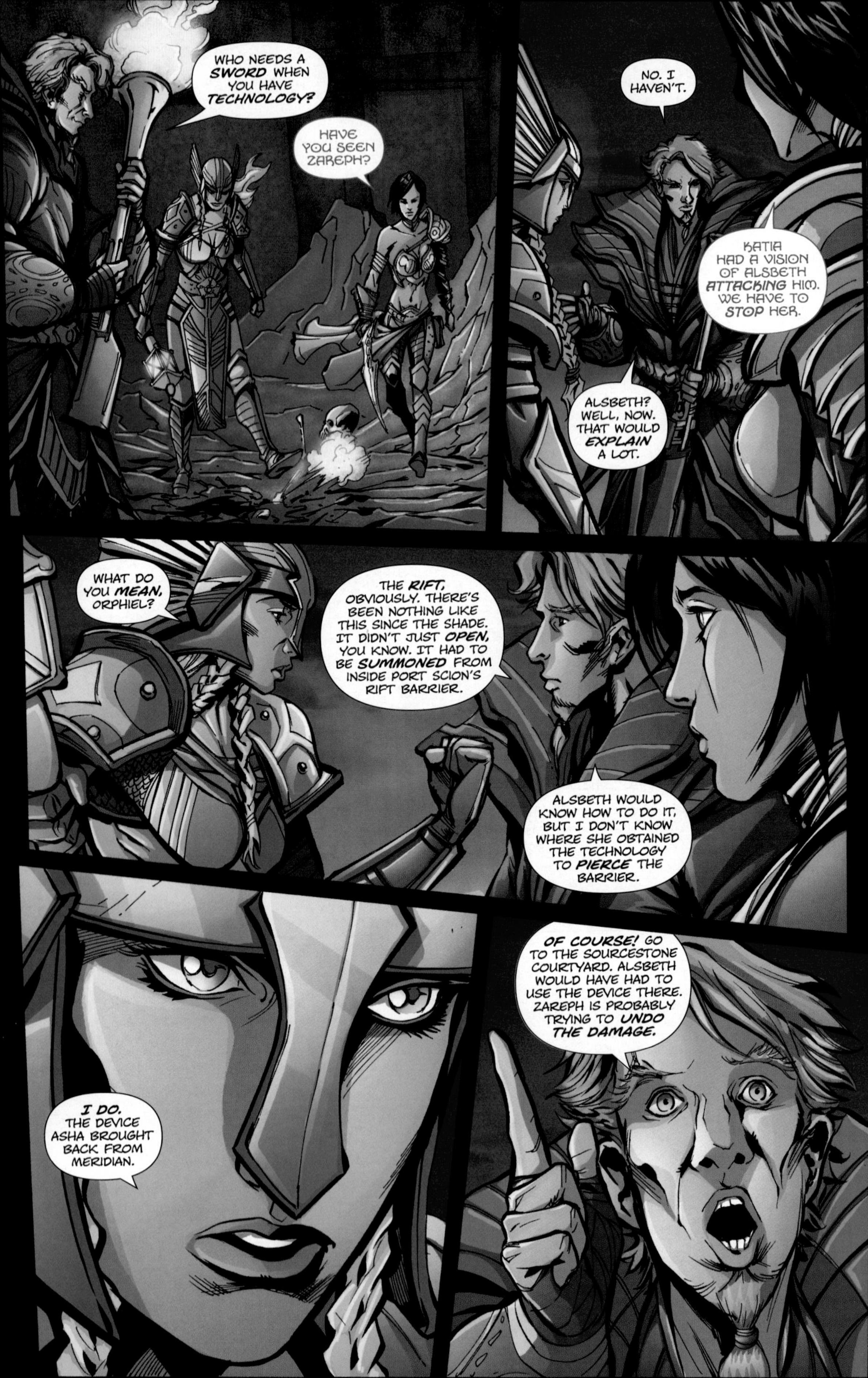
WHO NEEDS A SWORD WHEN YOU HAVE TECHNOLOGY?
HAVE YOU SEEN ZAREPH?
NO. I HAVEN'T.
KATIA HAD A VISION OF ALSBETH ATTACKING HIM. WE HAVE TO STOP HER.
ALSBETH? WELL, NOW. THAT WOULD EXPLAIN A LOT.
WHAT DO YOU MEAN, ORPHIEL?
THE RIFT, OBVIOUSLY. THERE'S BEEN NOTHING LIKE THIS SINCE THE SHADE. IT DIDN'T JUST OPEN, YOU KNOW. IT HAD TO BE SUMMONED FROM INSIDE PORT SCION'S RIFT BARRIER.
ALSBETH WOULD KNOW HOW TO DO IT, BUT I DON'T KNOW WHERE SHE OBTAINED THE TECHNOLOGY TO PIERCE THE BARRIER.
I DO. THE DEVICE ASHA BROUGHT BACK FROM MERIDIAN.
OF COURSE! GO TO THE SOURCESTONE COURTYARD. ALSBETH WOULD HAVE HAD TO USE THE DEVICE THERE. ZAREPH IS PROBABLY TRYING TO UNDO THE DAMAGE.

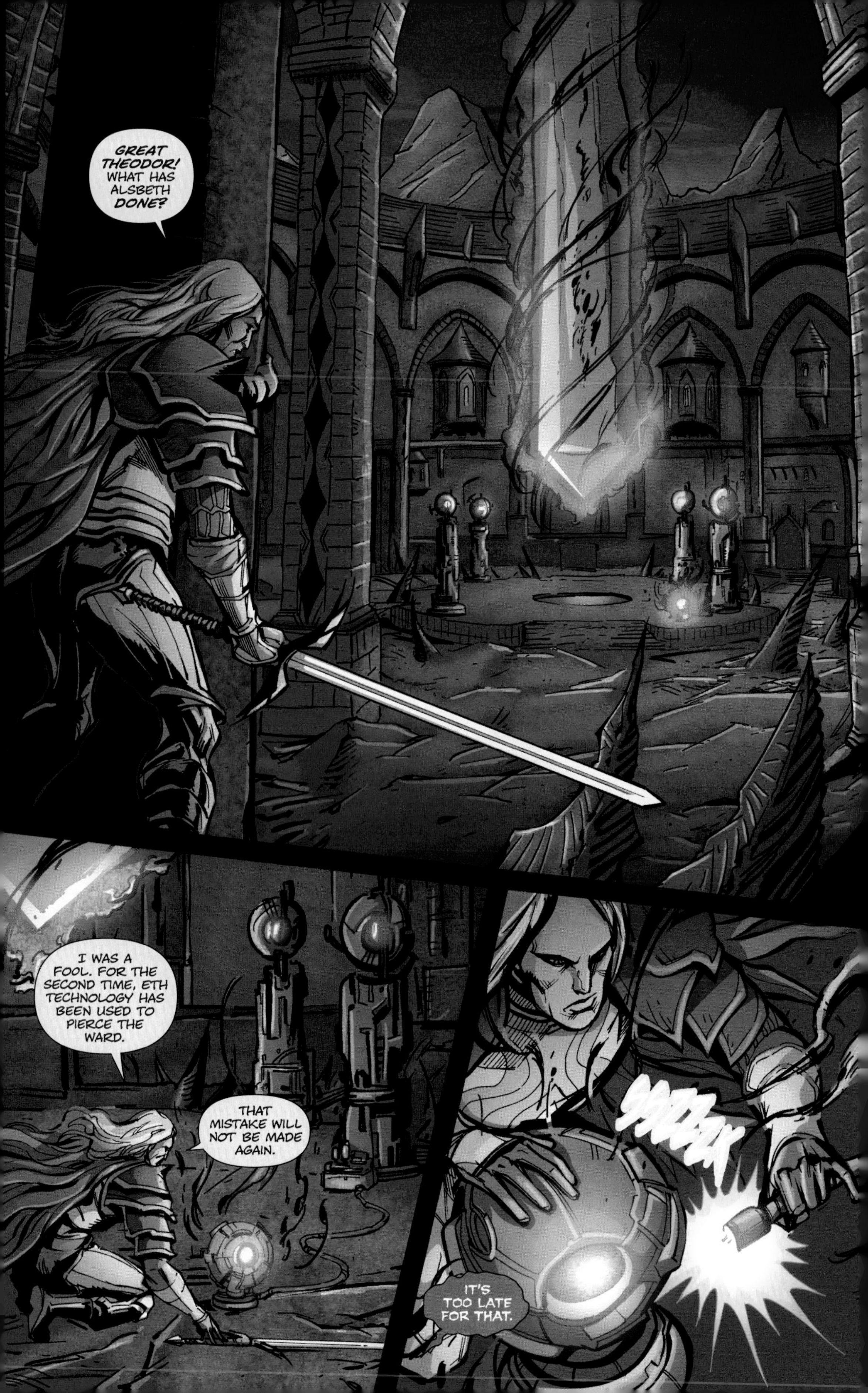
GREAT THEODOR! WHAT HAS ALSBETH DONE?
I WAS A FOOL. FOR THE SECOND TIME, ETH TECHNOLOGY HAS BEEN USED TO PIERCE THE WARD.
THAT MISTAKE WILL NOT BE MADE AGAIN.
IT'S TOO LATE FOR THAT.

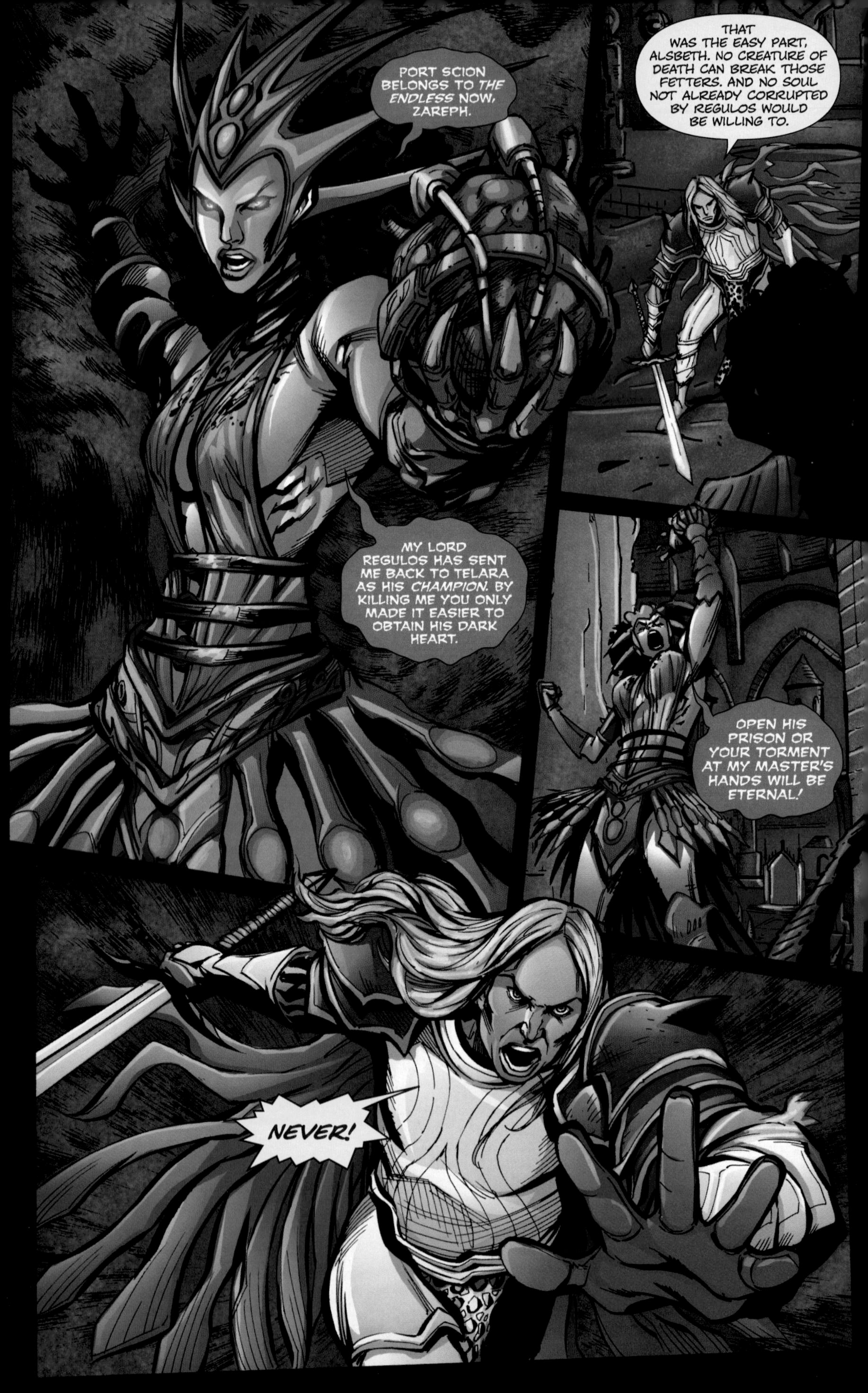
PORT SCION BELONGS TO THE ENDLESS NOW, ZAREPH.
THAT WAS THE EASY PART, ALSBETH. NO CREATURE OF DEATH CAN BREAK THOSE FETTERS. AND NO SOUL NOT ALREADY CORRUPTED BY REGULOS WOULD BE WILLING TO.
MY LORD REGULOS HAS SENT ME BACK TO TELARA AS HIS CHAMPION. BY KILLING ME YOU ONLY MADE IT EASIER TO OBTAIN HIS DARK HEART.
OPEN HIS PRISON OR YOUR TORMENT AT MY MASTER'S HANDS WILL BE ETERNAL!
NEVER!

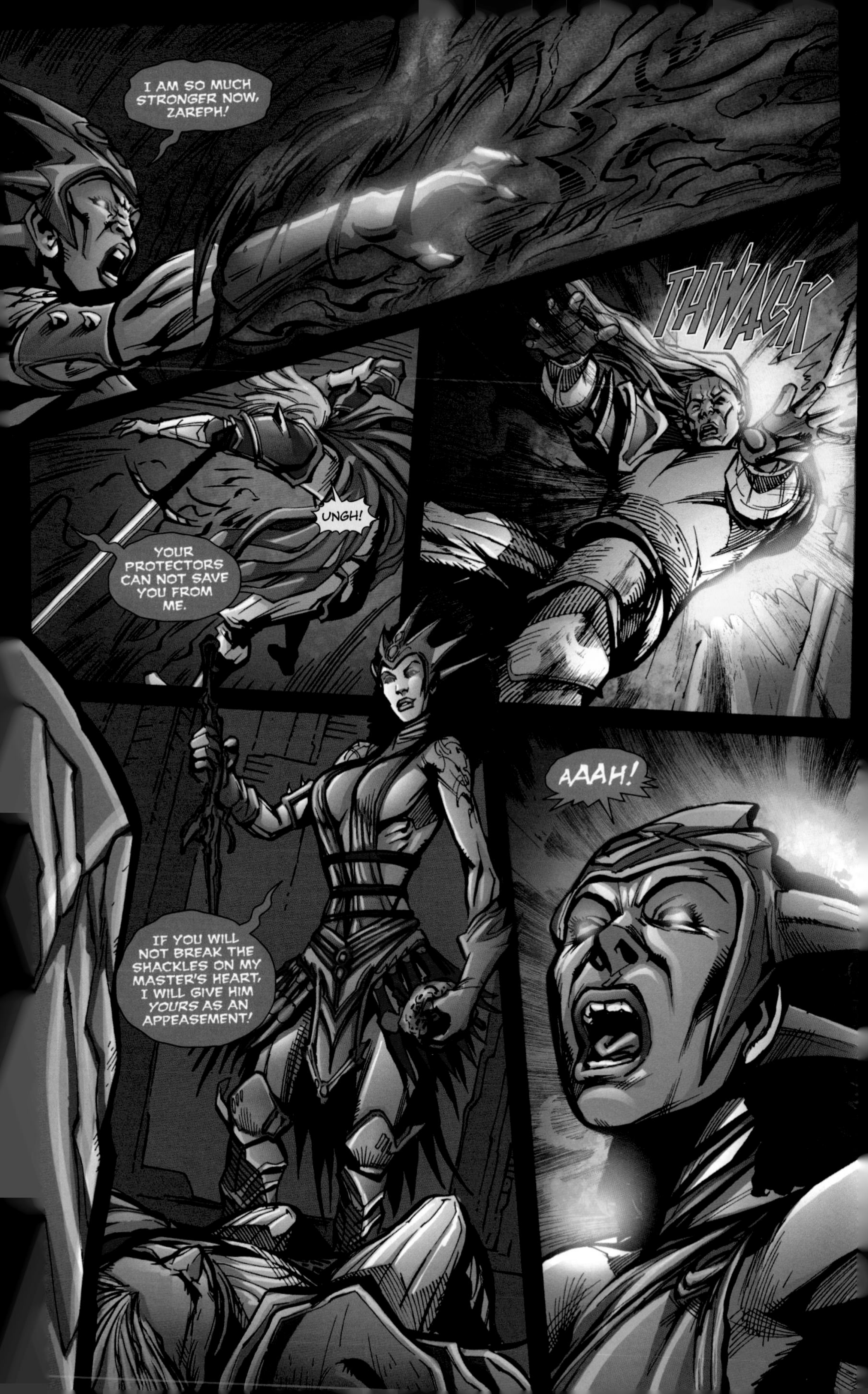
I AM SO MUCH STRONGER NOW, ZAREPH!
UNGH!
YOUR PROTECTORS CAN NOT SAVE YOU FROM ME.
THWACK
IF YOU WILL NOT BREAK THE SHACKLES ON MY MASTER'S HEART, I WILL GIVE HIM *YOURS* AS AN APPEASEMENT!
AAAH!

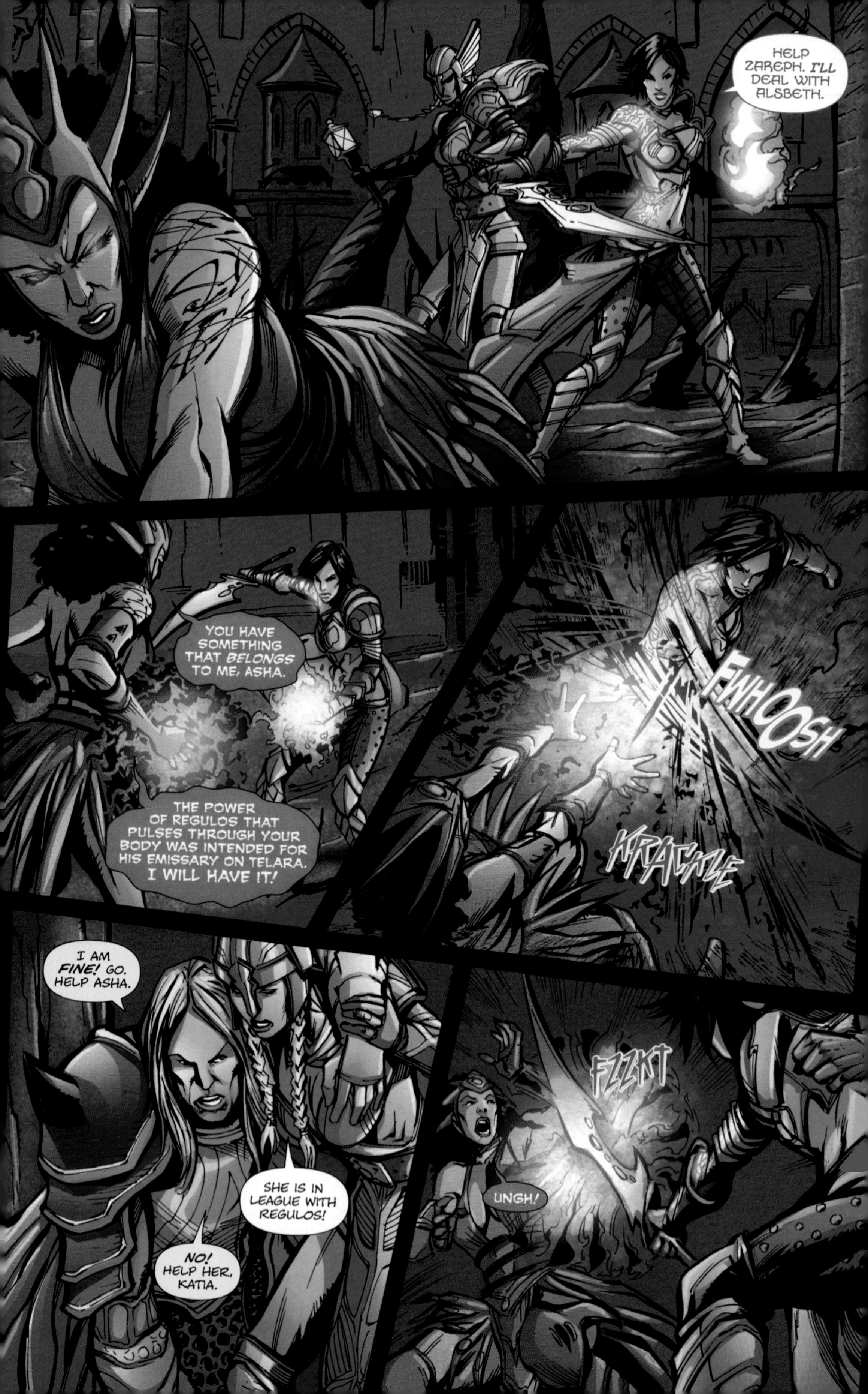

HELP ZAREPH. I'LL DEAL WITH ALSBETH.
YOU HAVE SOMETHING THAT BELONGS TO ME, ASHA.
THE POWER OF REGULOS THAT PULSES THROUGH YOUR BODY WAS INTENDED FOR HIS EMISSARY ON TELARA. I WILL HAVE IT!
FWHOOSH
KRACKLE
I AM FINE! GO. HELP ASHA.
SHE IS IN LEAGUE WITH REGULOS!
NO! HELP HER, KATIA.
FZZKT
UNGH!

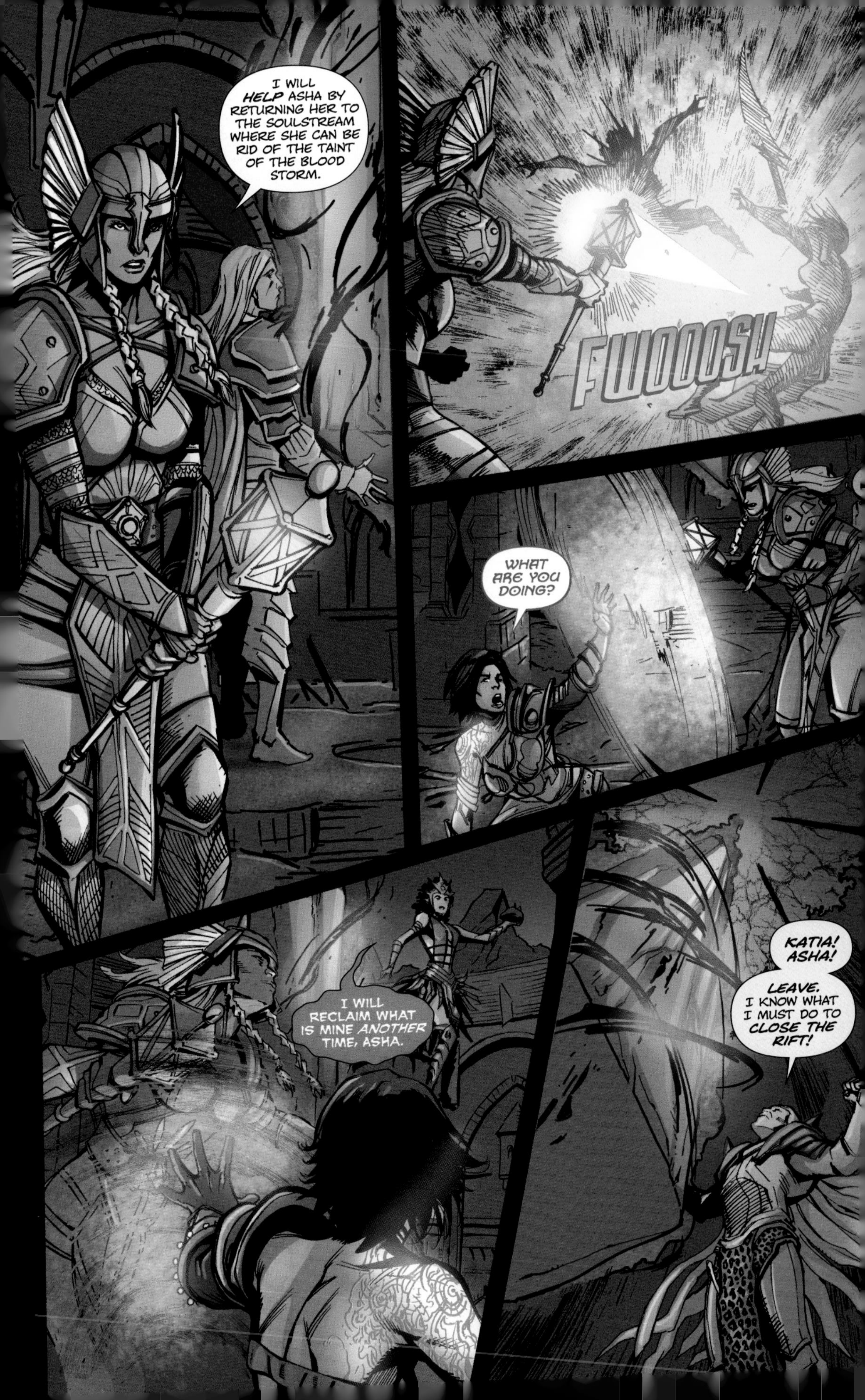
I WILL HELP ASHA BY RETURNING HER TO THE SOULSTREAM WHERE SHE CAN BE RID OF THE TAINT OF THE BLOOD STORM.
FWOOOSH
WHAT ARE YOU DOING?
I WILL RECLAIM WHAT IS MINE ANOTHER TIME, ASHA.
KATIA! ASHA!
LEAVE. I KNOW WHAT I MUST DO TO CLOSE THE RIFT!

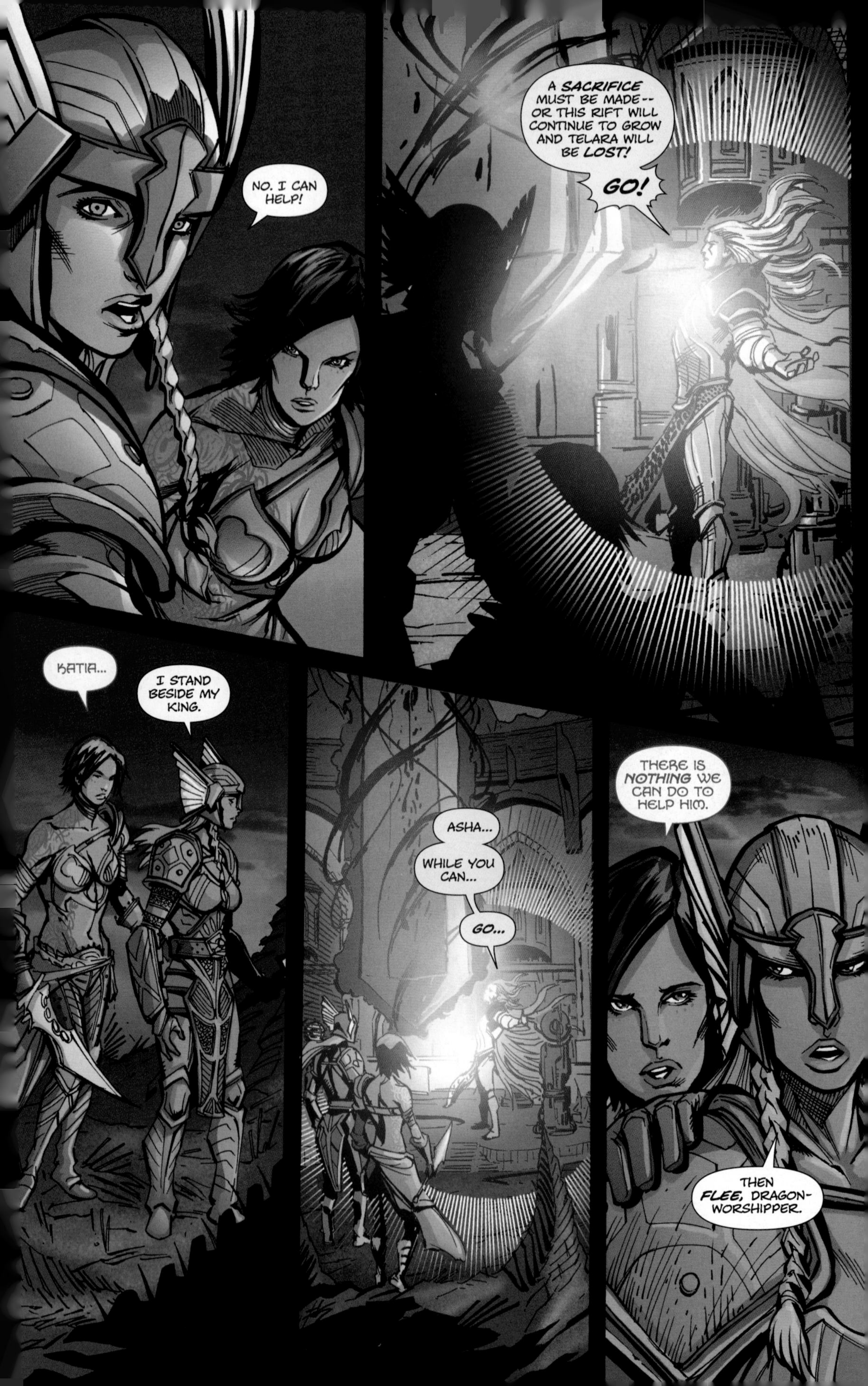
NO. I CAN HELP!
A SACRIFICE MUST BE MADE-- OR THIS RIFT WILL CONTINUE TO GROW AND TELARA WILL BE LOST!
GO!
KATIA...
I STAND BESIDE MY KING.
ASHA...
WHILE YOU CAN...
GO...
THERE IS NOTHING WE CAN DO TO HELP HIM.
THEN FLEE, DRAGON-WORSHIPPER.

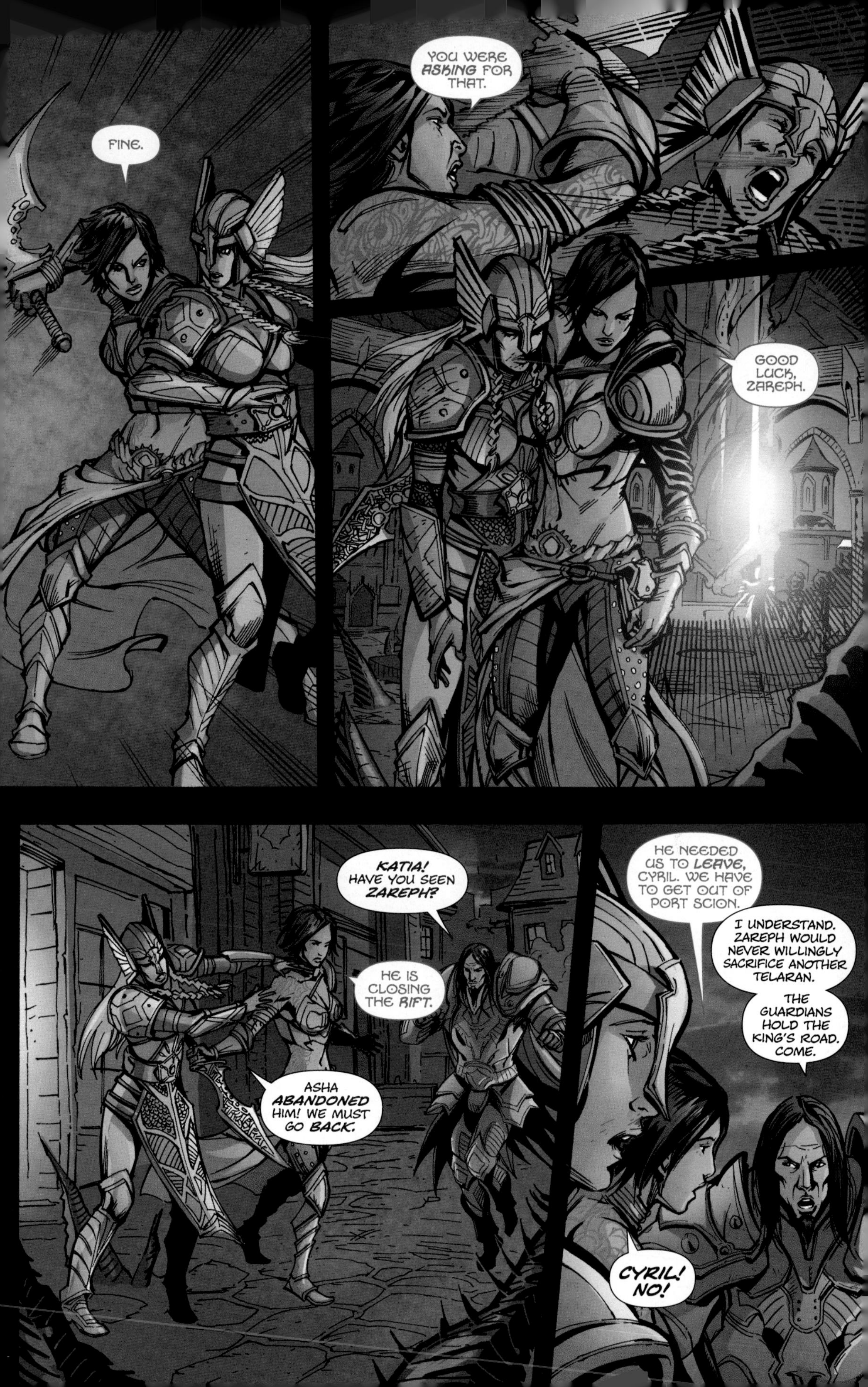
FINE.
YOU WERE ASKING FOR THAT.
GOOD LUCK, ZAREPH.
KATIA! HAVE YOU SEEN ZAREPH?
HE IS CLOSING THE RIFT.
ASHA ABANDONED HIM! WE MUST GO BACK.
HE NEEDED US TO LEAVE, CYRIL. WE HAVE TO GET OUT OF PORT SCION.
I UNDERSTAND. ZAREPH WOULD NEVER WILLINGLY SACRIFICE ANOTHER TELARAN.
THE GUARDIANS HOLD THE KING'S ROAD. COME.
CYRIL! NO!

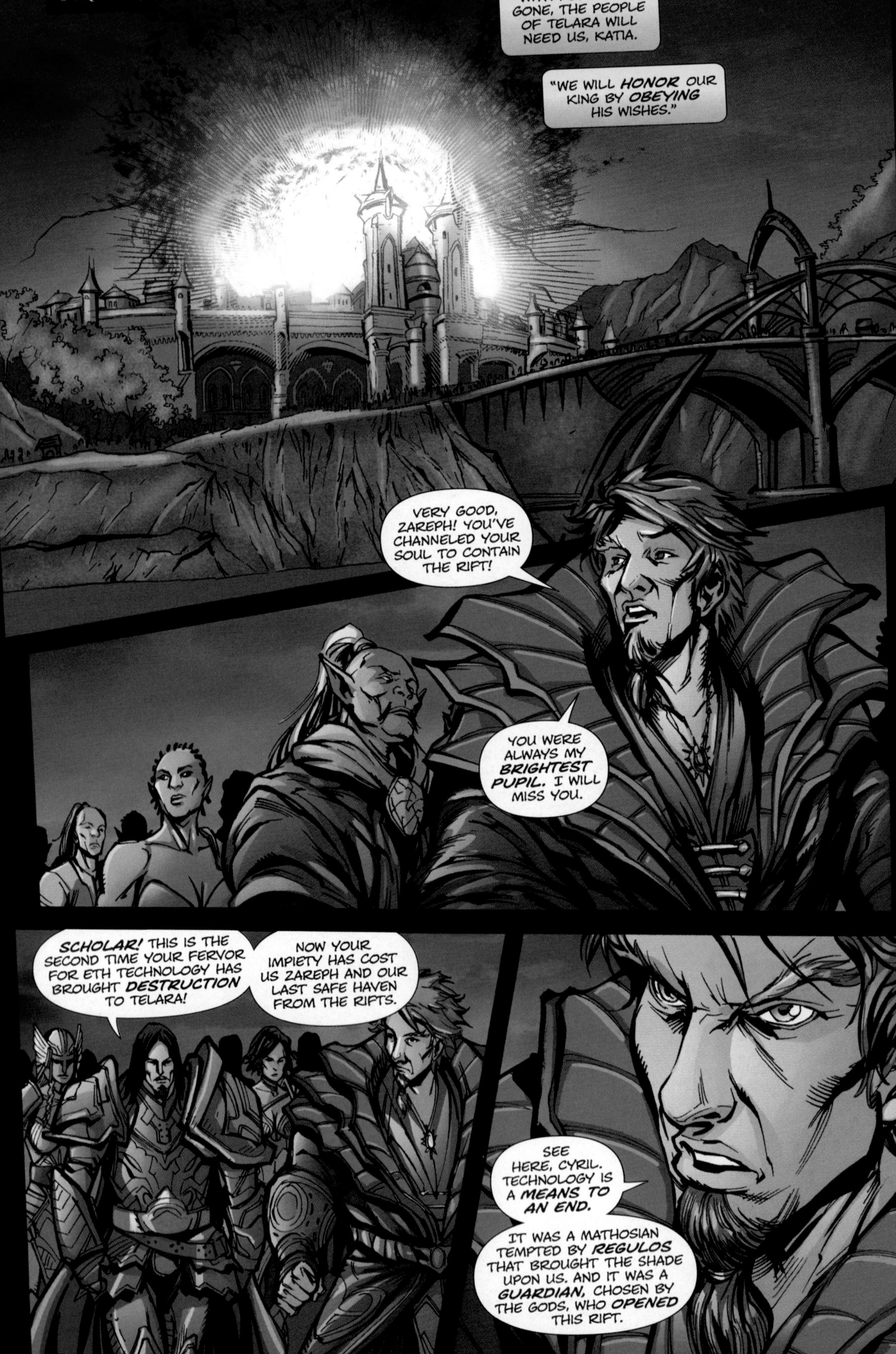
"WITH PORT SCION GONE, THE PEOPLE OF TELARA WILL NEED US, KATIA.
"WE WILL HONOR OUR KING BY OBEYING HIS WISHES."
VERY GOOD, ZAREPH! YOU'VE CHANNELED YOUR SOUL TO CONTAIN THE RIFT!
YOU WERE ALWAYS MY BRIGHTEST PUPIL. I WILL MISS YOU.
SCHOLAR! THIS IS THE SECOND TIME YOUR FERVOR FOR ETH TECHNOLOGY HAS BROUGHT DESTRUCTION TO TELARA!
NOW YOUR IMPIETY HAS COST US ZAREPH AND OUR LAST SAFE HAVEN FROM THE RIFTS.
SEE HERE, CYRIL. TECHNOLOGY IS A MEANS TO AN END.
IT WAS A MATHOSIAN TEMPTED BY REGULOS THAT BROUGHT THE SHADE UPON US. AND IT WAS A GUARDIAN, CHOSEN BY THE GODS, WHO OPENED THIS RIFT.

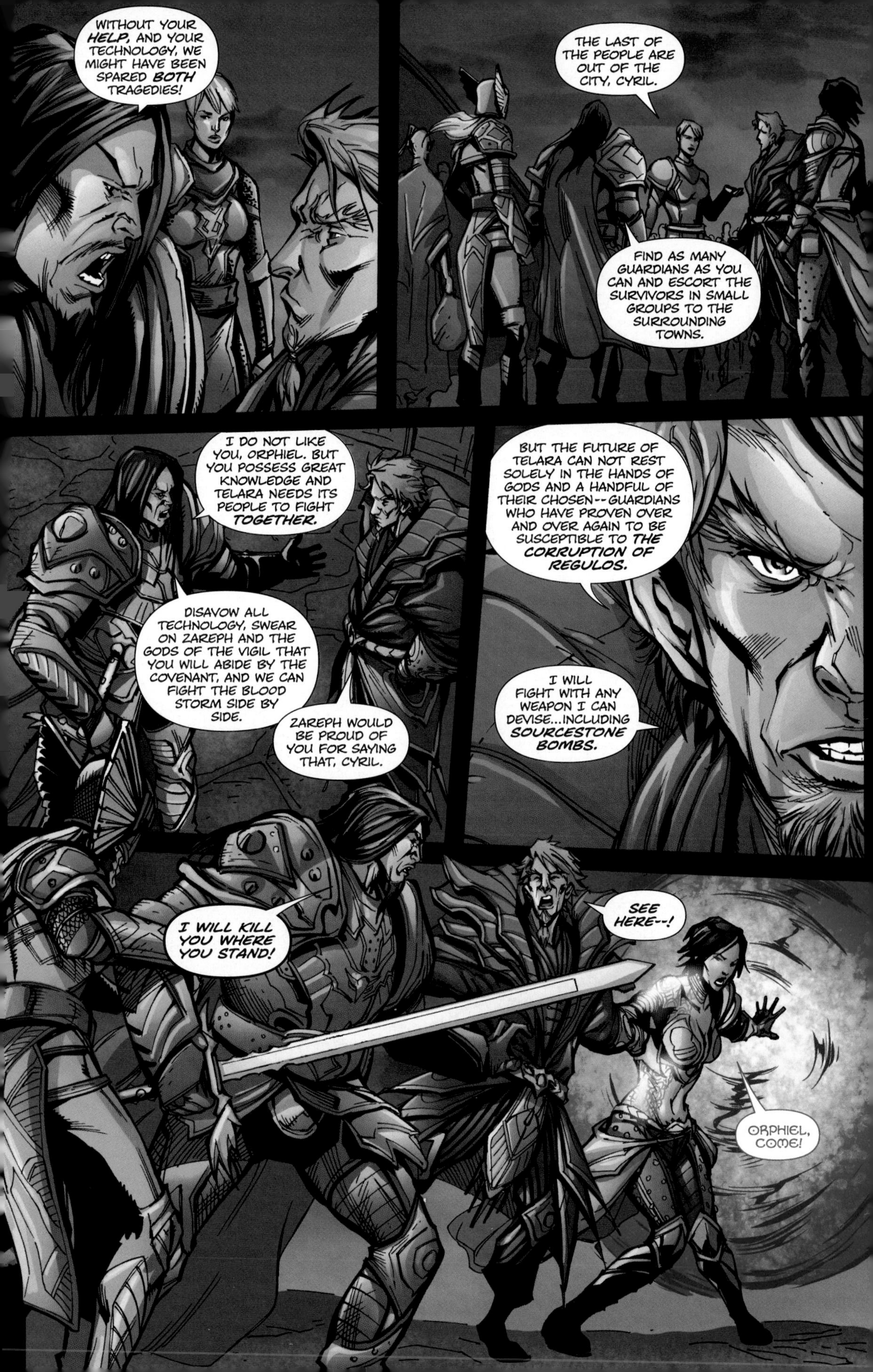
WITHOUT YOUR HELP, AND YOUR TECHNOLOGY, WE MIGHT HAVE BEEN SPARED BOTH TRAGEDIES!
THE LAST OF THE PEOPLE ARE OUT OF THE CITY, CYRIL.
FIND AS MANY GUARDIANS AS YOU CAN AND ESCORT THE SURVIVORS IN SMALL GROUPS TO THE SURROUNDING TOWNS.
I DO NOT LIKE YOU, ORPHIEL. BUT YOU POSSESS GREAT KNOWLEDGE AND TELARA NEEDS ITS PEOPLE TO FIGHT TOGETHER.
DISAVOW ALL TECHNOLOGY, SWEAR ON ZAREPH AND THE GODS OF THE VIGIL THAT YOU WILL ABIDE BY THE COVENANT, AND WE CAN FIGHT THE BLOOD STORM SIDE BY SIDE.
ZAREPH WOULD BE PROUD OF YOU FOR SAYING THAT, CYRIL.
BUT THE FUTURE OF TELARA CAN NOT REST SOLELY IN THE HANDS OF GODS AND A HANDFUL OF THEIR CHOSEN--GUARDIANS WHO HAVE PROVEN OVER AND OVER AGAIN TO BE SUSCEPTIBLE TO THE CORRUPTION OF REGULOS.
I WILL FIGHT WITH ANY WEAPON I CAN DEVISE...INCLUDING SOURCESTONE BOMBS.
I WILL KILL YOU WHERE YOU STAND!
SEE HERE--!
ORPHIEL, COME!

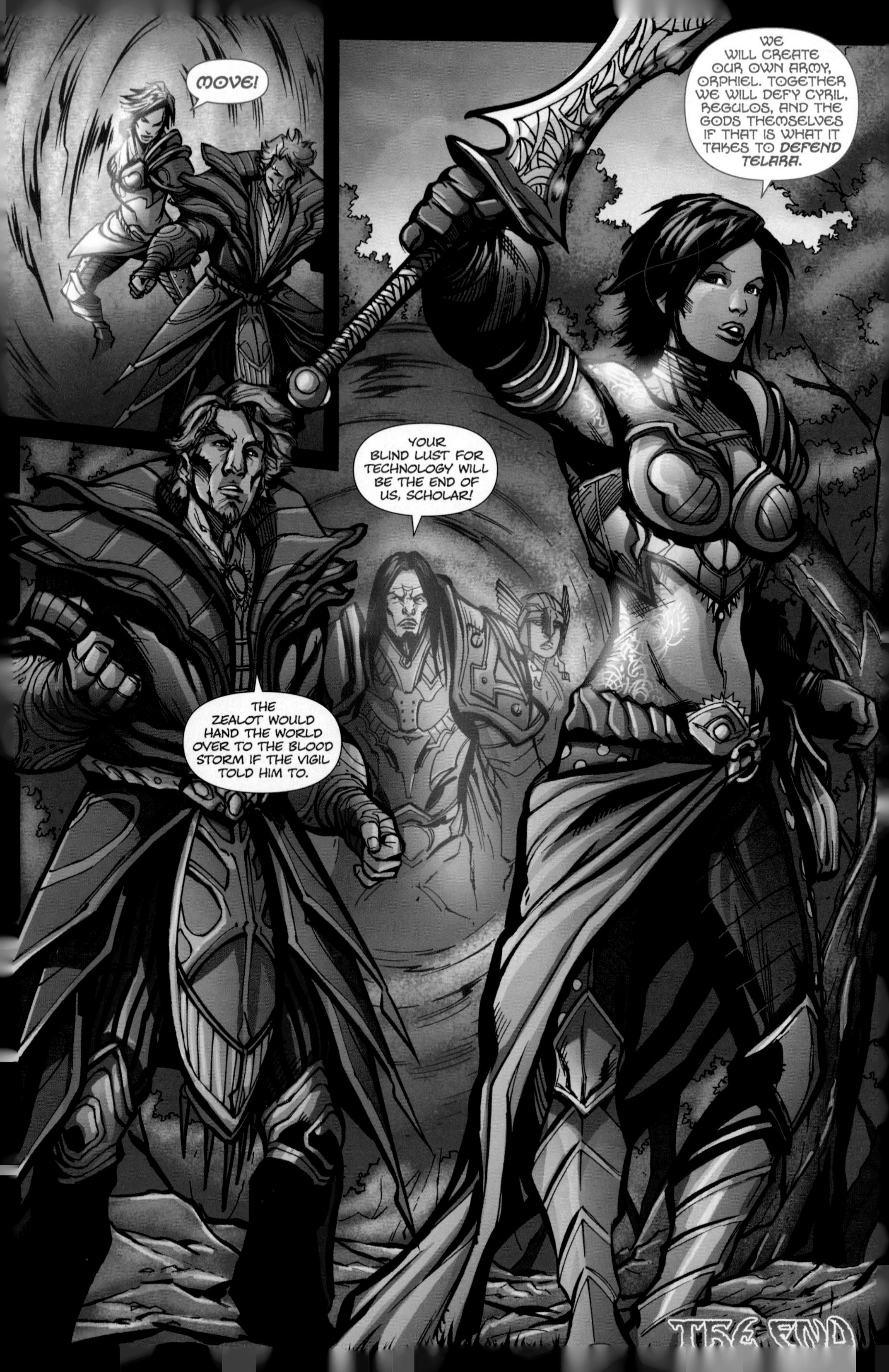
MOVE!
WE WILL CREATE OUR OWN ARMY, ORPHIEL. TOGETHER WE WILL DEFY CYRIL, REGULOS, AND THE GODS THEMSELVES IF THAT IS WHAT IT TAKES TO DEFEND TELARA.
YOUR BLIND LUST FOR TECHNOLOGY WILL BE THE END OF US, SCHOLAR!
THE ZEALOT WOULD HAND THE WORLD OVER TO THE BLOOD STORM IF THE VIGIL TOLD HIM TO.
THE END

THE HISTORY OF TELARA

Because the comic book series was released in advance of the game, the story utilized characters and concepts new to readers. In order to help them to become more familiar with Telara, each issue contained a two-page backup feature that provided further information about the history of this exciting world and some of its important figures, factions and entities. Get to know Telara better!

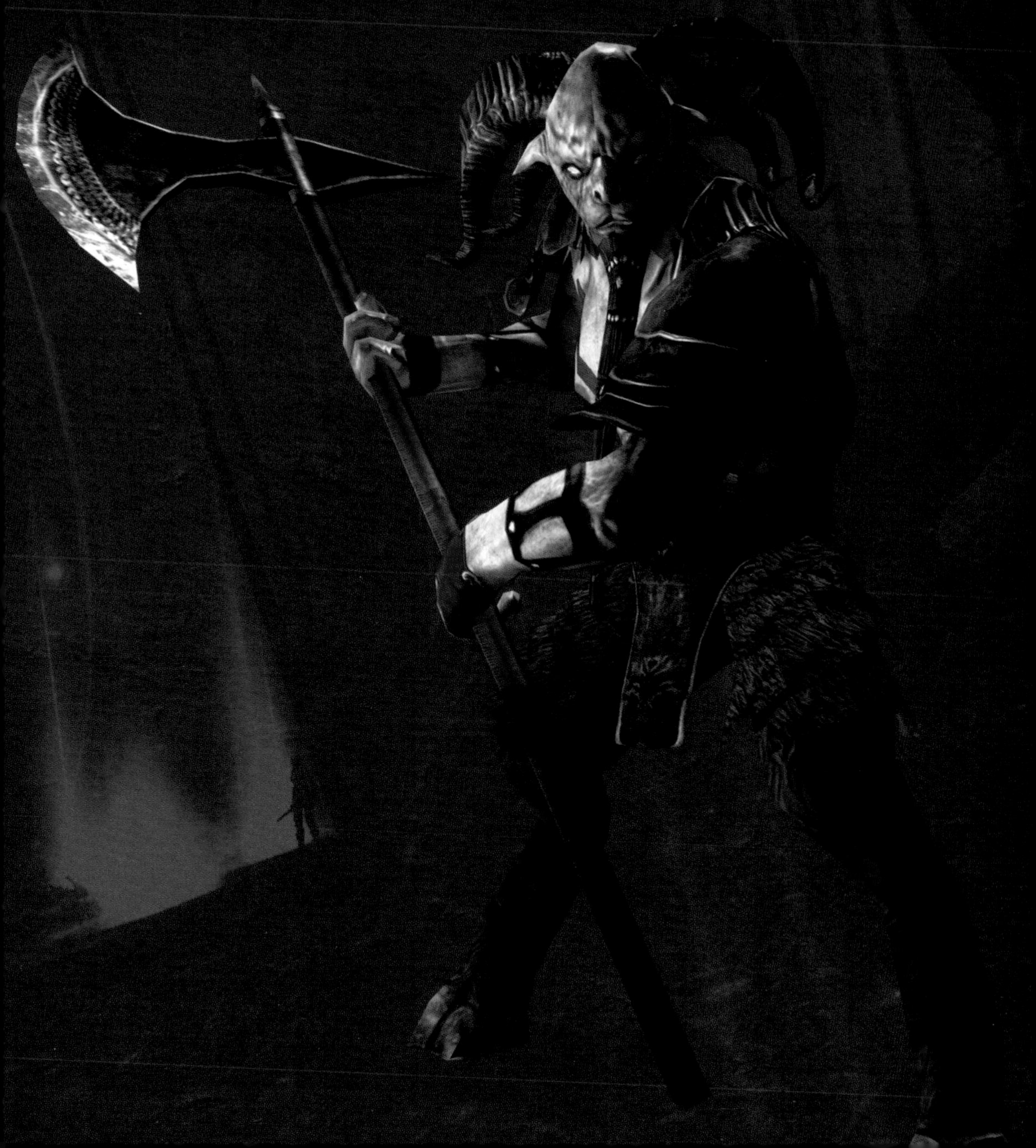

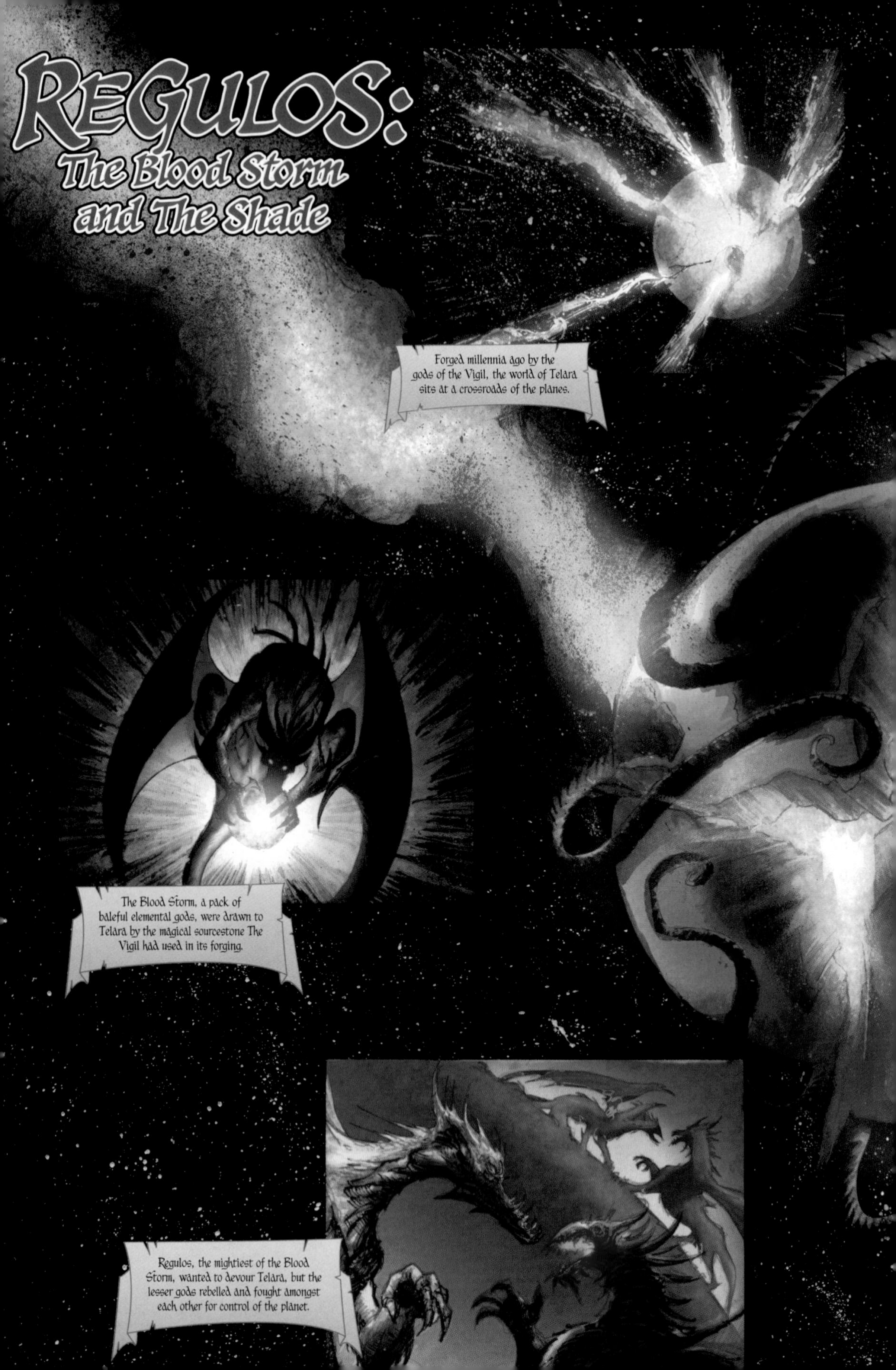

REGULOS:
The Blood Storm and The Shade
Forged millennia ago by the gods of the Vigil, the world of Telara sits at a crossroads of the planes.
The Blood Storm, a pack of baleful elemental gods, were drawn to Telara by the magical sourcestone The Vigil had used in its forging.
Regulos, the mightiest of the Blood Storm, wanted to devour Telara, but the lesser gods rebelled and fought amongst each other for control of the planet.

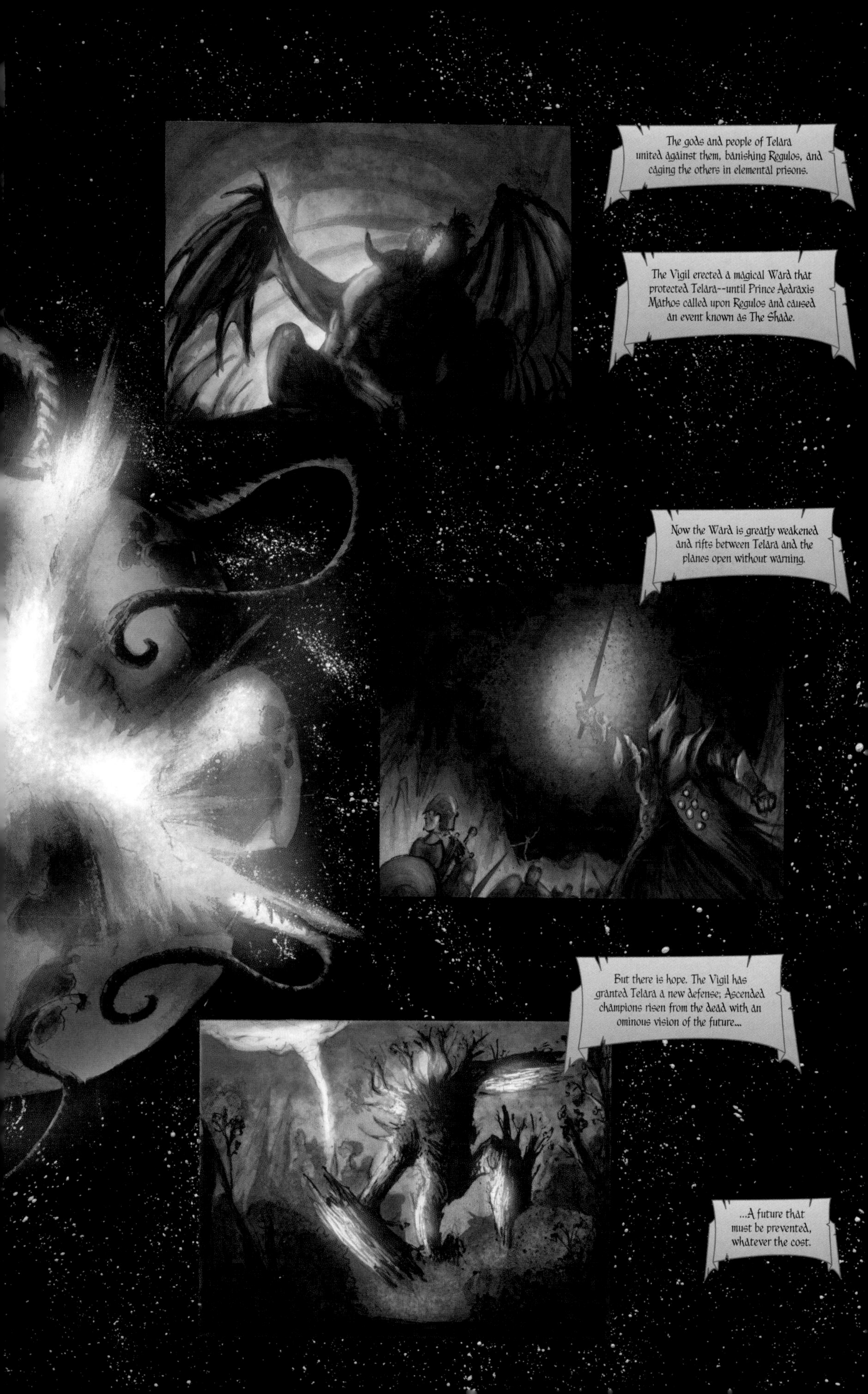
The gods and people of Telara united against them, banishing Regulos, and caging the others in elemental prisons.
The Vigil erected a magical Ward that protected Telara--until Prince Aedraxis Mathos called upon Regulos and caused an event known as The Shade.
Now the Ward is greatly weakened and rifts between Telara and the planes open without warning.
But there is hope. The Vigil has granted Telara a new defense; Ascended champions risen from the dead with an ominous vision of the future...
...A future that must be prevented, whatever the cost.

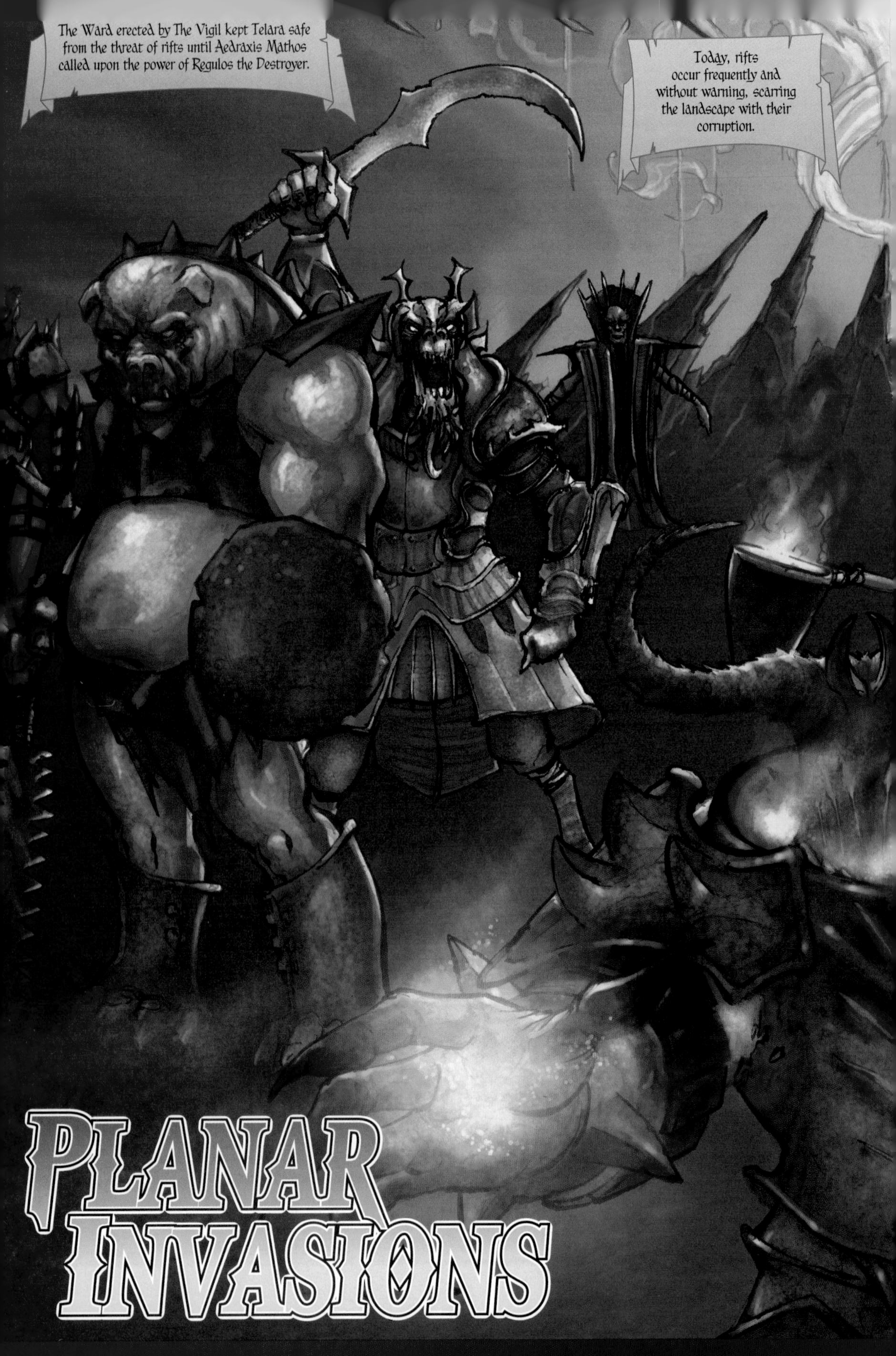
The Ward erected by The Vigil kept Telara safe from the threat of rifts until Aedraxis Mathos called upon the power of Regulos the Destroyer.
Today, rifts occur frequently and without warning, scarring the landscape with their corruption.
PLANAR INVASIONS

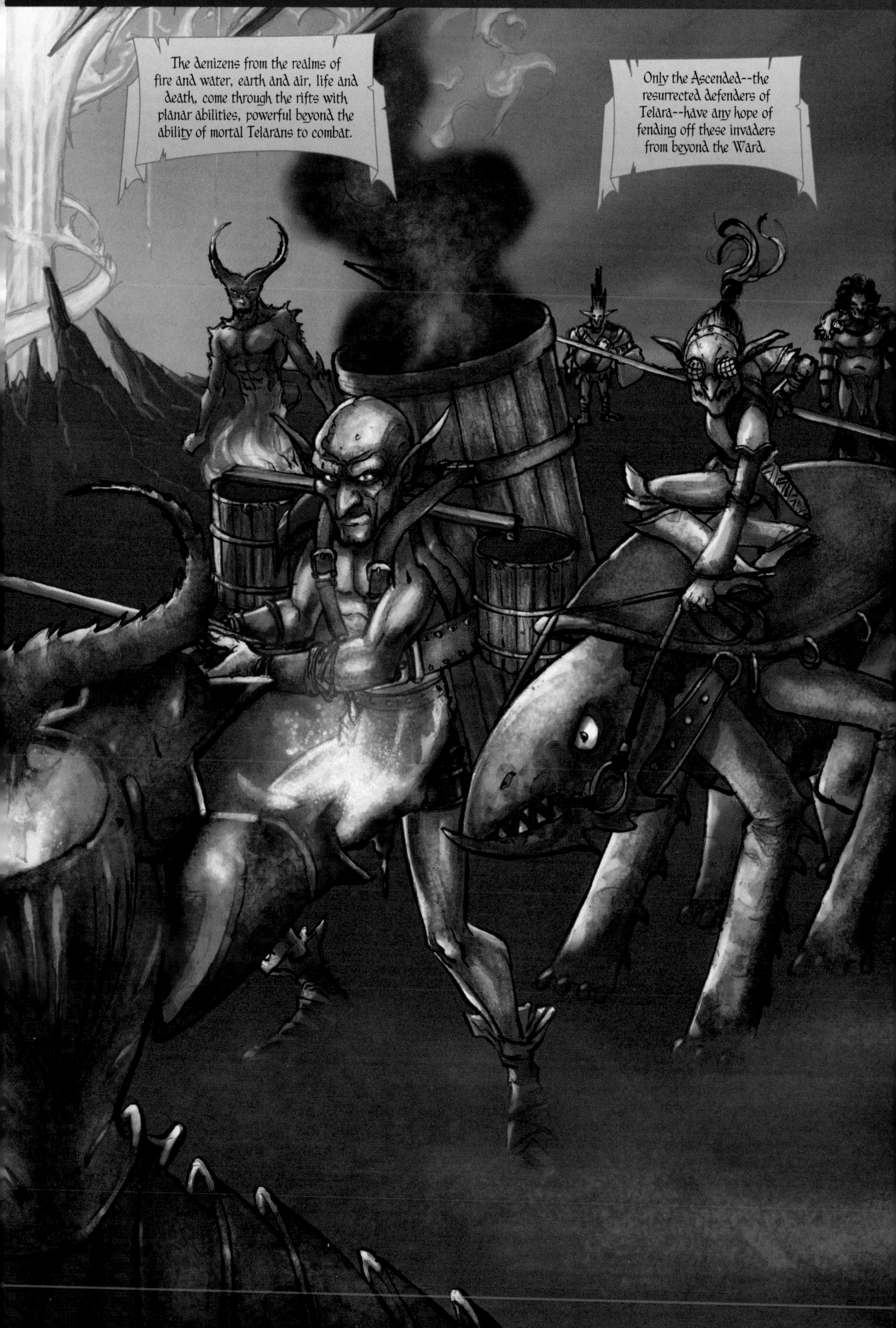
The denizens from the realms of fire and water, earth and air, life and death, come through the rifts with planar abilities, powerful beyond the ability of mortal Telarans to combat.
Only the Ascended--the resurrected defenders of Telara--have any hope of fending off these invaders from beyond the Ward.

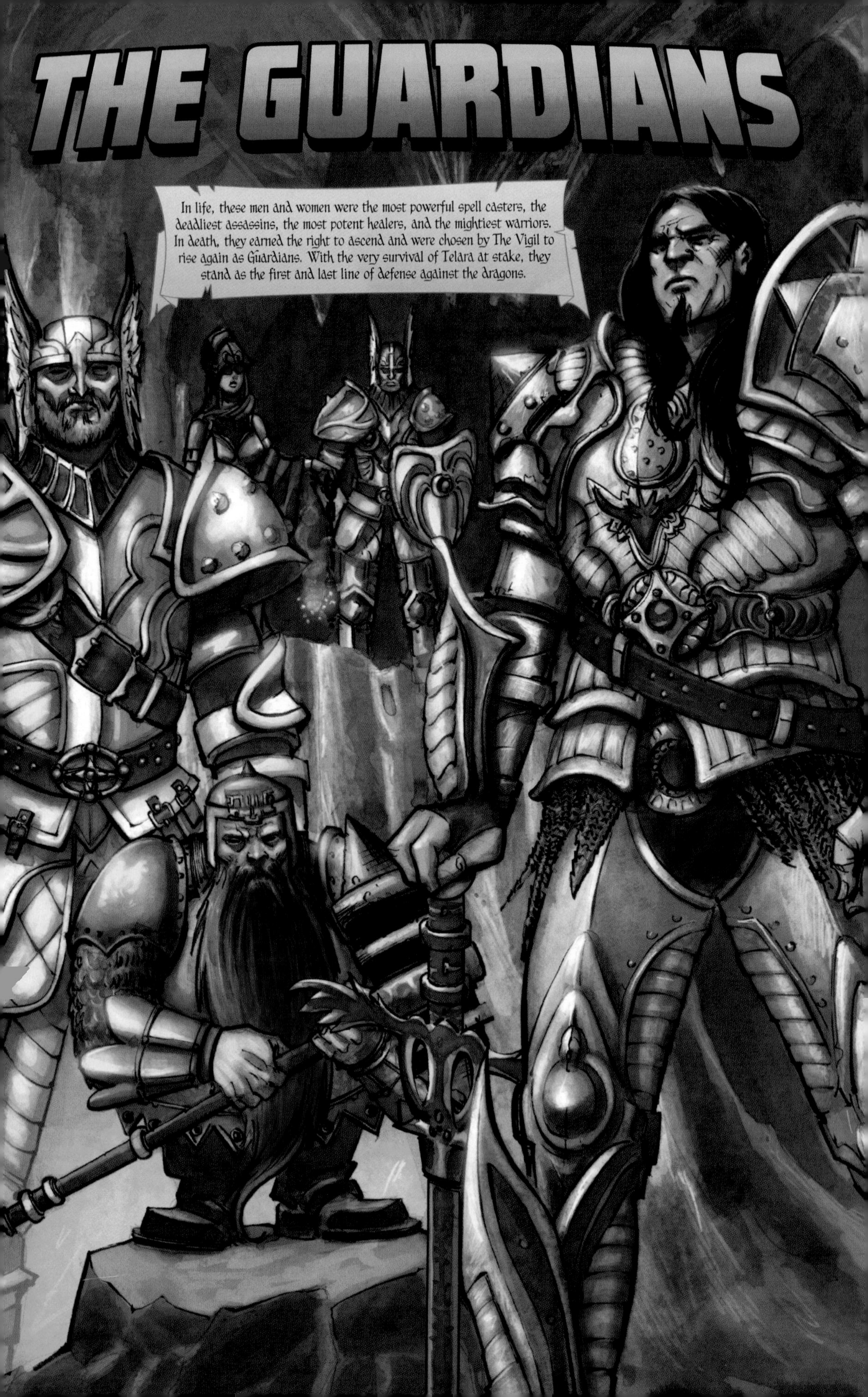
THE GUARDIANS
In life, these men and women were the most powerful spell casters, the deadliest assassins, the most potent healers, and the mightiest warriors. In death, they earned the right to ascend and were chosen by The Vigil to rise again as Guardians. With the very survival of Telara at stake, they stand as the first and last line of defense against the dragons.

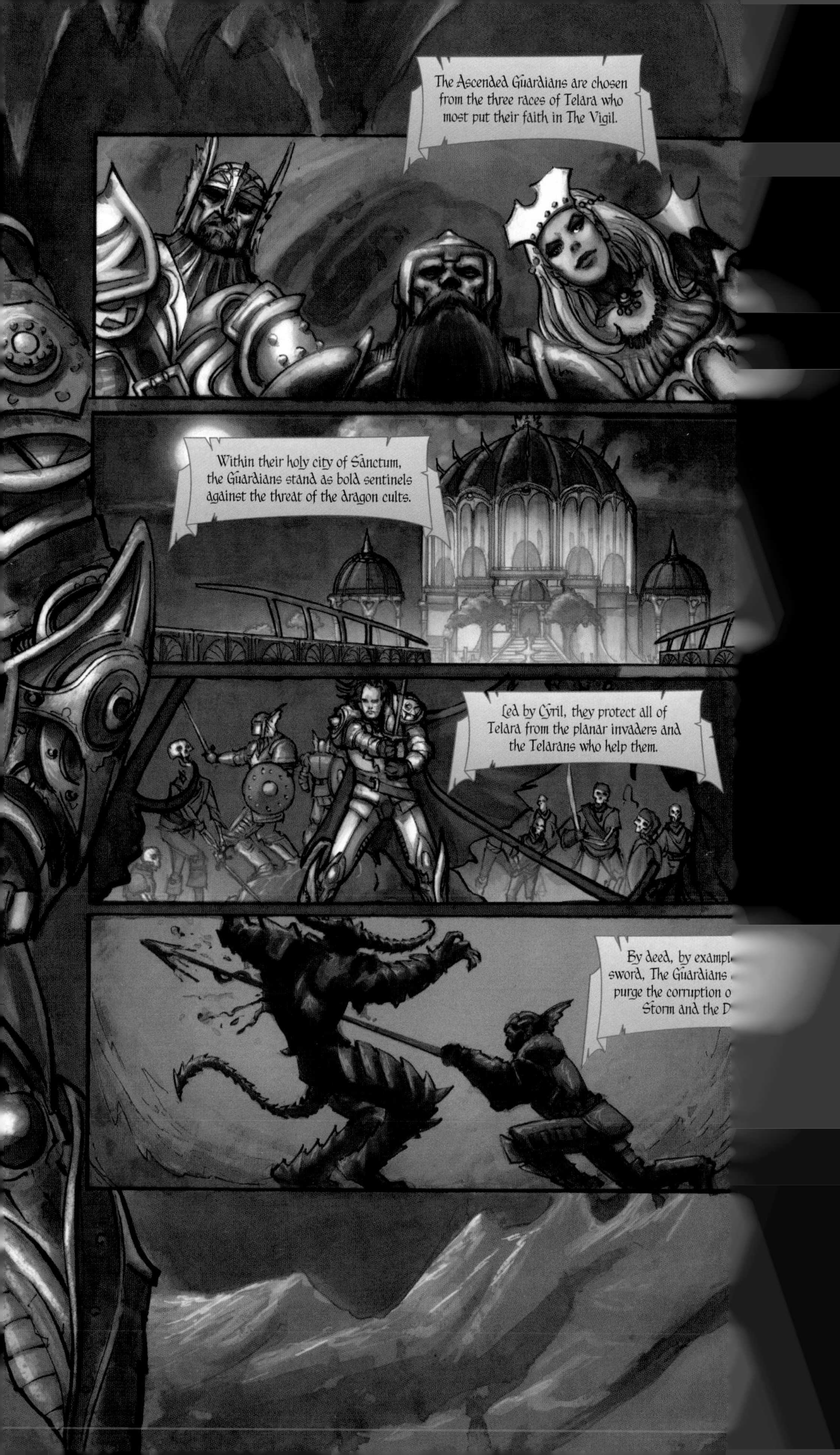
The Ascended Guardians are chosen from the three races of Telara who most put their faith in The Vigil.
Within their holy city of Sanctum, the Guardians stand as bold sentinels against the threat of the dragon cults.
Led by Cyril, they protect all of Telara from the planar invaders and the Telarans who help them.
By deed, by
sword, The Guardians
purge the corruption
Storm and the

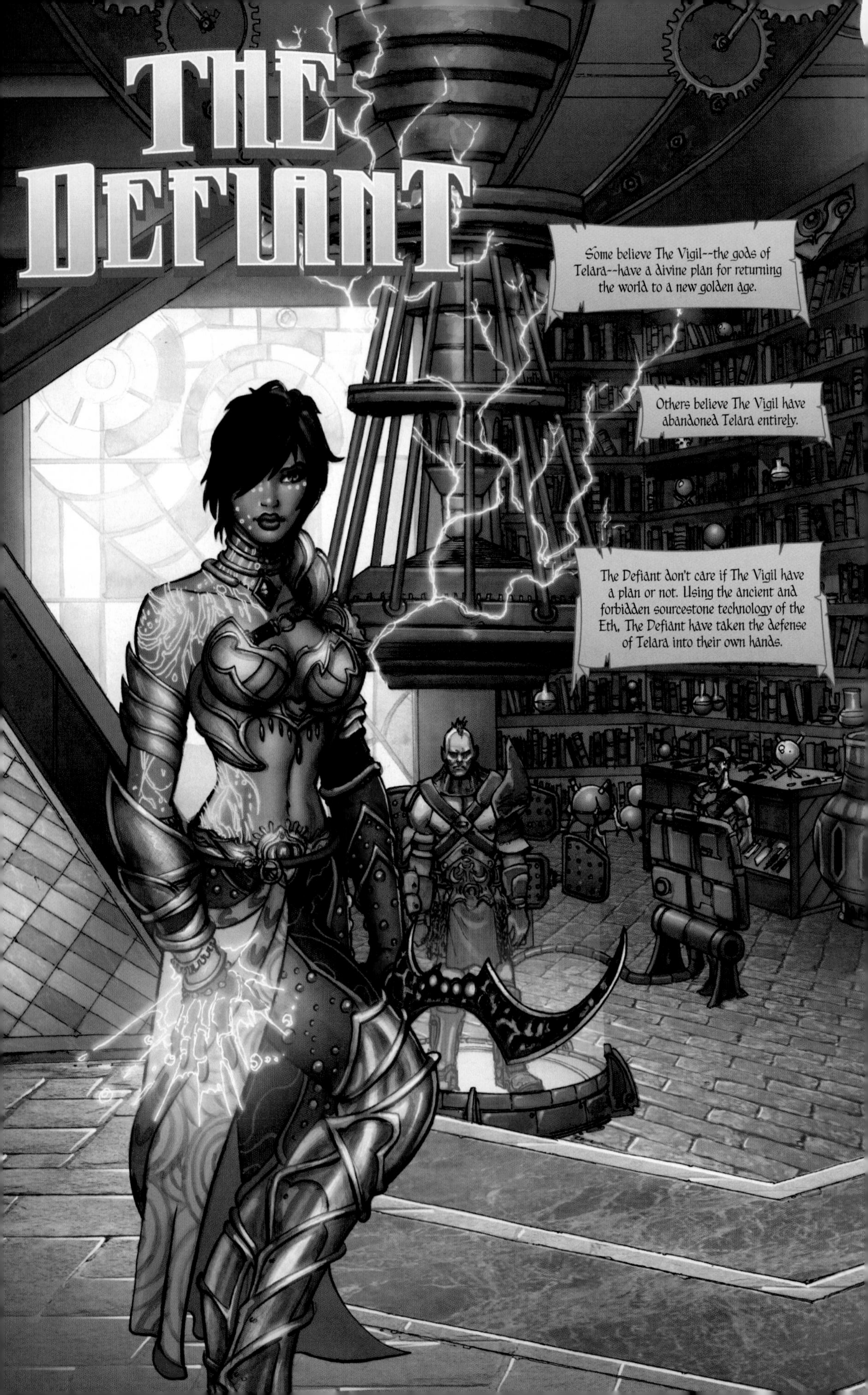
THE DEFIANT
Some believe The Vigil--the gods of Telara--have a divine plan for returning the world to a new golden age.
Others believe The Vigil have abandoned Telara entirely.
The Defiant don't care if The Vigil have a plan or not. Using the ancient and forbidden sourcestone technology of the Eth, The Defiant have taken the defense of Telara into their own hands.

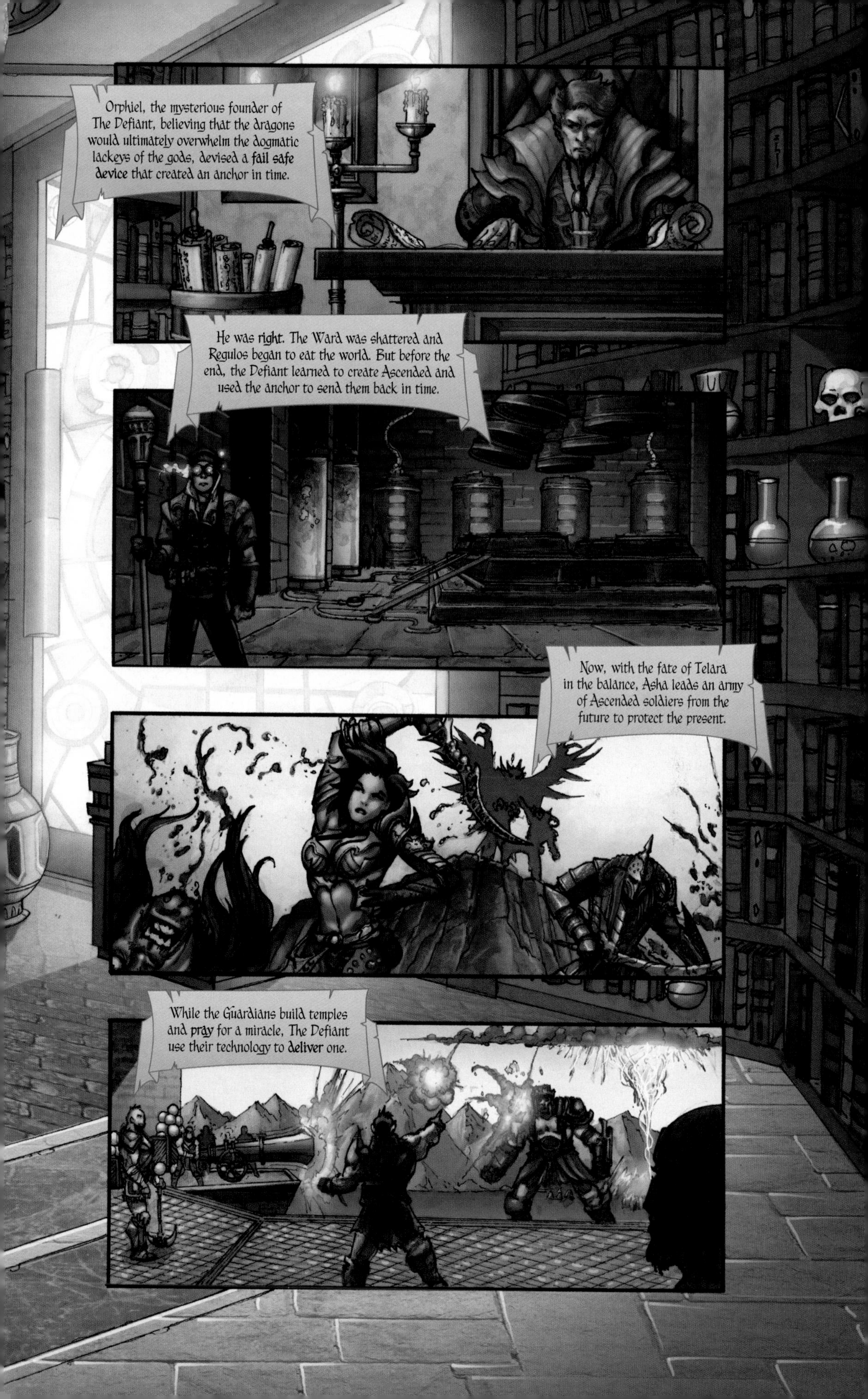
Orphiel, the mysterious founder of The Defiant, believing that the dragons would ultimately overwhelm the dogmatic lackeys of the gods, devised a fail safe device that created an anchor in time.
He was right. The Ward was shattered and Regulos began to eat the world. But before the end, the Defiant learned to create Ascended and used the anchor to send them back in time.
Now, with the fate of Telara in the balance, Asha leads an army of Ascended soldiers from the future to protect the present.
While the Guardians build temples and pray for a miracle, The Defiant use their technology to deliver one.

A great disaster has compromised the Ward between Telara and the six elemental planes. Rifts occur when two planes intersect over a tear in the Ward, allowing passage between different dimensions. Rifts are doorways for inter-dimensional invasion, though they may grant otherworldly power to those brave enough to seize the opportunity.

Nowhere in Telara is truly safe. Invasions can happen anywhere. Some are drawn to experience these phenomena for themselves, while others snap into action to defend Telara from unknown dangers.

Join legions of adventurers in RIFT™, a new Massively Multiplayer Online Role Playing Game set in a fantasy world being torn apart. Rifts sunder reality across the land and release powerful forces that threaten Telara's very existence.

Each breach brings with it new enemies, events and treasures, and changes the world dynamically around you.

Play with your friends across vast lavishly detailed environments, or take them on head-to-head in challenging Player versus Player (PvP) combat as you battle to obtain the secrets of the planes. Build and advance your character, choosing from six distinct races and utilizing an amazing new class system with nearly limitless possibilities.

The rifts have divided the people and endangered the world. Whether you fight to seal the rifts forever or harness their power for your own gain, epic adventures lie ahead.

KEY FEATURES

FULL-FEATURED

Guilds, dungeons, raids, auctions, crafting, a vibrant economy, Player vs. Player combat, and more!

DEEPER GAMEPLAY

New features like Guild Quests and Artifact Collections enhance your gaming experience by giving you earned achievements that matter.

HIGHLY ACCESSIBLE
HD GRAPHICS

Play a game that has stunning visuals on virtually any computer, even if your PC isn't state-of-the-art.

WORLD AS YOUR ADVERSARY

Extra-planar creatures surge into the world from rifts, turning bastions of safety into frenzied battlefields. Defeat these monsters and earn unique rewards, or use them to your advantage by forcing enemies to engage them. Your choices impact others!

8 PRIMAL FORCES

Creatures from the planes of Air, Earth, Fire, Water, Life, and Death battle for control of the world of Telara! Two warring factions—the Guardians and the Defiant—face off against each other and fight creatures from the planes as they seek to save the world.

PVP COMBAT

Battle others in exhilarating Player vs. Player combat! Earn PvP ranks, titles, loot, and unique souls to further enhance your character. Head to four cross-server Warfronts and fight others in world PvP.

BUILD YOUR CLASS

No other game lets you build your class the way RIFT™ does. Specialize in a single class or pick and choose abilities from many to create a character uniquely suited to your play-style— and have fun while you experiment!

CHOOSE YOUR ROLE

Each character can have up to four different roles, so you can choose different classes for every situation! You might have one for PvP and another for raids; or perhaps you want a high-damage or high-defense build. The choice is yours to mix and match as you see fit!

THE HISTORY OF TELARA

ARRIVAL OF THE BLOOD STORM

Millennia ago, the gods forged a world from sourcestone and peopled it with many races. All lived in harmony until he coming of the Blood Storm, a pack of baleful ods embodying the six essential forces: Life, Death, Air, Fire, Water, and Earth.

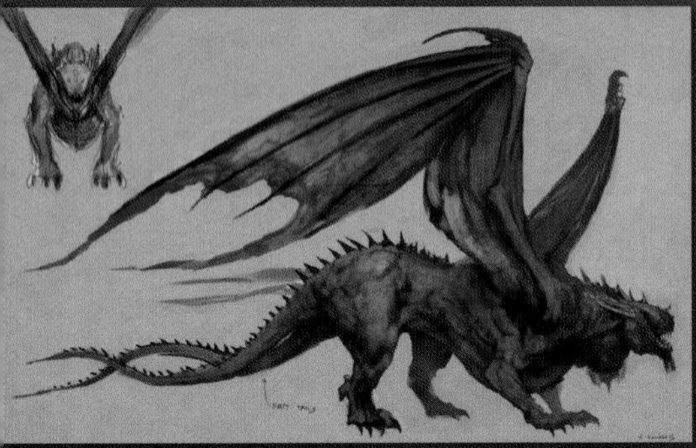

The Blood Storm ravaged the universe, consuming every world they encountered. At their head was Regulos the Destroyer, Eater of Worlds and he embodiment of death. When they came upon Telara, the lesser Blood Storm rebelled against heir leader.

ust when Telara was at their mercy, the Blood Storm manifested as great dragons and fell to nfighting. The lesser dragons fought each other to rule the world, and against Regulos to keep him from devouring their prize. Telara's people seized the

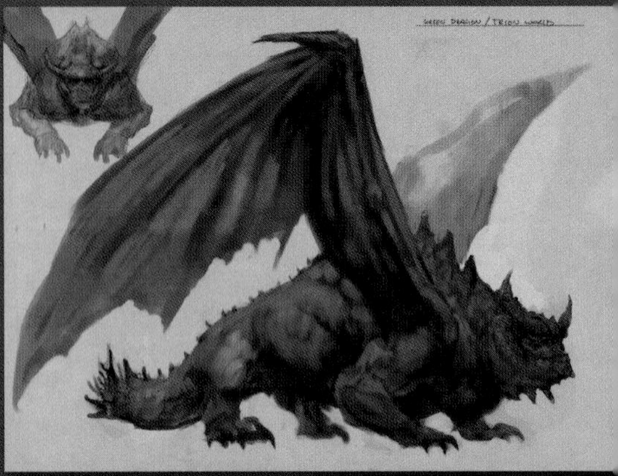

opportunity to slay Regulos's physical form, banish his spirit, and lock the five lesser dragons in elemental prisons. With help from the Vigil mages erected the Ward to seal Telara off from the planes and keep the Blood Storm at bay.

THE AGE OF MEN

Two great human civilizations flourished and fel in the aftermath of the Blood Storm War. First rose the technomagical Empire of Eth. As their knowledge and power grew, the Eth pushed the boundaries of the Ward. But dragon cults bent on releasing the Blood Storm infiltrated their eldritch laboratories. The Eth destroyed their machines and their civilization rather than see their accomplishments used to free Regulos.

The Mathosian Empire filled the gap left by the Eth. Disavowing their predecessors' pursuit of technology, the Mathosians pledged themselves to the principles of duty, honor, and justice. Telara prospered for centuries, until the death of King Jostir Mathos, and the civil war between his twin sons, Zareph and Aedraxis.

Aedraxis, eldest by seconds, was corrupted by the dragon cults and became an avatar of Regulos. In the brothers' final battle, Aedraxis used ancient Eth technology to pierce the barrier between the planes, calling on the dragon to overcome Zareph. Black tendrils of Regulos's power flooded through the opening, annihilating the opposing armies—including wretched Aedraxis—and leaving Telara devastated.

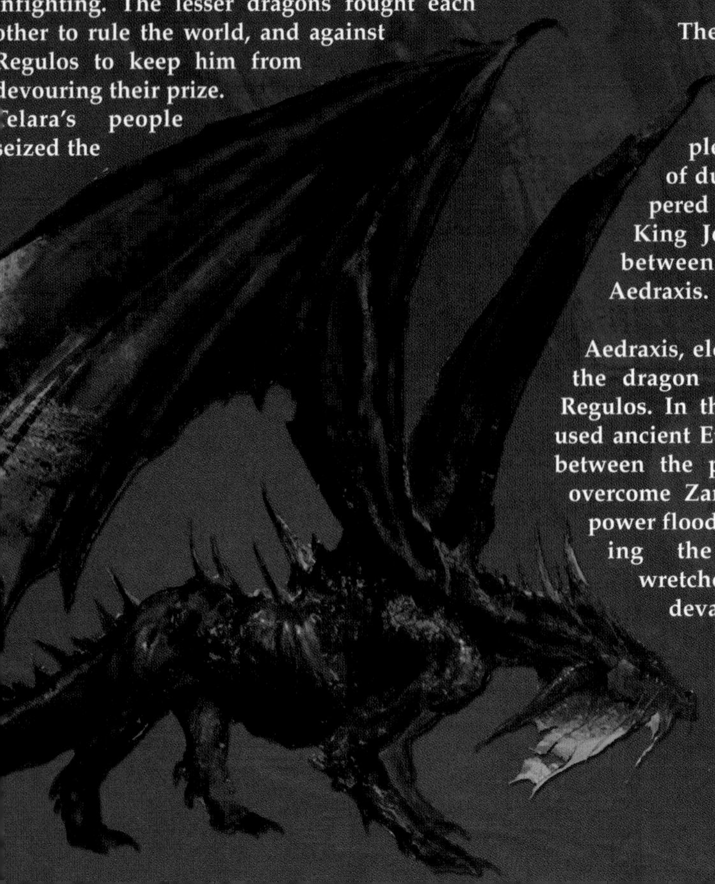

CRACKS IN THE WARD

Zareph escaped the touch of Regulos and led the survivors to Port Scion. But the Ward had been compromised, allowing rifts to form: doorways

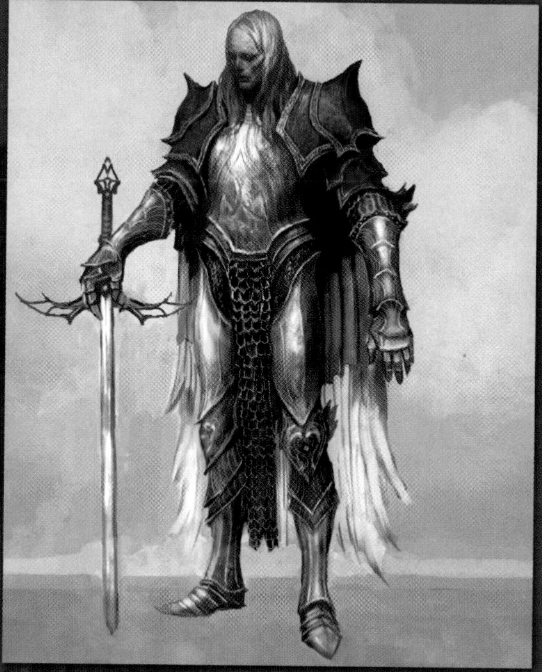

between Telara and the planes. Even mighty Port Scion eventually fell to the Planar threat, and the last safe haven from the rifts was sealed and lost. What remains of the Ward is all that stands between Telara and utter destruction. No place is safe. Rifts grow more numerous by the day and the Blood Storm stir in their prisons, marshalling their minions on Telara and the planes.

But there is cause for hope. Two powerful factions field reborn champions called the Ascended, defending Telara against all threats from the planes.

The Guardians, led by the legendary Cyril Kalmar, are a holy order of Mathosians, High Elves, and Dwarves, resurrected on the battlefield through the will of the gods. The Defiant, a collective of Eth, rugged Bahmi, and Kelari Elves, have returned from a nightmare future to save Telara with machines powered by sourcestone.

While both groups would save Telara, each desires to establish a new empire in

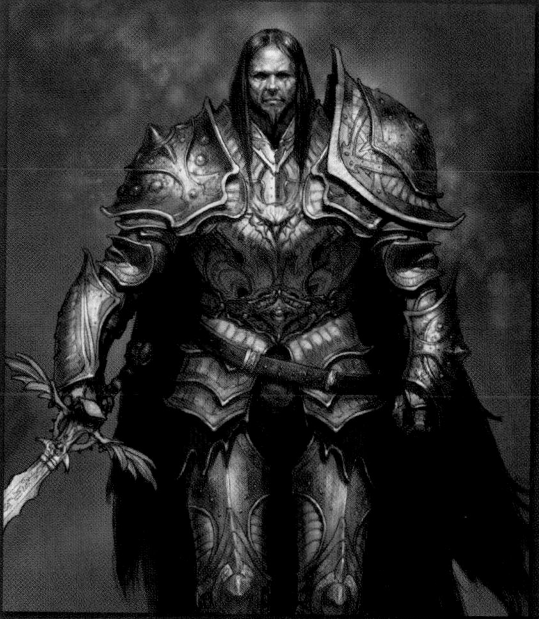

its own image. The Guardians seek a world of honor, tradition, and devotion to the Vigil, while the Defiant envision bustling mechamagical cities from whose spires the ambitious can seize power from the planes.

Time grows short. The dragon cults gain power by the day, exploiting the conflict between the Defiant and Guardians to weaken the Ward even further.

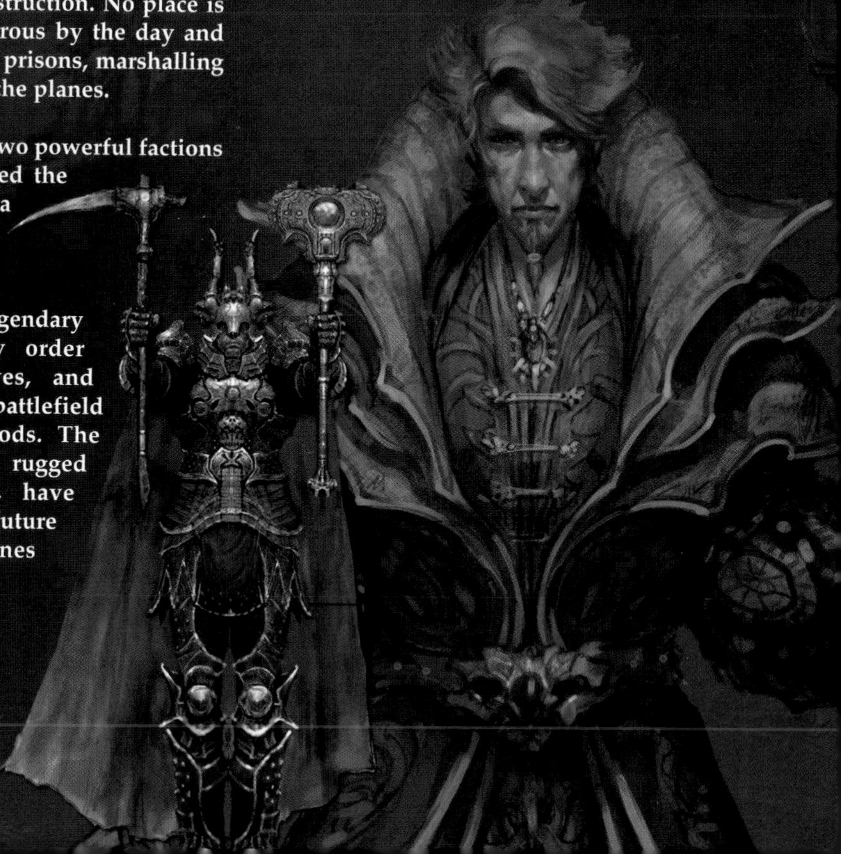

THE GUARDIANS

As the first Ascended champions to return to Telara, the Guardians represent the sincere belief that the gods of the Vigil have not abandoned Telara, but are working an intricate plot for the final battle of good against evil—the Day of Judgment! The Guardians have a destiny as part of this divine plan to save the world.

The Guardians seek redemption for the catastrophic events their leaders brought upon the world. Only their holy power and unending resolve can defeat the dragons. If those who fall under their rule feel the Guardians are overly judgmental and controlling, they will come to understand that this is in everyone's best interest. The Guardians seek to save Telara, not just battle its monsters.

Following a holy prophecy handed down on the eve of their resurrection, the Guardians maintain that a world-breaking convergence of all the planes is nigh, and that only the faithful can stave off doom and restore harmony to Telara. To this crusade the Guardians have sworn themselves, and they are perfectly willing to stop the Defiant's heretical experiments from saving Regulos the trouble of destroying Telara.

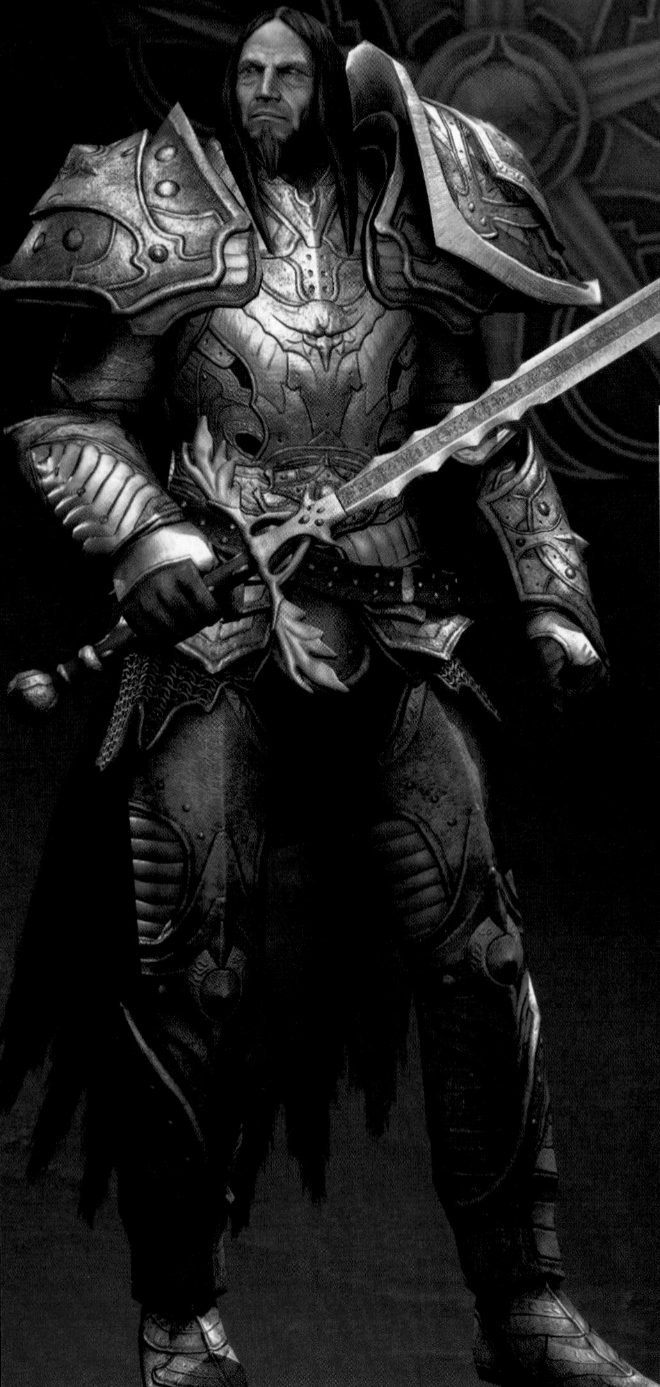

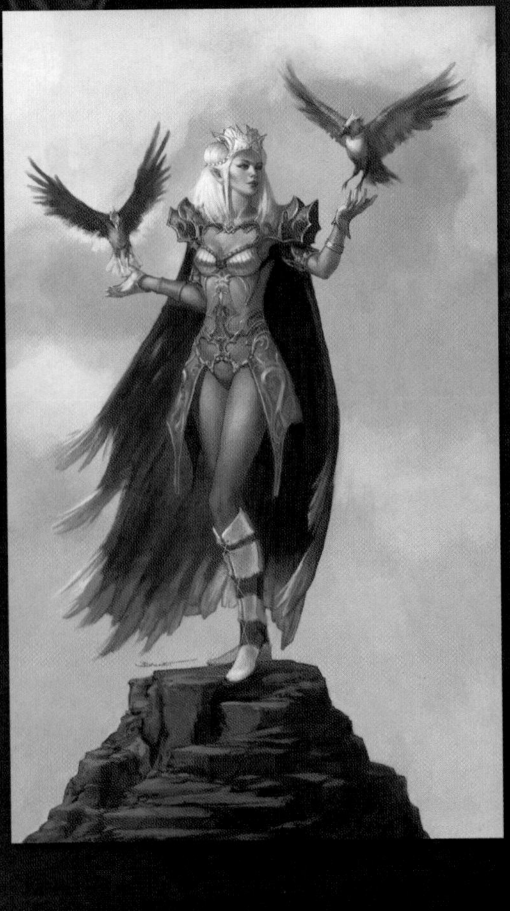

THE DEFIANT

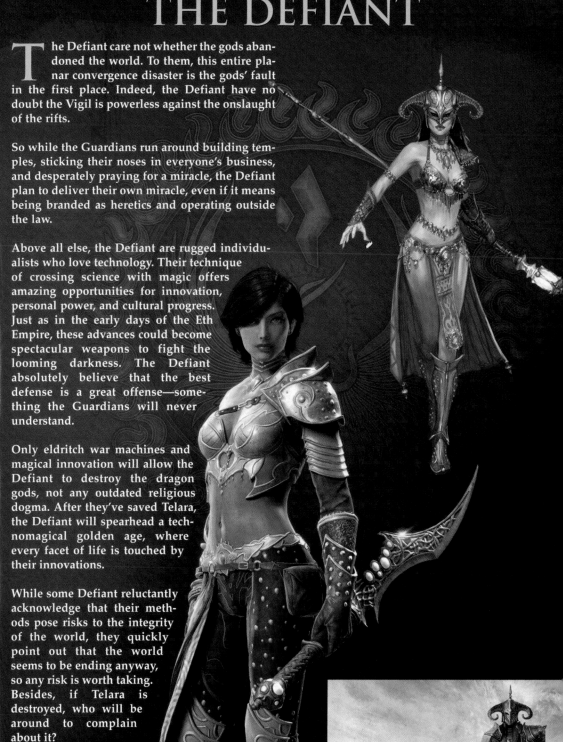

The Defiant care not whether the gods abandoned the world. To them, this entire planar convergence disaster is the gods' fault in the first place. Indeed, the Defiant have no doubt the Vigil is powerless against the onslaught of the rifts.

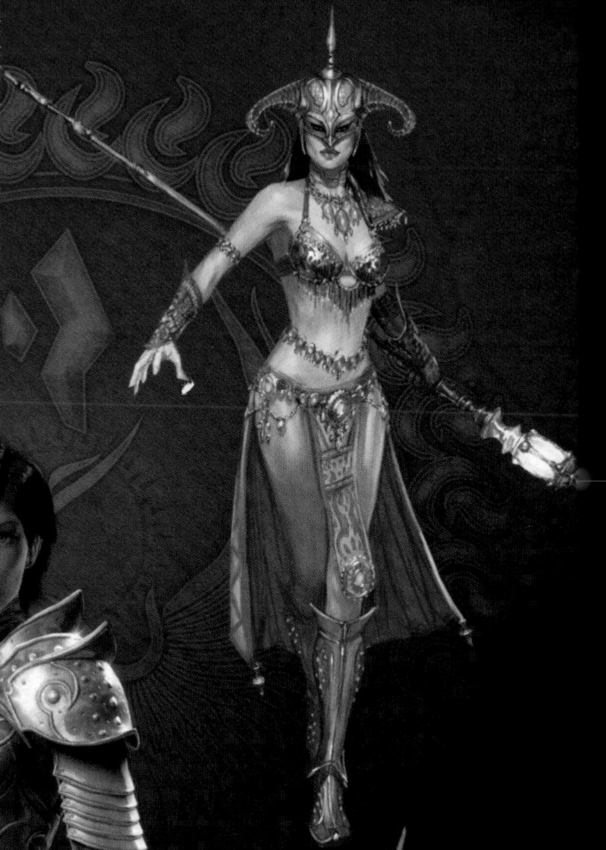

So while the Guardians run around building temples, sticking their noses in everyone's business, and desperately praying for a miracle, the Defiant plan to deliver their own miracle, even if it means being branded as heretics and operating outside the law.

Above all else, the Defiant are rugged individualists who love technology. Their technique of crossing science with magic offers amazing opportunities for innovation, personal power, and cultural progress. Just as in the early days of the Eth Empire, these advances could become spectacular weapons to fight the looming darkness. The Defiant absolutely believe that the best defense is a great offense—something the Guardians will never understand.

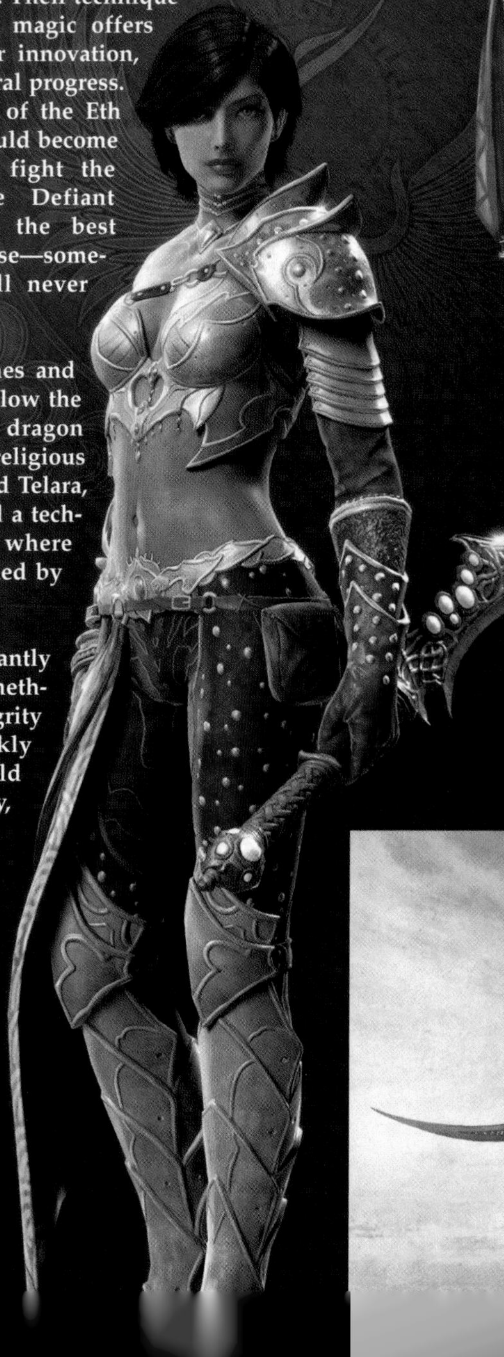

Only eldritch war machines and magical innovation will allow the Defiant to destroy the dragon gods, not any outdated religious dogma. After they've saved Telara, the Defiant will spearhead a technomagical golden age, where every facet of life is touched by their innovations.

While some Defiant reluctantly acknowledge that their methods pose risks to the integrity of the world, they quickly point out that the world seems to be ending anyway, so any risk is worth taking. Besides, if Telara is destroyed, who will be around to complain about it?

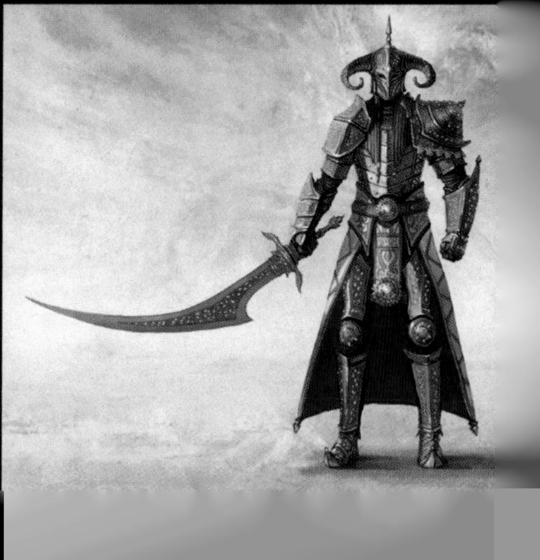

INVASION FROM BEYOND

Rifts are tearing Telara apart. A disastrous magic explosion during the final battle of the Mathosian Civil War has left the veil between Telara and the elemental planes fractured and torn.

Telaran scholars, priests, and historians strive to unlock the mysteries of these treacherous portals. It is believed that Regulos, the dragon god of extinction, personally works to weaken the Ward, and intensify the rifts' disruptions.

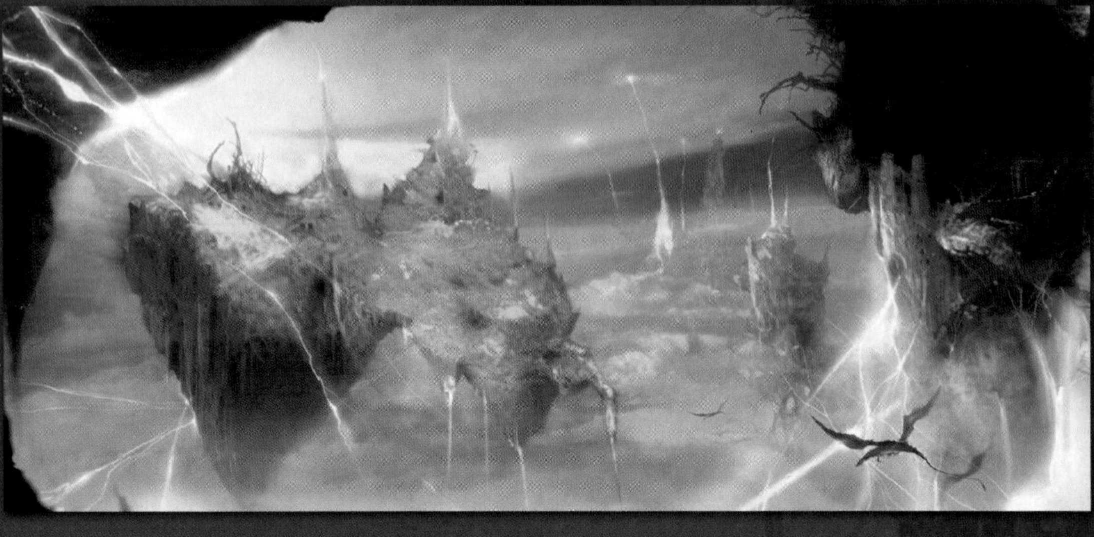

Rifts occur when a fissure forms in the Ward, opening a doorway for violent planar invasions to descend upon Telara's lands and people. Invasions can occur anywhere and at any time, and their dire threat to the world is growing. Two major factions, the Guardians and the Defiant, have emerged to save Telara from the rifts. Both factions work in different ways to preserve Telara's future, and each seeks to undermine the other.

Powerful magic has been used to study the rifts, and some scholars even risk opening the portals on purpose, often resulting in great tragedy. Still, there is much to learn by observing these dangerous gateways.

One thing is certain—if the rifts do not come to an end, the world of Telara surely will.

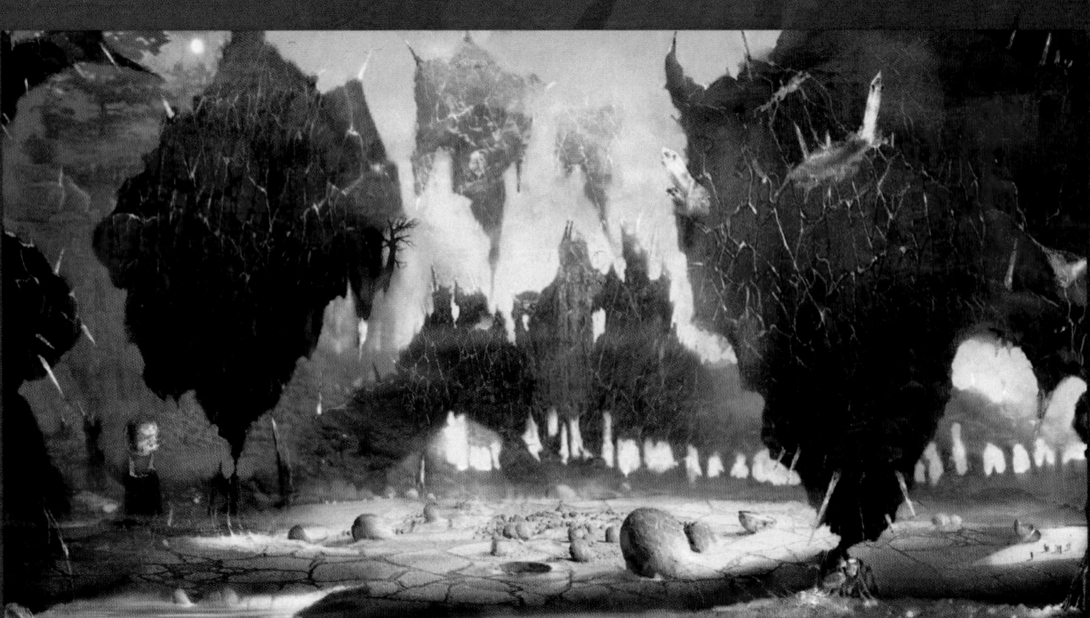